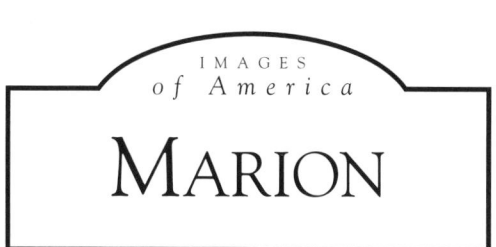

IMAGES
of America

MARION

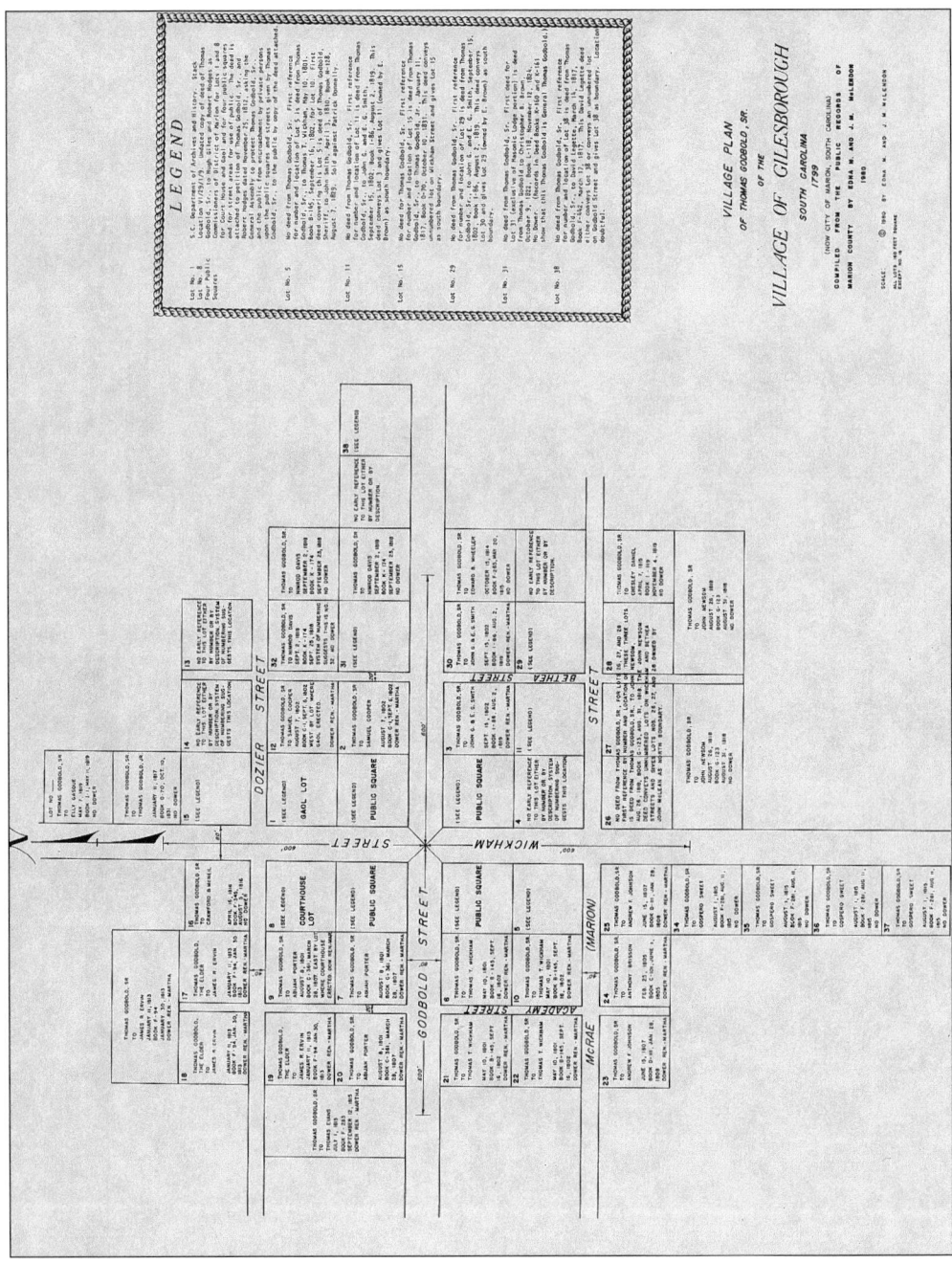

This is "the Village Plan, Village of Gilesborough." This map was reprinted with permission from Mr. Malcolm McLendon.

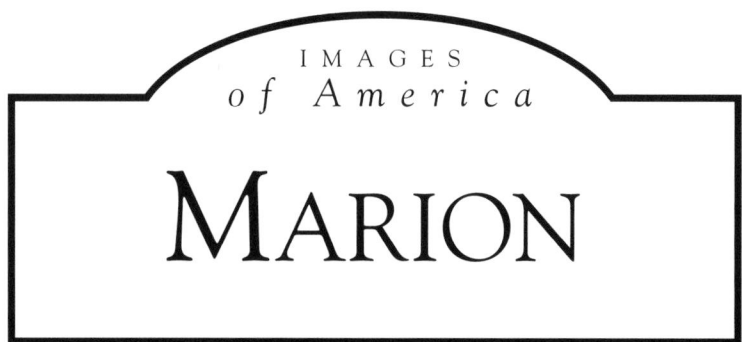

IMAGES
of America

MARION

Historic Marion Revitalization Association

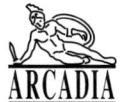

ARCADIA

Published by Arcadia Publishing,
an imprint of Tempus Publishing, Inc.
2 Cumberland Street
Charleston, SC 29401

Printed in Great Britain.

Library of Congress Catalog Card Number applied for.

For all general information contact Arcadia Publishing at:
Telephone 843-853-2070
Fax 843-853-0044
E-Mail arcadia@charleston.net

For customer service and orders:
Toll-Free 1-888-313-BOOK

Visit us on the internet at http://www.arcadiaimages.com

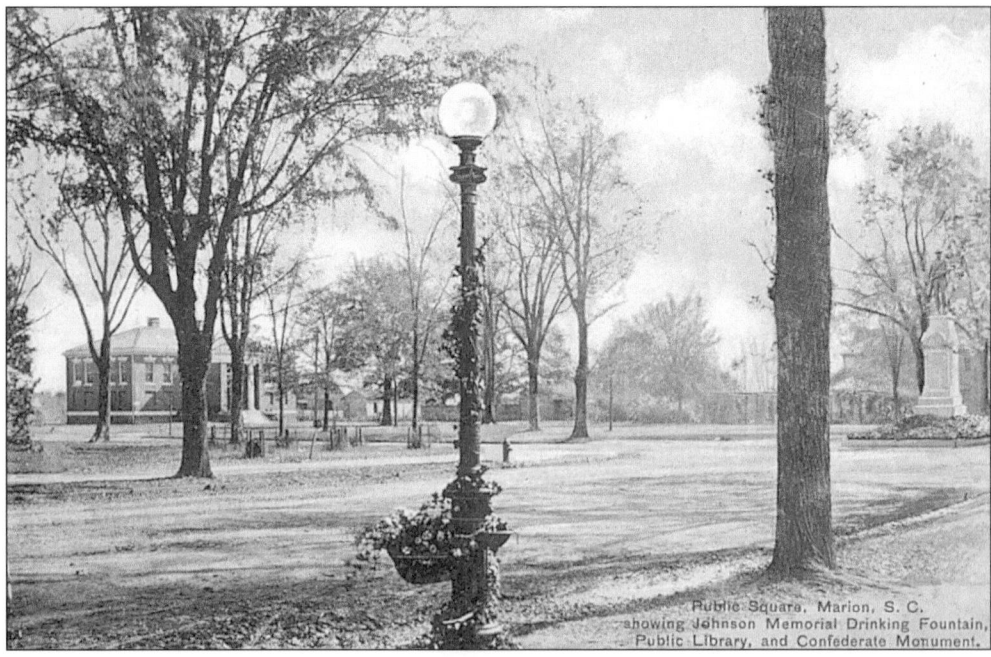

This is the Public Square in Marion, South Carolina. This view shows the Johnson Memorial Drinking Fountain, the Marion County Public Library, and the Confederate Monument.

CONTENTS

Introduction   8

1.   At Home, at Church, at School   9

2.   All Dressed Up with Places to Go   45

3.   Doin' Business   57

4.   Draggin' Main   79

5.   Travelin'   97

6.   Workin' and Playin'   111

Acknowledgments   128

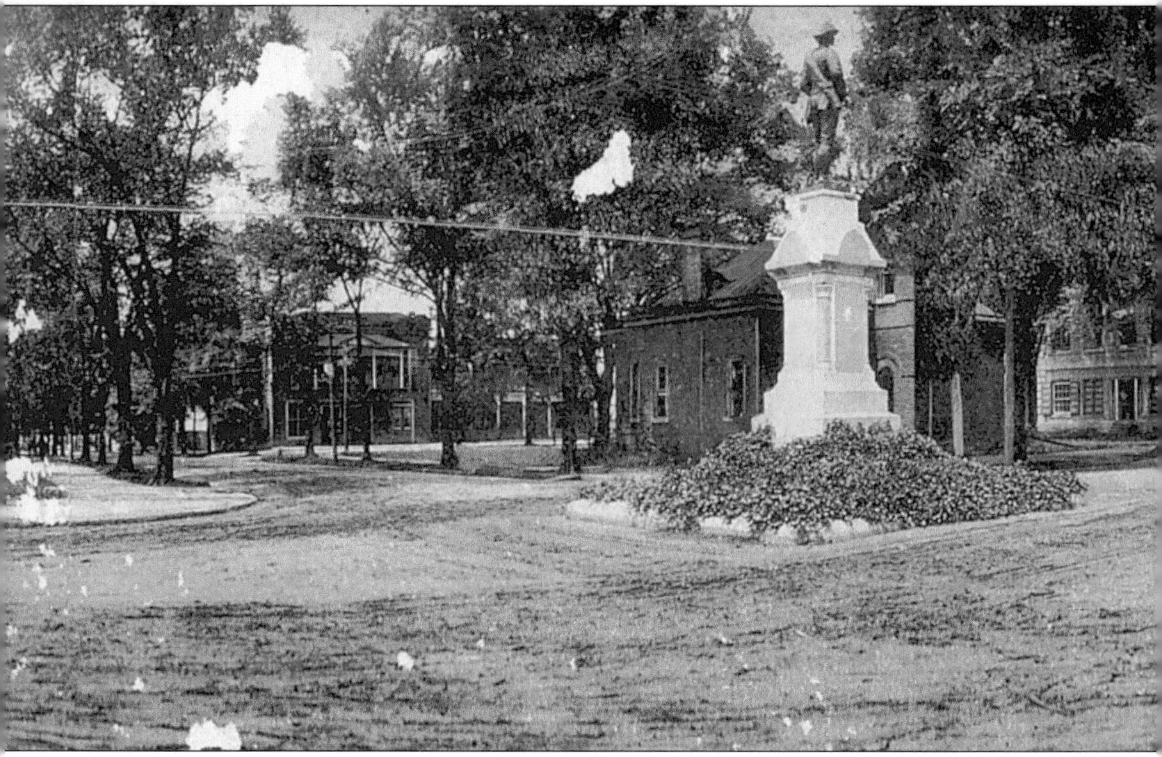

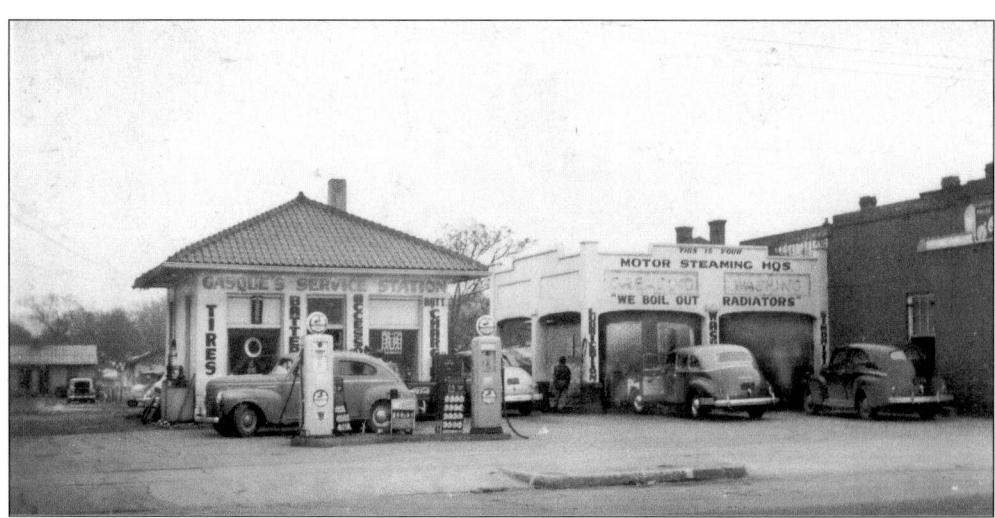

This is a photograph of the intersection of what we know as Godbold and Main Streets. These dirt roads were allegedly American Indian trails that led north to south from Ports Ferry to

Gasque's Service Station, at 214 North Main Street, was located between Alpert's Department Store and Marion Cleaners. Eventually, a Mobile gas station was located on the site. In 1974, Colonial State Bank was constructed on this Main Street site.

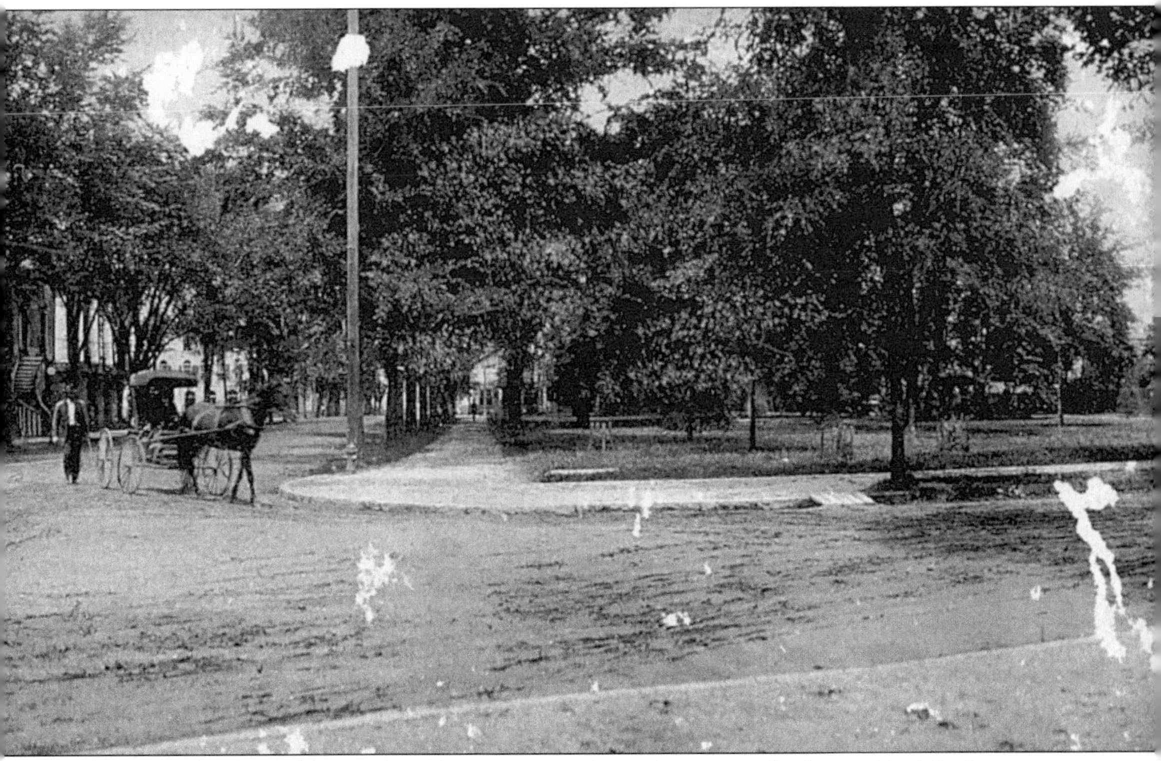

Smith's Mill on Catfish Creek and east to west from Newsome's Bridge to Catfish Causeway. (Photo courtesy of Mary Pace Proctor.)

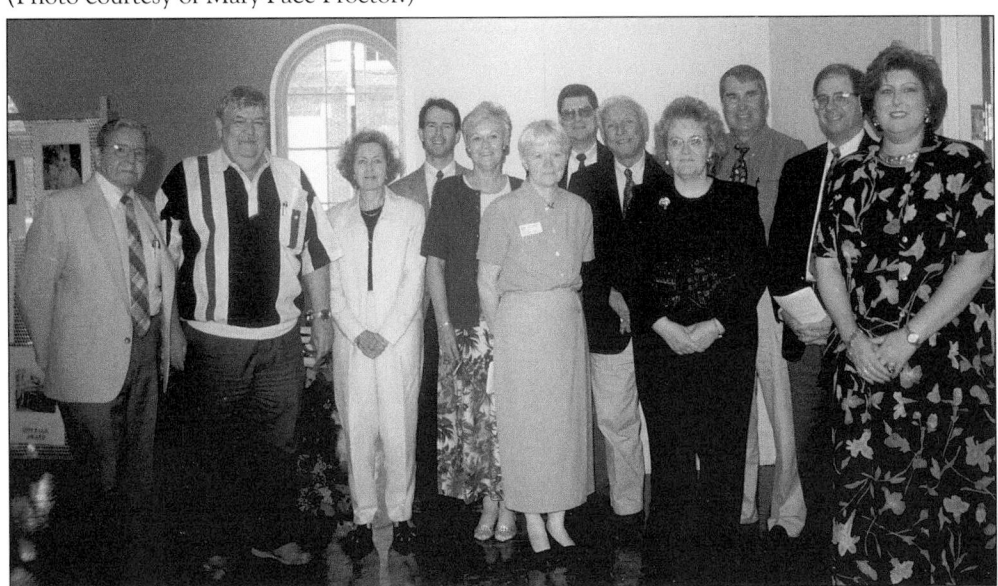

The Board of Directors for the Historic Marion Revitalization Association is pictured here. From left to right are as follows: F.T. Zeman, Demont Ammons, Ann Hooks, Ashley Brady, Laura White, Judy Johnson (Ex-officio), Mike Jackson (President), William Thompson, Jane Edwards (Ex-officio), Frazier Waldrop (Ex-officio), Bill Johnson, and Melody Wagner. Jack Hulon and Leon Sturkey are not pictured.

INTRODUCTION

We advertised for treasured pictures, and each came in with its own story. No matter how small or faded, they recreated our past. Recorded here is more than a century of life in Marion, South Carolina. These are the images photographed—our homes, churches, and schools. There are lumber mills, mercantile stores, wringer washing machines, cotton gins, tobacco warehouses, the fire horses, graduations, and watermelon cutting. We meet in the crossroads near places called home, proud to be photographed.

These memories were taken from old family albums, from dusty attic trunks, and from ribbon-tied shoeboxes, and some were still framed and proudly displayed. Using photographs solicited from all over Marion, this pictorial is a group effort to recreate and build a collected memory of Marion, "that pretty little town on the way to the beach." We invite you to ponder.

This book is dedicated to all who are proud to have called Marion home.

Mike Jackson, HMRA Board President
Betty C. Owens, HMRA Executive Director
The Book Committee, Historic Marion Revitalization Association

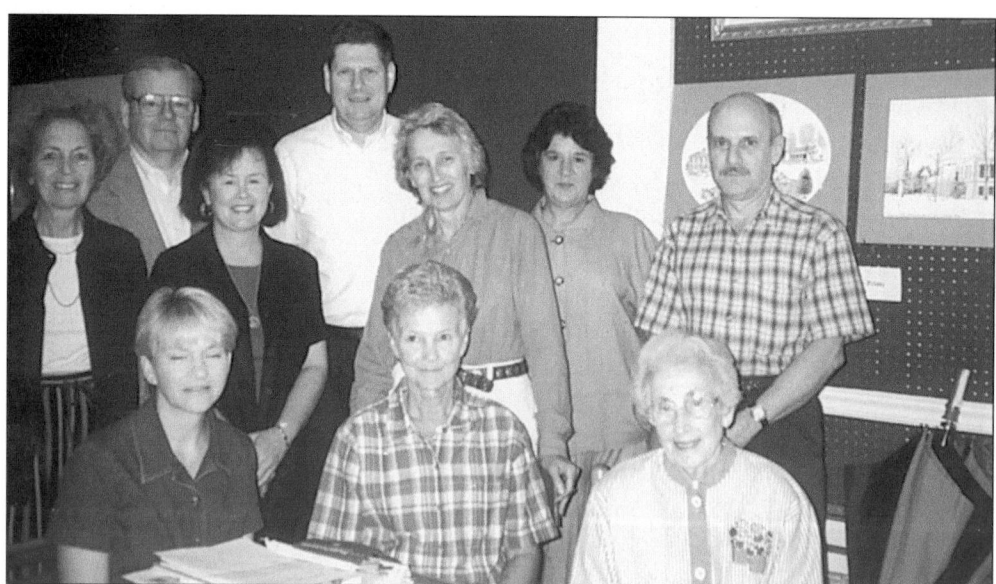

Shown here is the Book Committee for this photographic history of Marion, South Carolina. Pictured, from left to right, are as follows: (seated) Laney Baumrind, Nancy Askins, and Elizabeth McIntyre; (second row) Ann Hooks, Betty C. Owens (HMRA Executive Director), and Bonita McLaurin; (back row) Tommy Lett, Mike Jackson (HMRA Board President), Patsy Ammons (HMRA Assistant), and Maxcy Foxworth. Suzanne Gasque McIntyre is not pictured.

One
AT HOME, AT CHURCH, AT SCHOOL

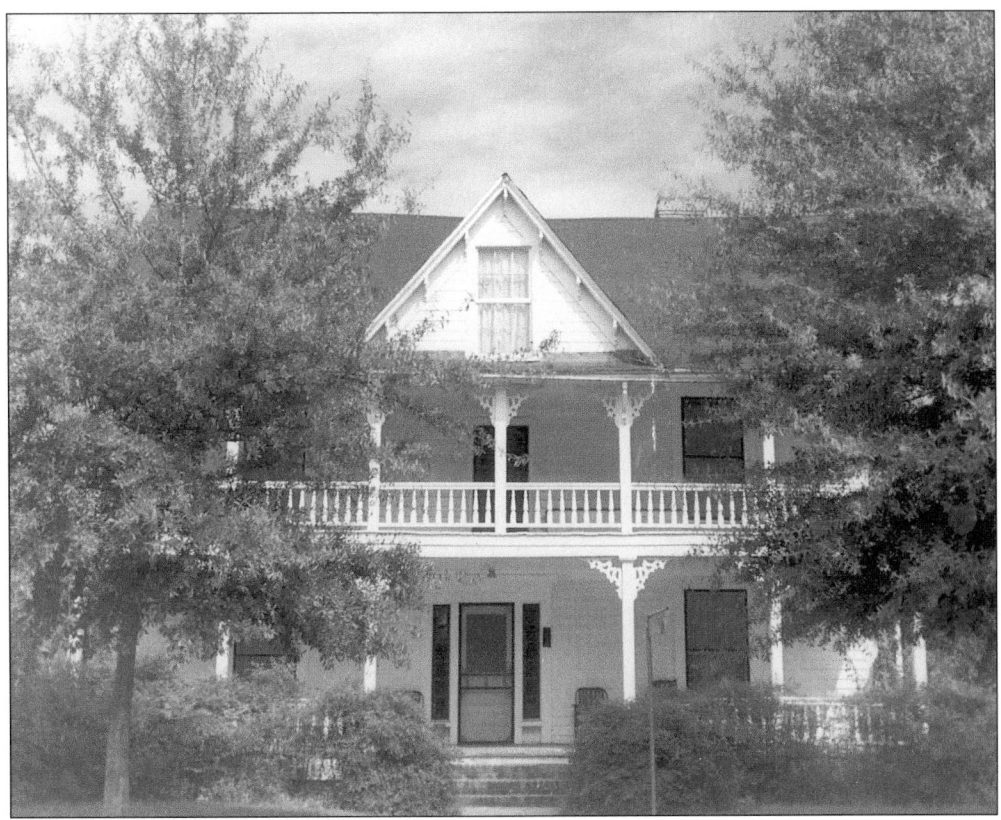

The Godbold house at 109 East Dozier Street is the oldest house in Marion. Painted on an attic wall is the date 1804 and the name Thomas Godbold. Thomas Godbold gave land for a public square, courthouse, and jail. Often called Marion's first developer, he laid out the surrounding town with great foresight. Remodeled in 1870, the home was later a popular boardinghouse operated by Mrs. Henry Davis. (Photo courtesy of Libby Owens Stanley.)

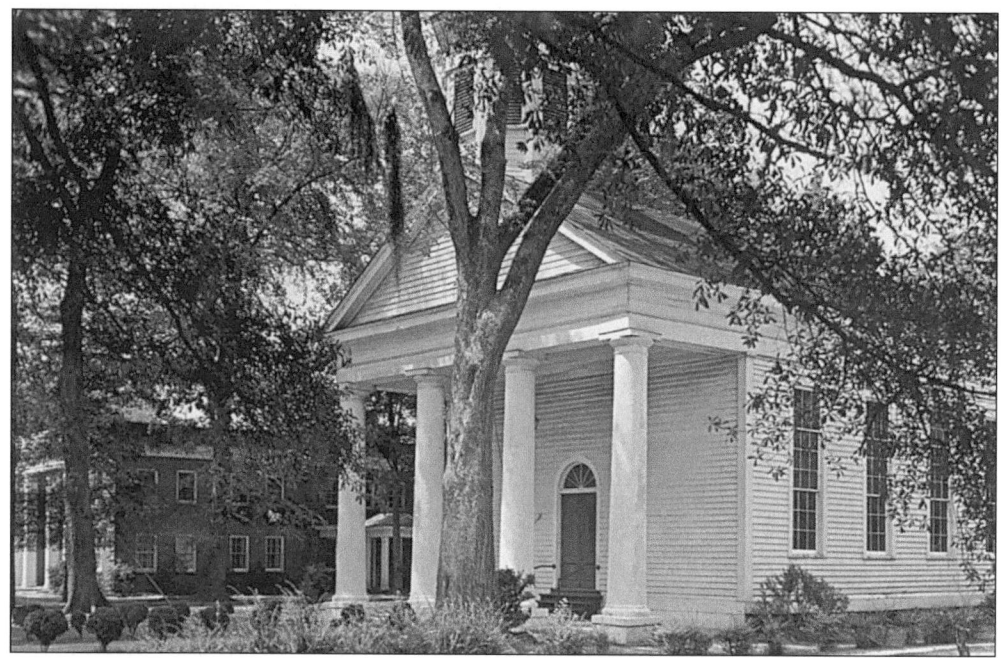

The Marion Presbyterian Church on South Main Street was built in 1852 and is the oldest church building in Marion County. The educational building was built *c.* 1950 and housed a kindergarten operated by the church. (Photo courtesy of Valerie Baumrind Bonatis.)

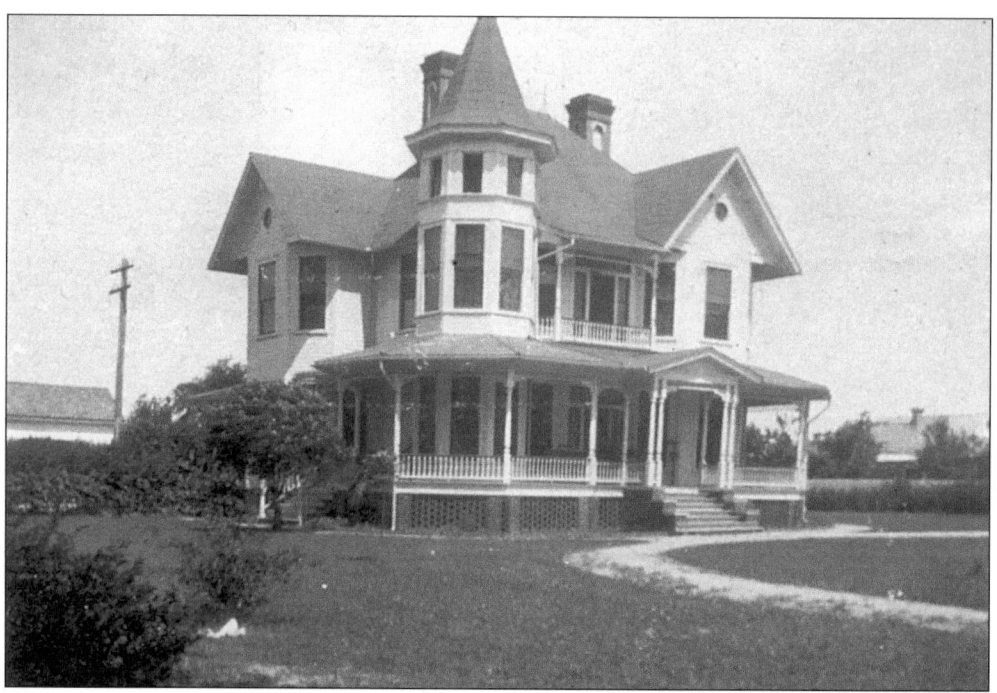

Built by James Stackhouse and sold to William S. Foxworth in 1907, this Queen Anne–style house stood just north of the Presbyterian Church on South Main Street until it was demolished about 1960. (Photo courtesy of William Thompson.)

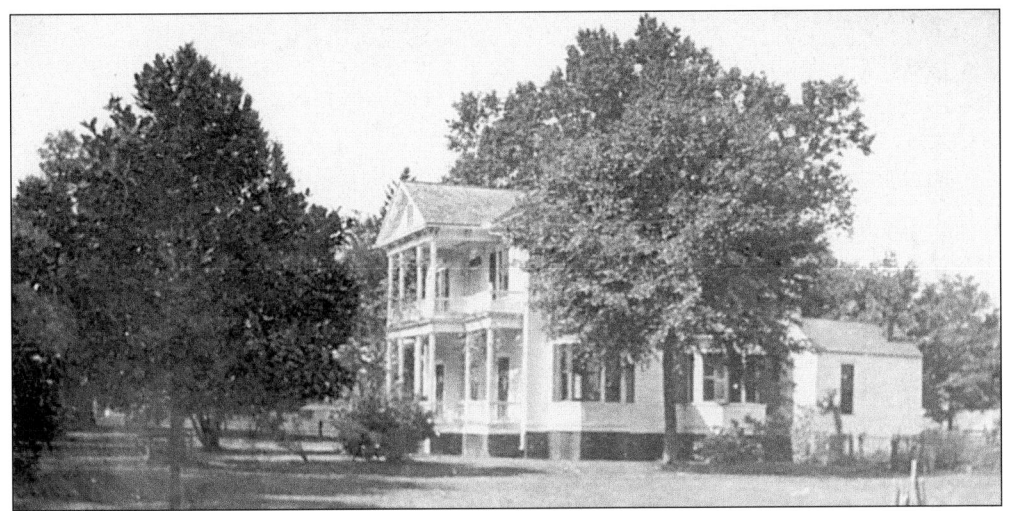

This house on South Main Street was built in 1858 by Robert Reaves and was later home to the Samuel Evans family and the O.K. Laroque family. The Marion Presbyterian Church used it as a youth center before its demolition in early 1970. (Photo courtesy of Suzanne Gasque McIntyre.)

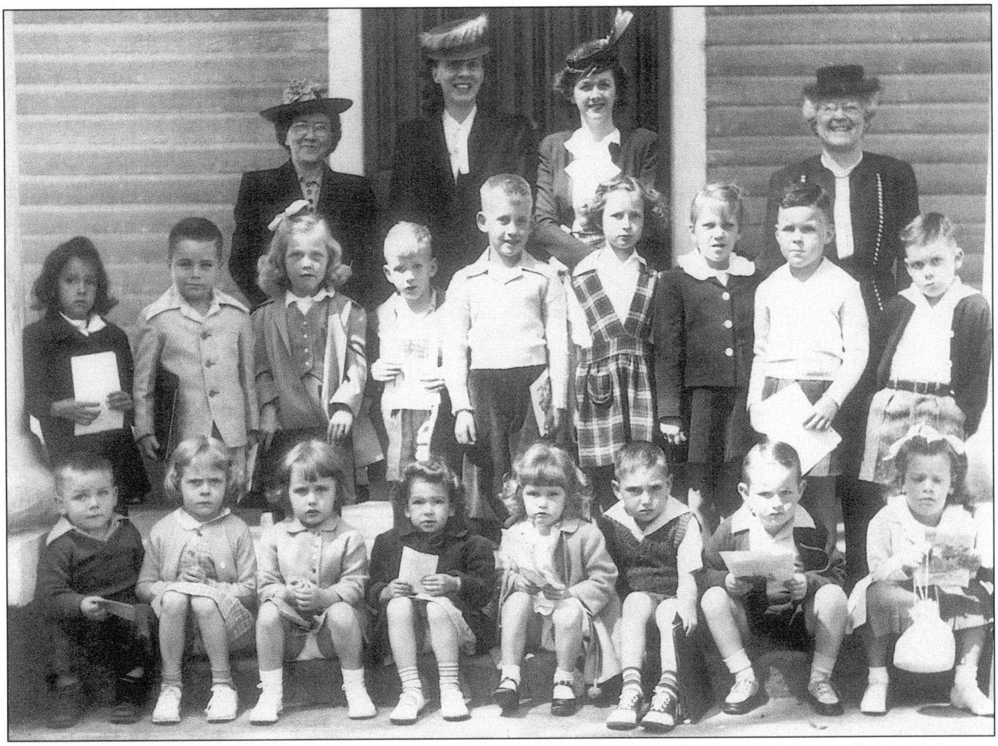

Seen here is a gathering of Sunday school classes and teachers in front of the Marion Presbyterian Church. This photograph of Rally Day in 1946 includes Billy Wallace, Ann Carol Gasque, Harriet Foxworth, Patsy Zeman, Bruce Stanton, Blakely McIntyre, Elaine McCormick, Eleanor Zeman, Charles Jones, Julie Ann Rogers, Jamie Mickie, Betty Langston, Reggie Rowell, Rawlings Hubbard, Tommy Hughes, Miss Lyle Hay, Flora Hughes, and Edna Hughes. (Photo courtesy of Libby Stanley.)

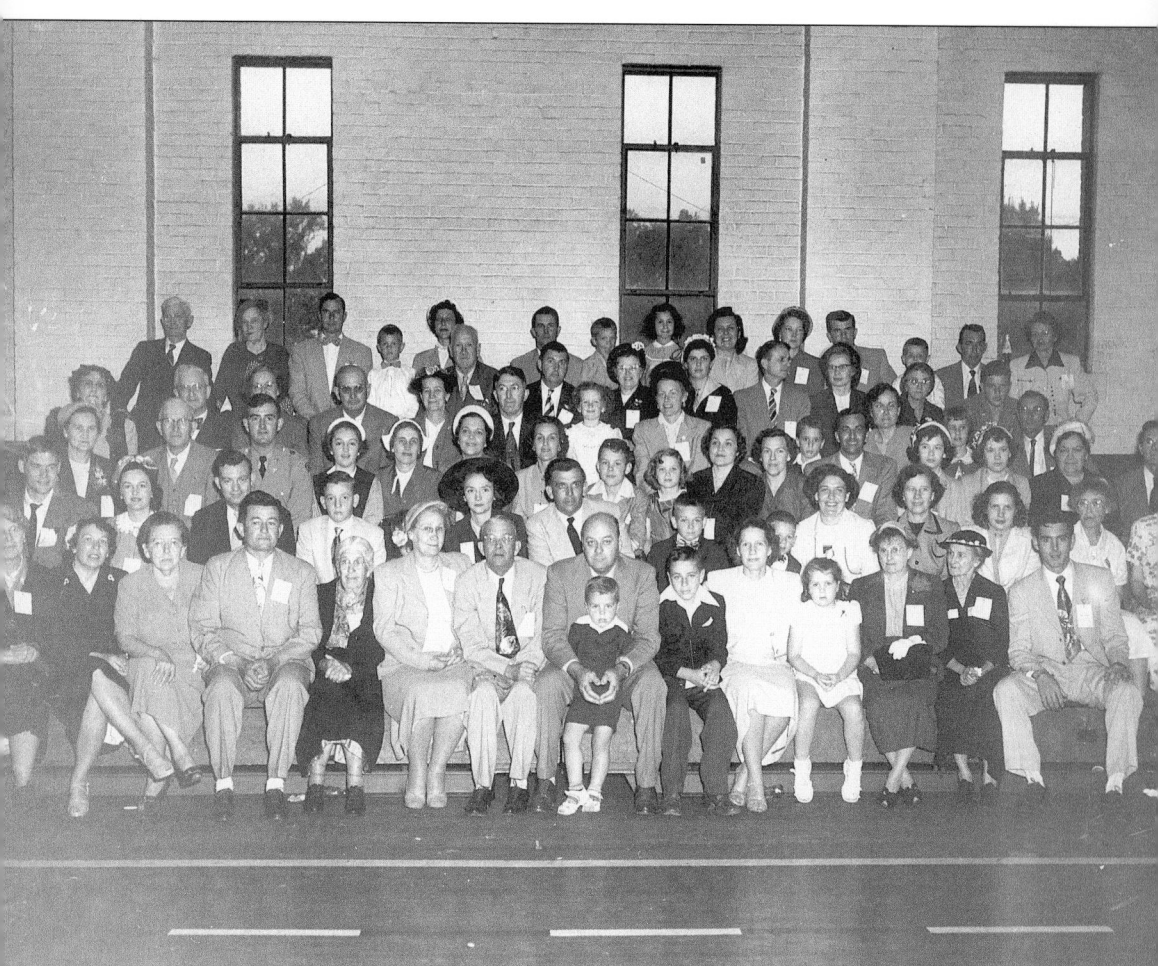

Gathered in the old National Guard Armory on Willcox Avenue are McIntyre descendants at the 1952 Presbyterian Church Centennial. The following people are, from left to right, as follows: (row one) Kate Dunlop, Marie Harrelson Blanton, Eulene Miller McIntyre, Blake McIntyre, Kate McIntyre Davis, Mollie Pace Stanley, Foster Stanley, Howard Jones, Evans Jones, Christine Evans Jones, Cheryl Jones, Elizabeth McIntyre Corley, Lora McIntyre Foxworth, and Julian Vaughn; (row two) Archie McIntyre, Virginia Shackelford McIntyre, Tommy Blanton, Jimmy Blanton, Ricky McIntyre, Dorothy Stewart McIntyre, Freddy McIntyre, Billy Wallace, Jimmy Rhett Wallace, Jannes McIntyre Wallace, Ella Davis Wall, Pansy Lane Stanley, unidentified, and unidentified; (row three) Margaret Boatwright McIntyre, Archie McIntyre, Duncan C. McIntyre, Thalia Salmon, Elizabeth McIntyre, Mary Sale Salmon, "LaLa" Owens Hubbard, Rawlings Hubbard, "Tootie" Hubbard, Libby Owens Stanley, Sophie Owens Neale, Hal Stanley, Margaret Frierson, Catherine Frierson, Mary Bowman Frierson, and William Frierson; (row four) Daisy McIntyre Brown, Baker McIntyre, Ann Redfern McIntyre, Duncan McIntyre, Julise McIntyre Johnson, Frank Salmon, Maree McIntyre, Maree Johnson McIntyre, Maxcy Foxworth, Clyde Evans Foxworth, Harriet Foxworth, and Richard Foxworth; (row five) James Johnson, J.C. McIntyre, unidentified, Roseanne Stanley, George McIntyre, Elizabeth Watson McIntyre, Sarah Foxworth Jordan, and Capers Jordan; (row six) Hampton McIntyre Sr., Clara Stubbs McIntyre, Hampton McIntyre Jr., Hampton McIntyre, Evelyn Collins McIntyre, Johnny McIntyre, Miller McIntyre, Phillip McIntyre, and Sue McDaniel McIntyre. (Photo courtesy of Ginny McIntyre.)

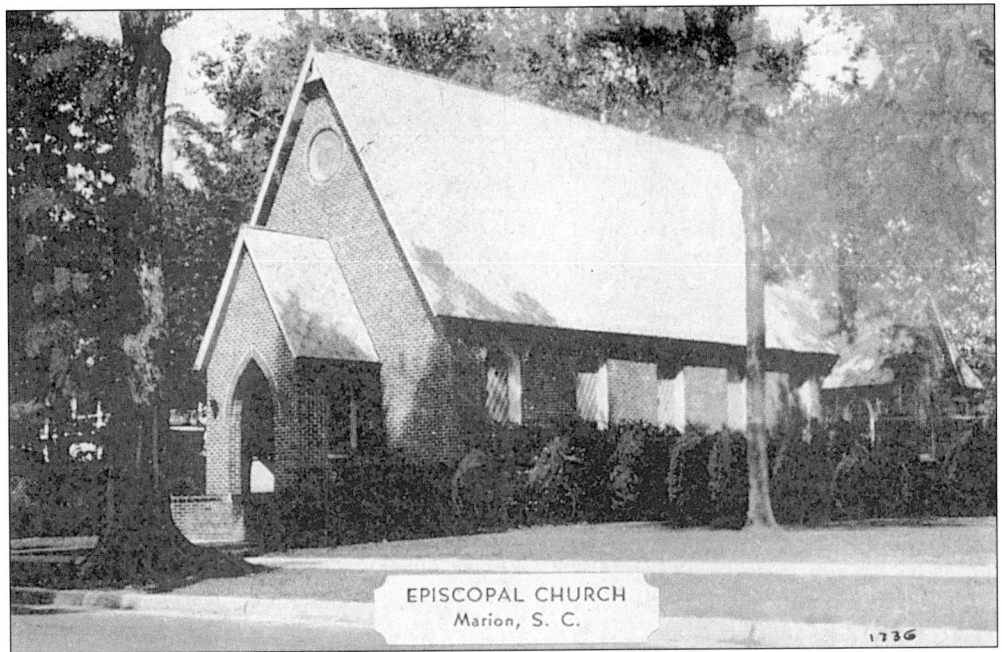

The Episcopal Church of the Advent of Marion was organized in 1867. Erected in 1880 and brick veneered in 1928, the church looks the same today. (Photo courtesy of Valerie Baumrind Bonatis.)

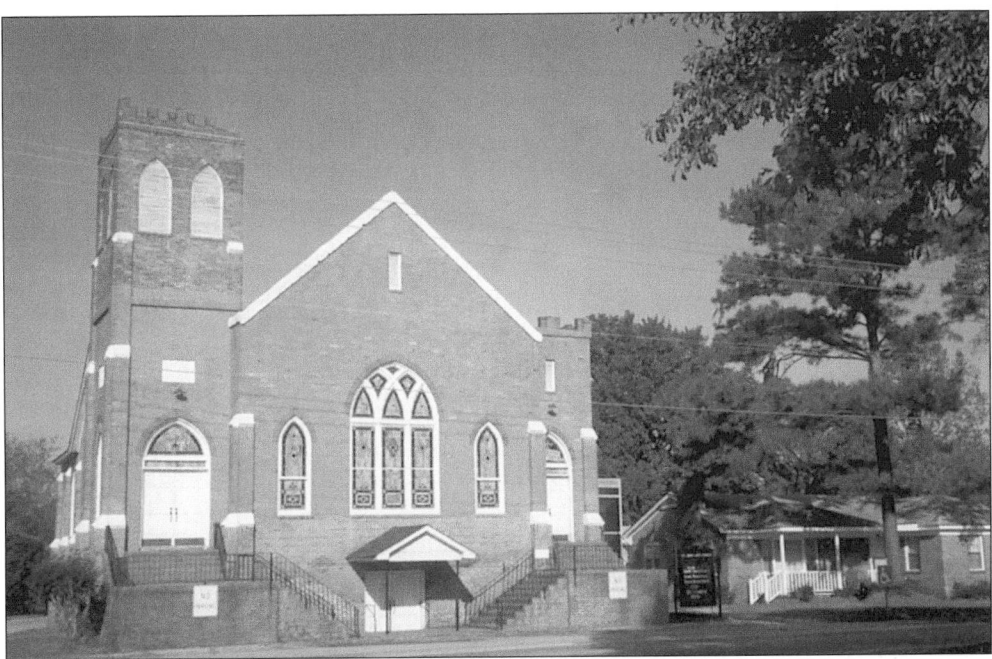

Saint John A.M.E. Church is located on Mill Street. The tower to the left of the facade and the pointed stained-glass windows give the structure a Gothic influence. (Photo courtesy of Dr. James Blake.)

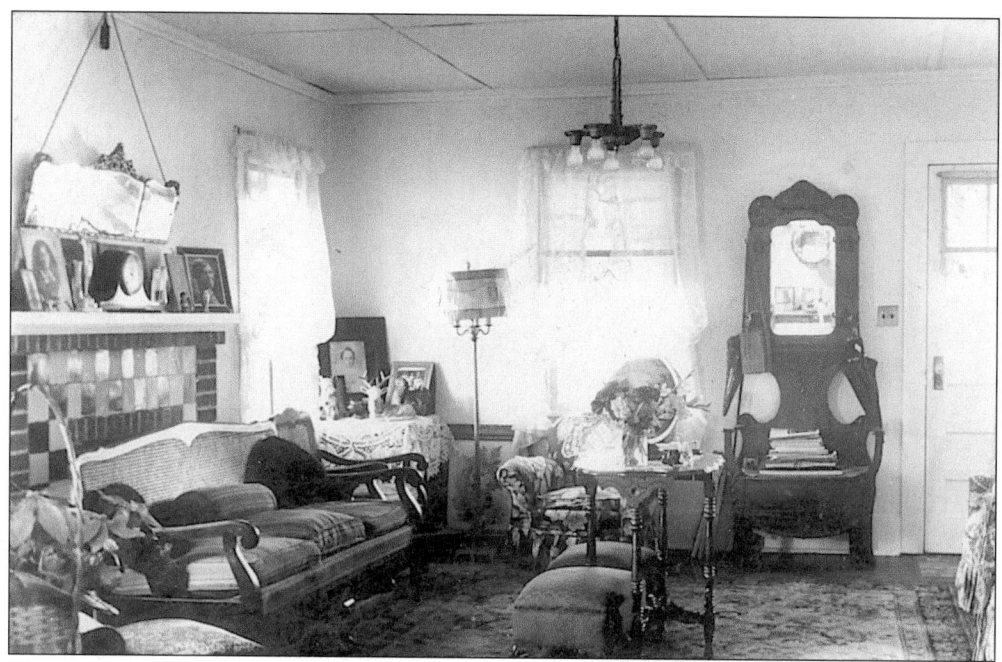

Illustrating home decor of the late 1920s is the interior of the Henry L. Jackson home on South Main Street. (Photo courtesy of Poiette McGill.)

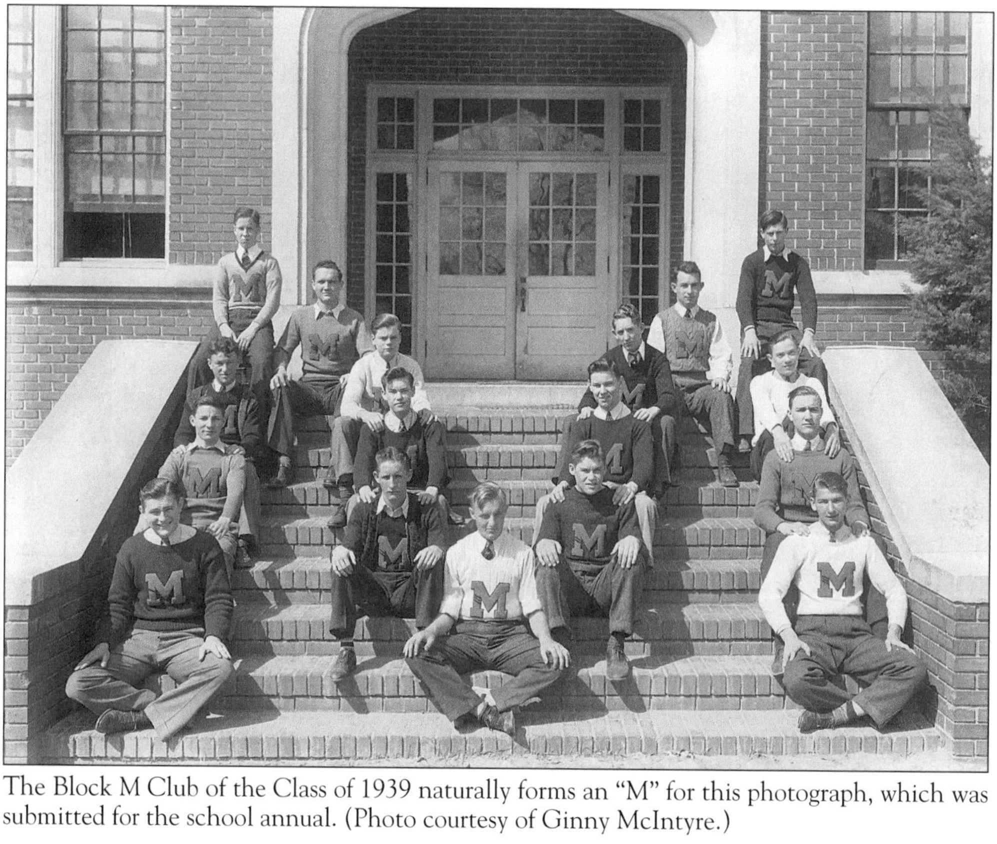

The Block M Club of the Class of 1939 naturally forms an "M" for this photograph, which was submitted for the school annual. (Photo courtesy of Ginny McIntyre.)

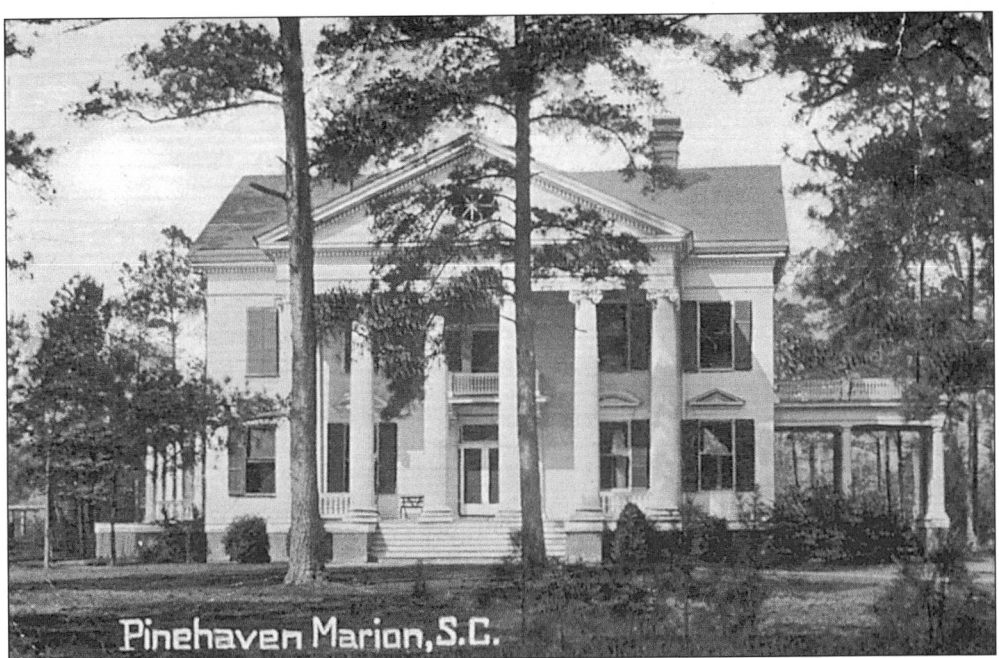

Pinehaven, the home of Judge Charles A. Woods, was built in the early 1900s on South Main Street and was torn down in later years to construct the home of Mr. and Mrs. Buddy Collins. (Photo courtesy of Margaret E. Wood.)

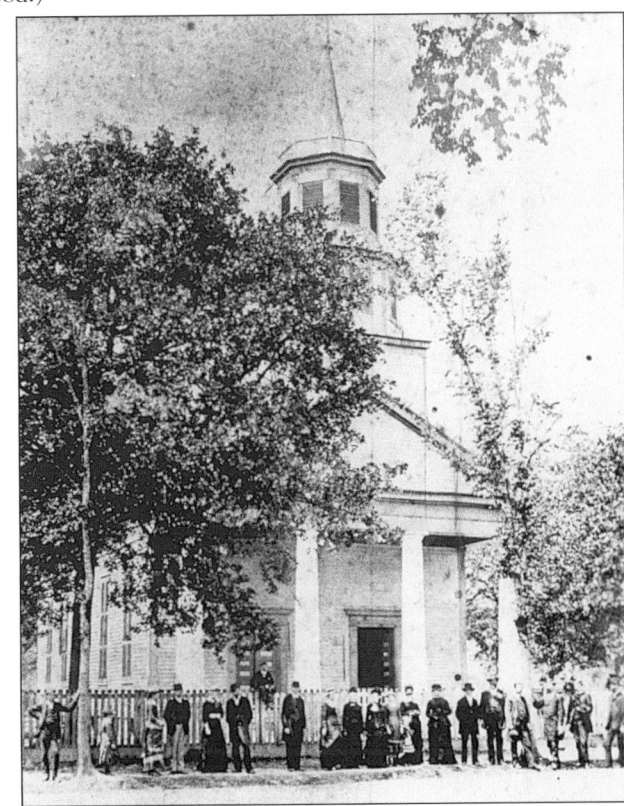

Here, remembering the Sabbath Day, are members of the Baptist Church on the southwest corner of Main and Baptist Streets. This church was built in 1851 and demolished when a new sanctuary was built in 1910 at the present site. (Photo courtesy of Suzanne Gasque McIntyre.)

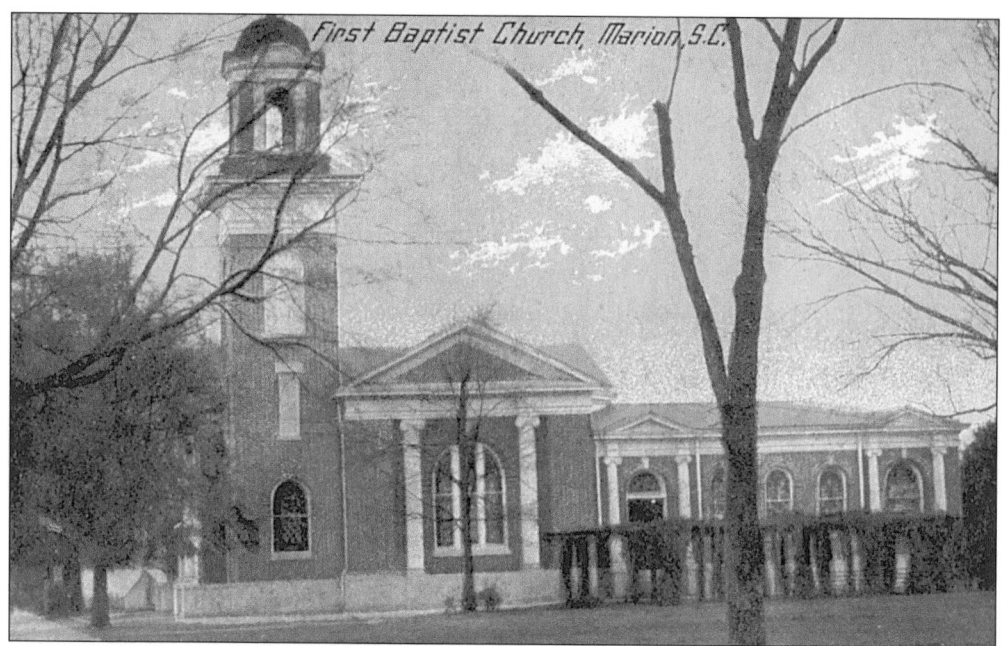

This First Baptist Church was built in 1910 at the present site and was torn down and replaced in 1966 with the present structure. (Photo courtesy of Valerie Baumrind Bonatis.)

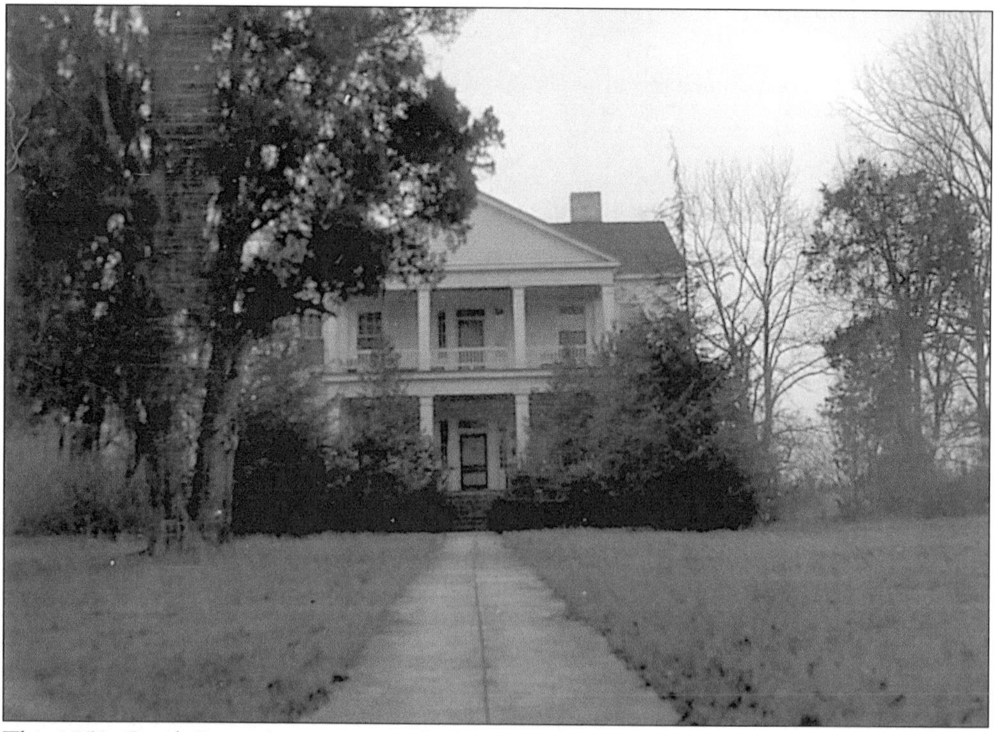

This 1850s Greek Revival structure was built on Presbyterian Street as a town house by Major S.F. Gibson. It was later purchased by George Norwood, who gave it to his daughter, Louisa N. Mullins, as a wedding gift. This house was destroyed by fire in the 1980s. (Photo courtesy of Mitzi Winesett.)

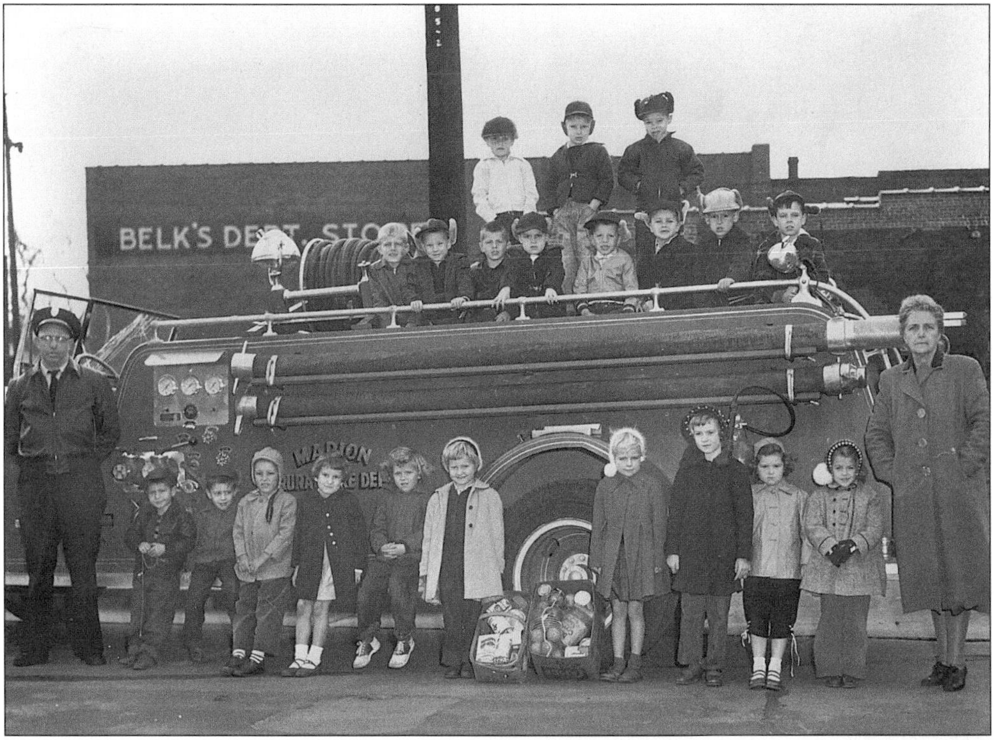

Mrs. Maggie Evans and her mid-1950s kindergarten class have been collecting food for Thanksgiving distribution. J.V. Rowell will reward them with a ride on the fire truck. (Photo by Lewis-Paige Studio; courtesy of Margaret E. Wood.)

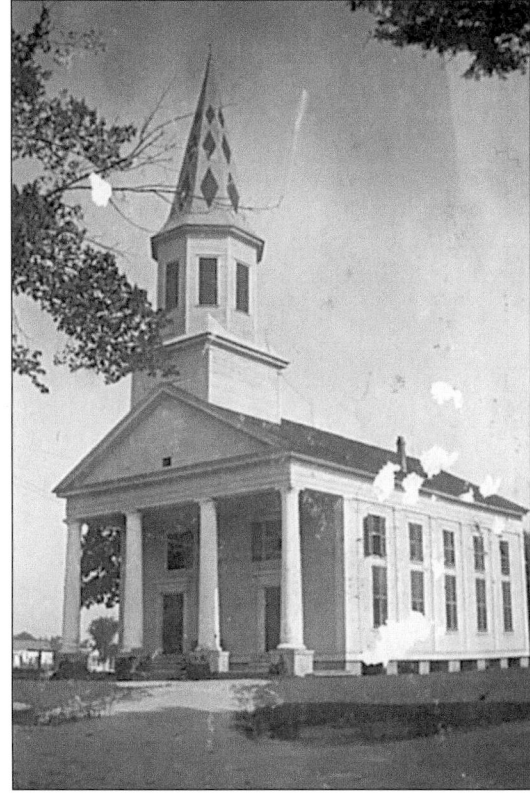

This early Marion Methodist Episcopal Church was completed in 1853 on the northwest corner of Godbold and Pine Streets. (Photo courtesy of Mike McLendon.)

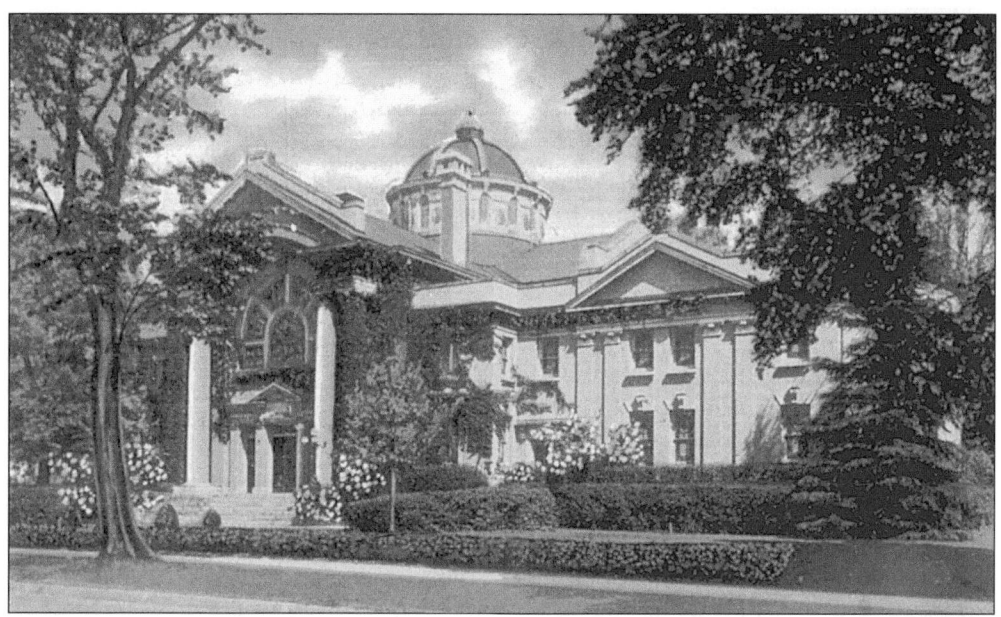

This 1957 photograph shows the Methodist Episcopal Church, which was built in 1912, before additions were made. (Photo courtesy of Valerie Baumrind Bonatis.)

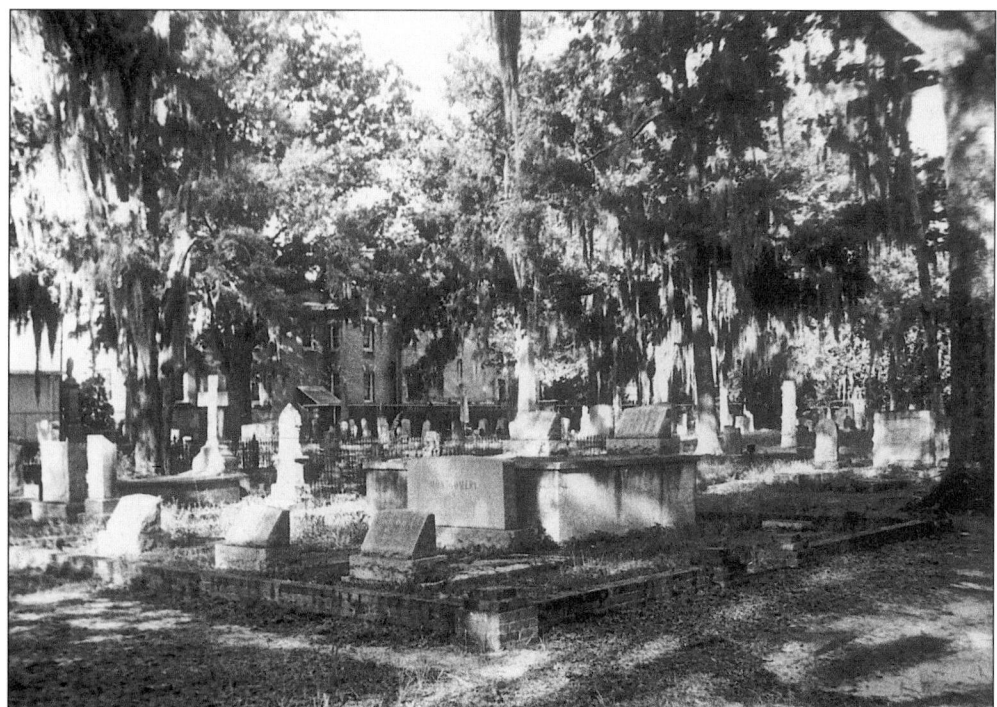

The Old Town Cemetery, or Old Marion Cemetery, is located behind the First United Methodist Church on the corner of Oak and Arch Streets. (Photo courtesy of Suzanne Gasque McIntyre.)

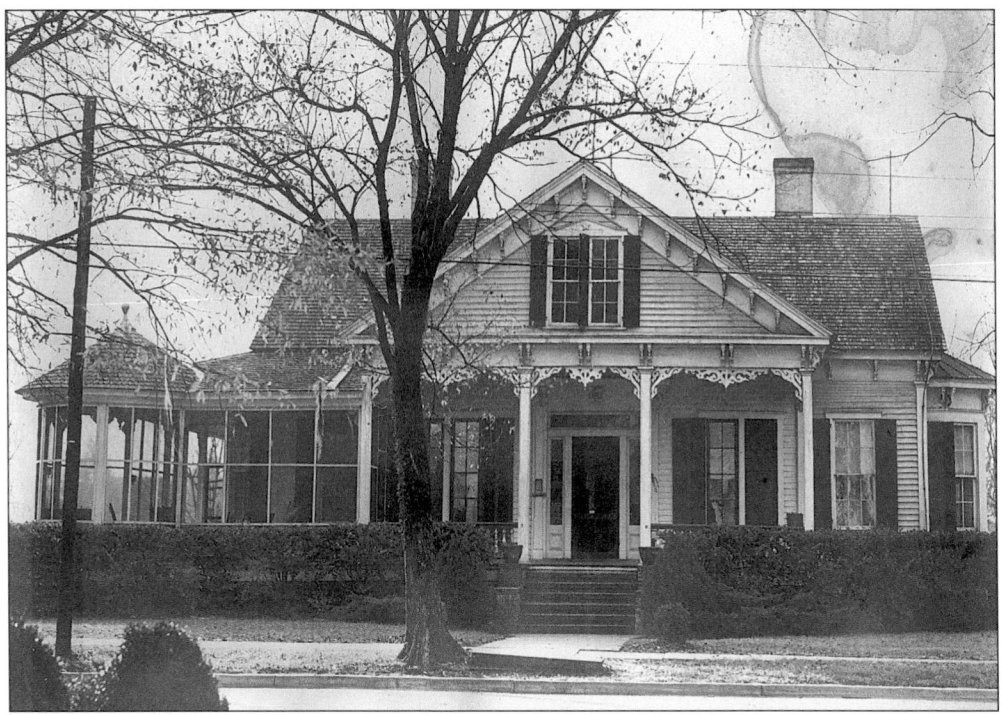

This home at 314 East Godbold Street was built in 1876 by Gabriella Owens and purchased in 1902 by Boyd Jones. (Photo courtesy of Billy Cornelius.)

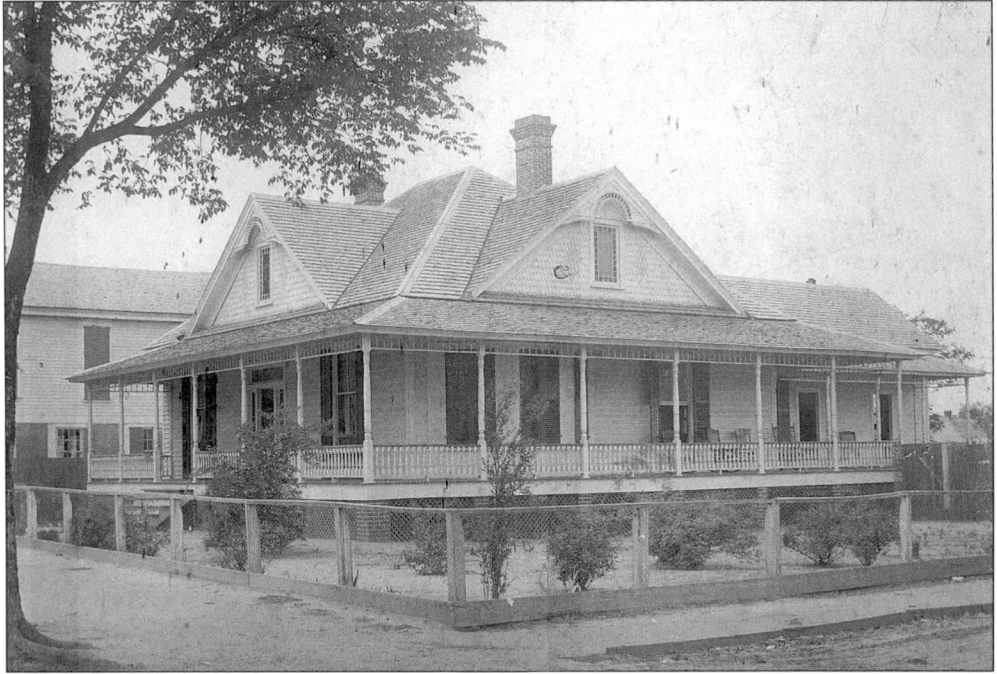

This Victorian cottage was the home of C.L. Pace at the corner of Godbold and Pine Streets prior to its burning. The Clinton Lodge can be seen in the background. (Photo courtesy of Rudy Pace.)

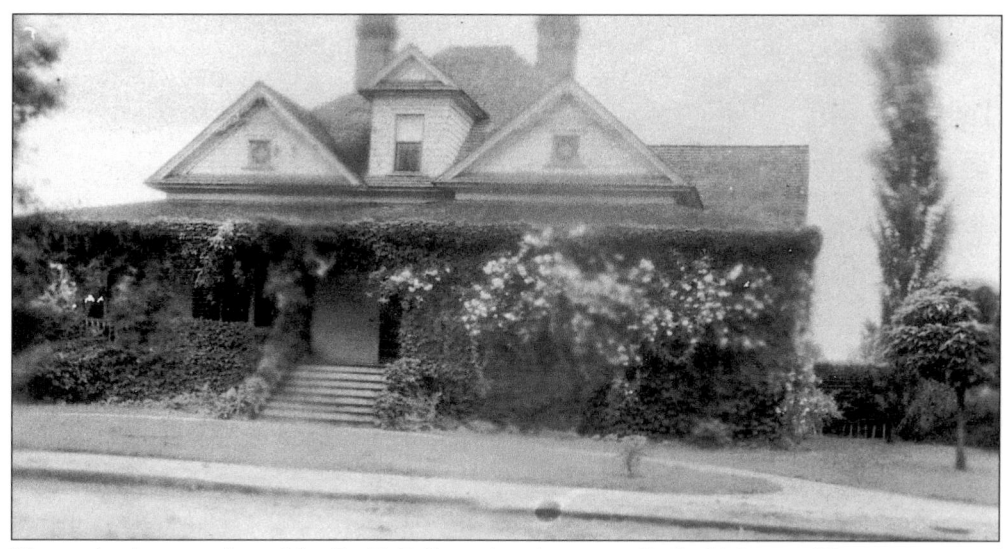

This early photograph is of the Dr. T.C. Easterling home on Godbold Street. (Photo courtesy of Suzanne Gasque McIntyre.)

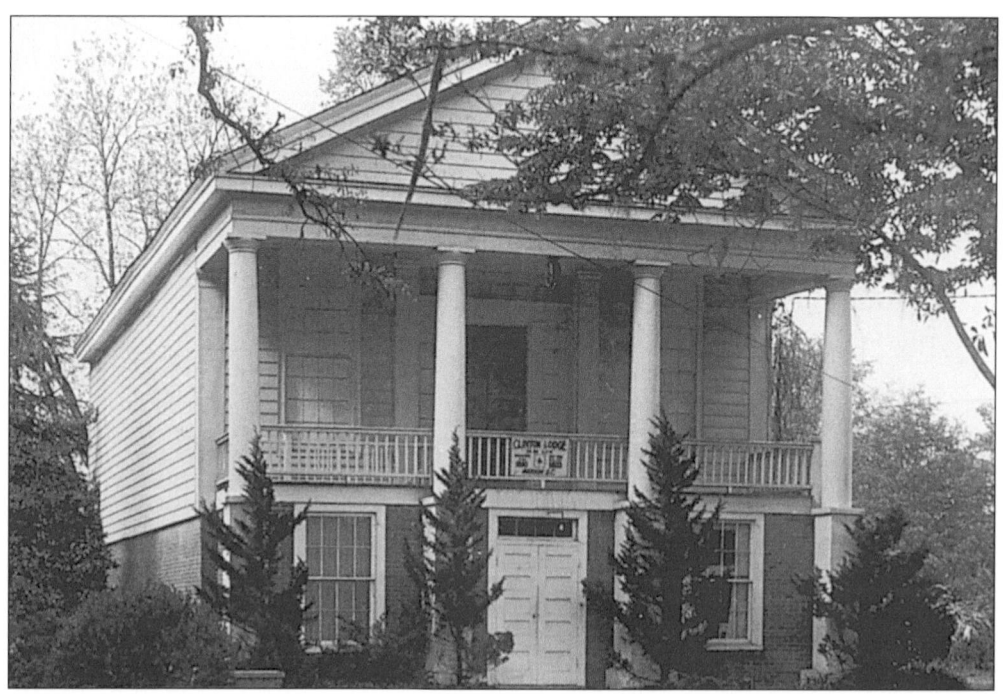

The Clinton Lodge at 203 East Godbold Street was erected from 1822 to 1823 on a lot deeded to Lodge No. 25 on October 8, 1822, by Thomas Godbold. The lodge was also used by the Marion Academy Society for classrooms in the late 1800s. (Photo courtesy of Libby Stanley.)

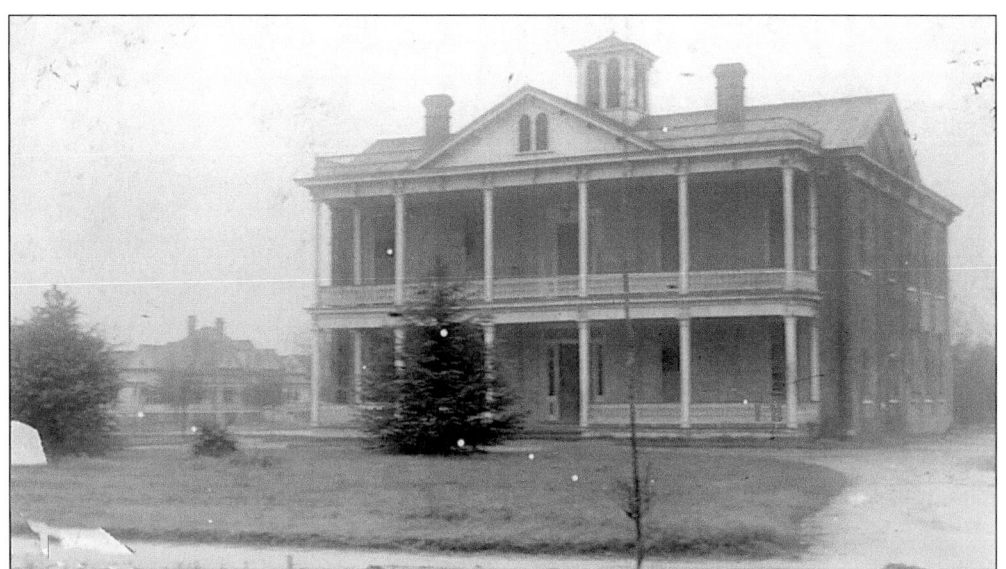

Built in 1886, the old Marion Academy became the first complete graded school in old Marion District. (Photo courtesy of Mike McLendon.)

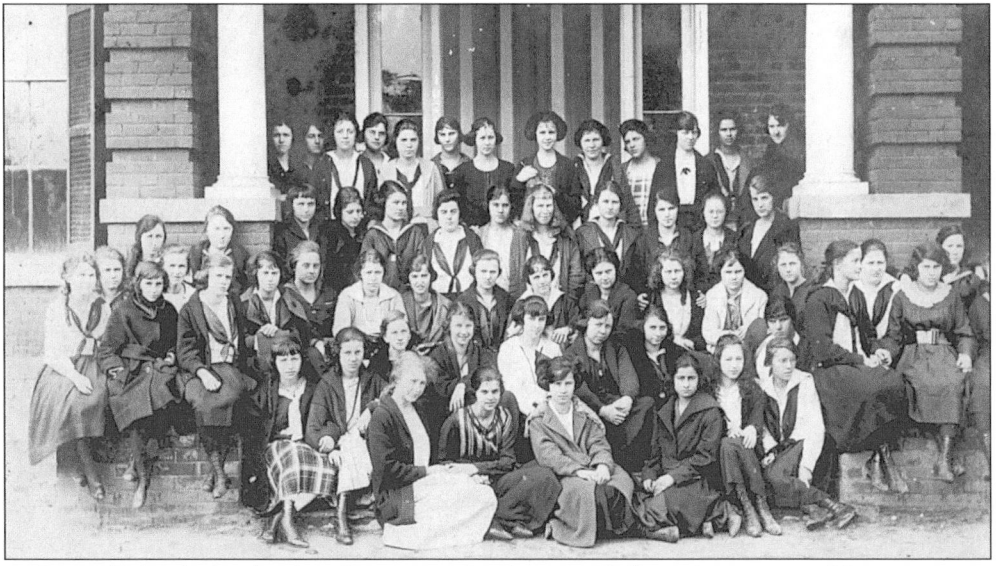

Girls enrolled in high school at the Marion Academy on Willcox Avenue posed for a picture in 1923. Those in the photograph include Helen McMillan, Jessie Stanley, Ella Davis, Hester Schulmeyer, Frances Porter, Lois Sidney Jones, Kakie Walker, Jessie Phillips, Thelma Hennecy, Gladys Jolly, Myrtle Smith, Ida Jane Mace, Mary Cross, Lou Norwood, Aura Phillips, Pearl White, Beulah Williams, Isla Williams, Iris Hennecy, Lillie Stalvey, Letha Mae Herring, Mary White, Alice Hodges, Hazel Brown, Mildred Rogers, Tattie Baker, Esther Soloman, Leila Stone, Gladys McLucas, Thelma Rogers, Paula Gasque, Mary Orr, Katherine Smith, H.B. Coleman, Tot Smith, Va Foxworth, Wilma Jenkins, Mary Davis, Louise Lupo, Ruby Braswell, Azilee Snipes, Esther Finger, Yetta Lienvand, Esther Shumacher, Libby Rogers, Polly Guerry, Helen Witcover, Margaret Guerry, Dora Herbert, Unie Davis, Catherine Layton, J.B. Pace, Elizabeth Rogers, Rhoda McDuffie, and Harriet McLellan. (Photo courtesy of Suzanne Gasque McIntyre.)

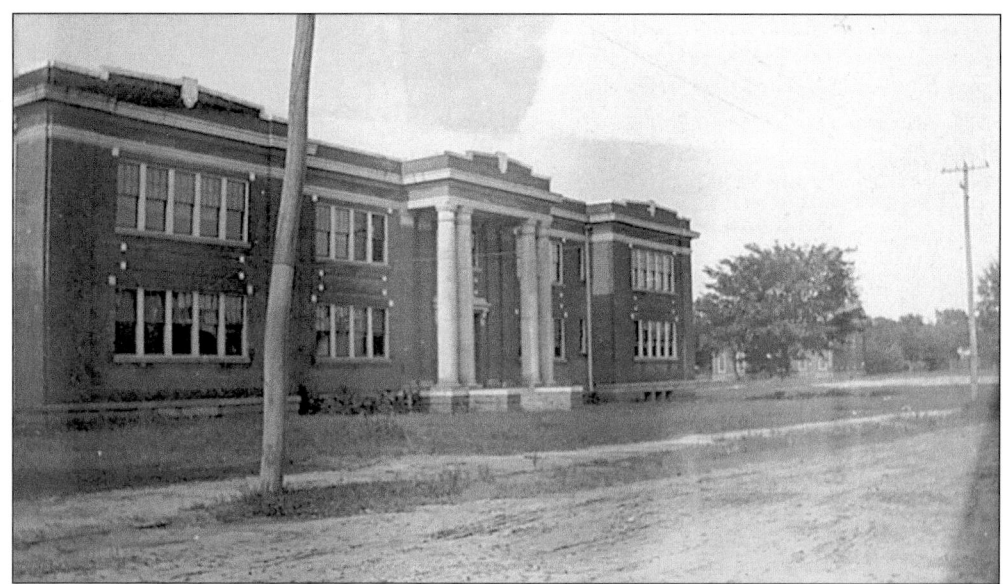

Marion Grammar School, built about 1905, stood on Godbold Street facing the end of Second Avenue. It was demolished in the 1970s. (Photo courtesy of Ginny McIntyre.)

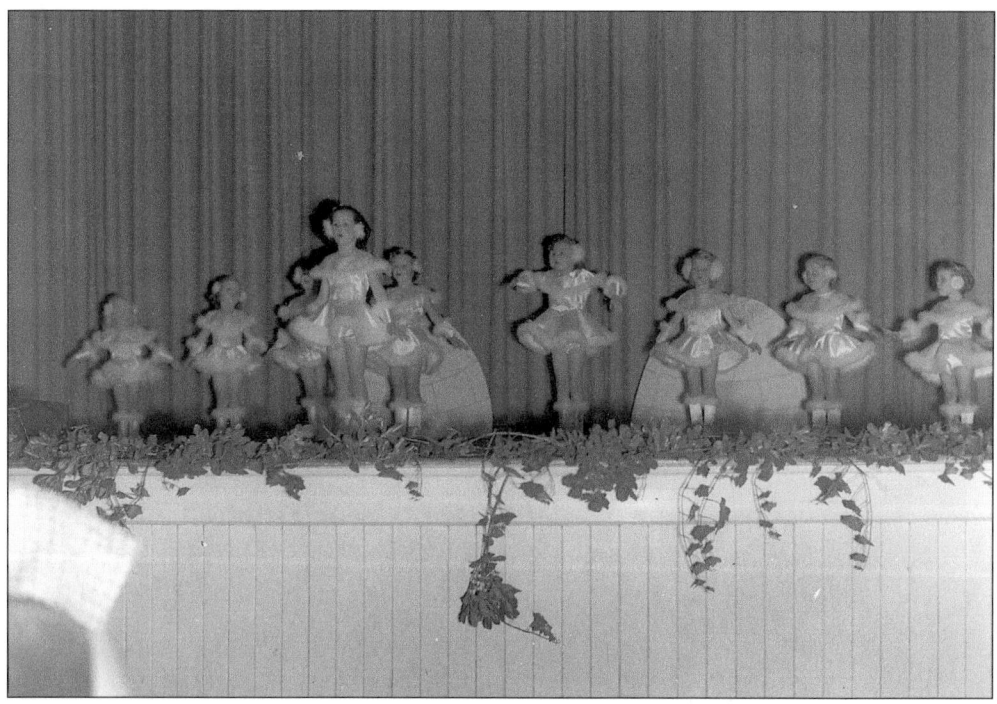

The Marion Grammar School Auditorium was the scene of many community activities from the time it was built in 1905 until it was demolished in the mid-1970s. (Photo courtesy LeeAnne E. Owens.)

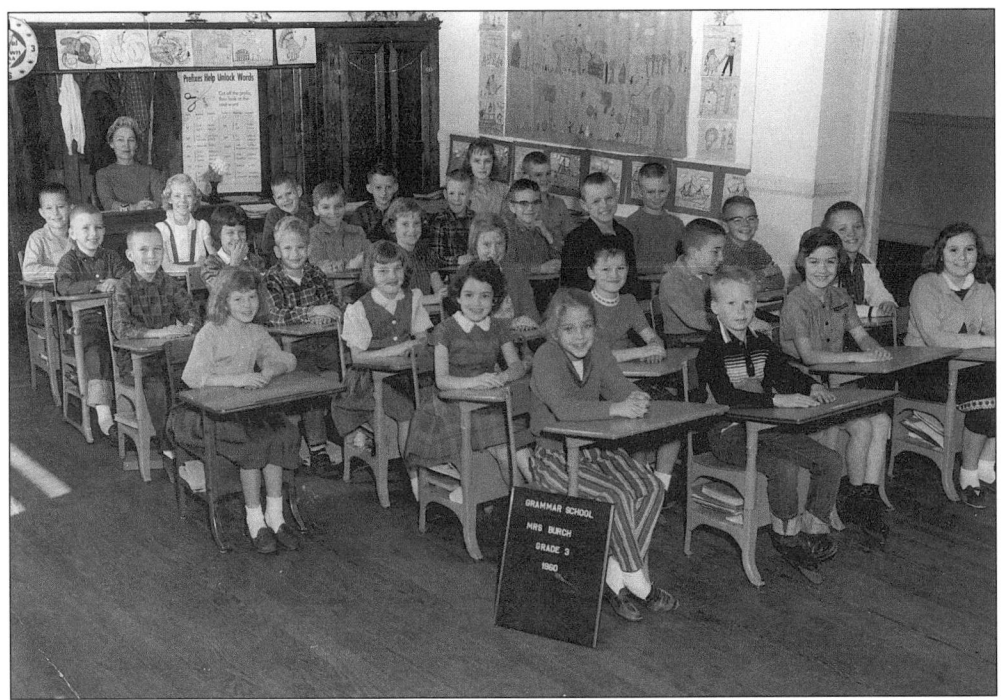

Mrs. Elizabeth Burch's third-grade class in 1960 features a typical classroom in Marion Grammar School. (Photo courtesy of Mike Jackson.)

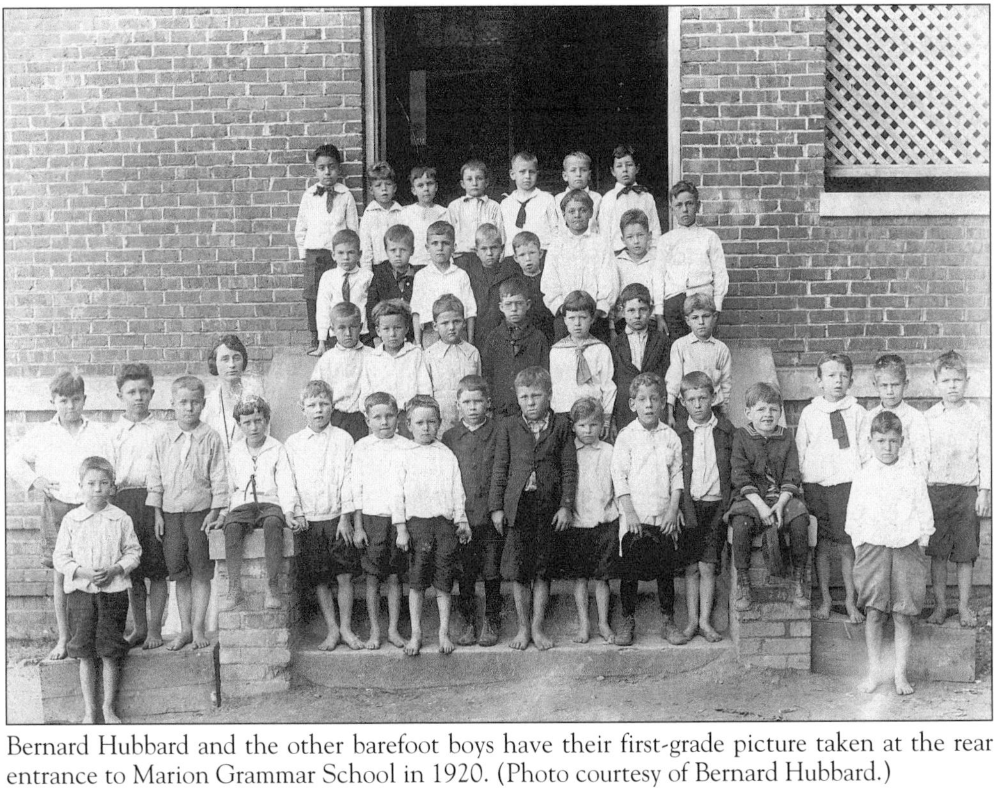

Bernard Hubbard and the other barefoot boys have their first-grade picture taken at the rear entrance to Marion Grammar School in 1920. (Photo courtesy of Bernard Hubbard.)

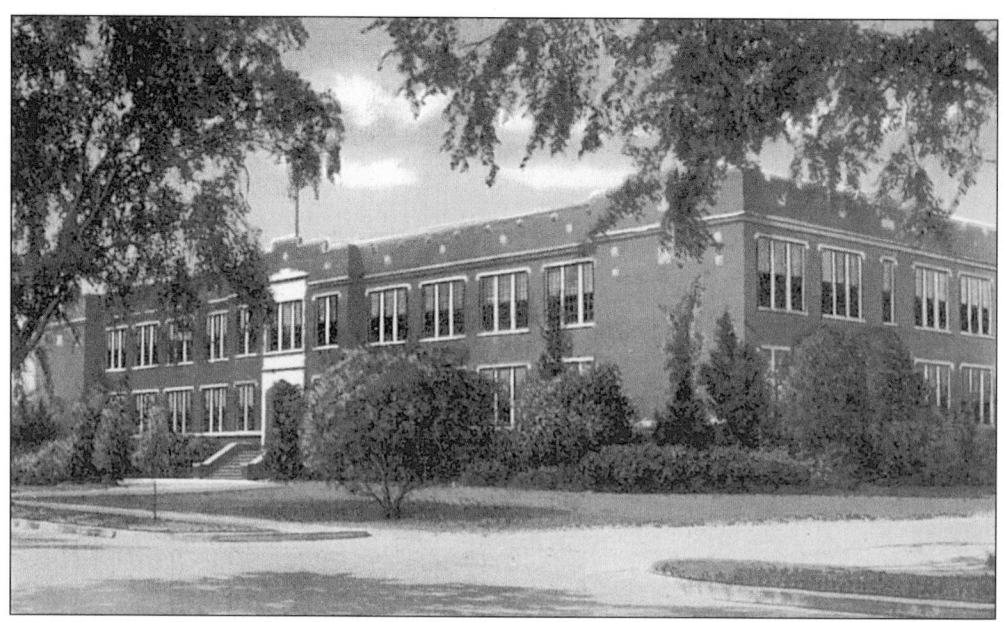

The Marion High School, at 719 North Main Street, opened in September 1924, with Dr. T.C. Easterling as superintendent and Mr. C.B. Seaborn as principal. (Photo courtesy of Valerie Baumrind Bonatis.)

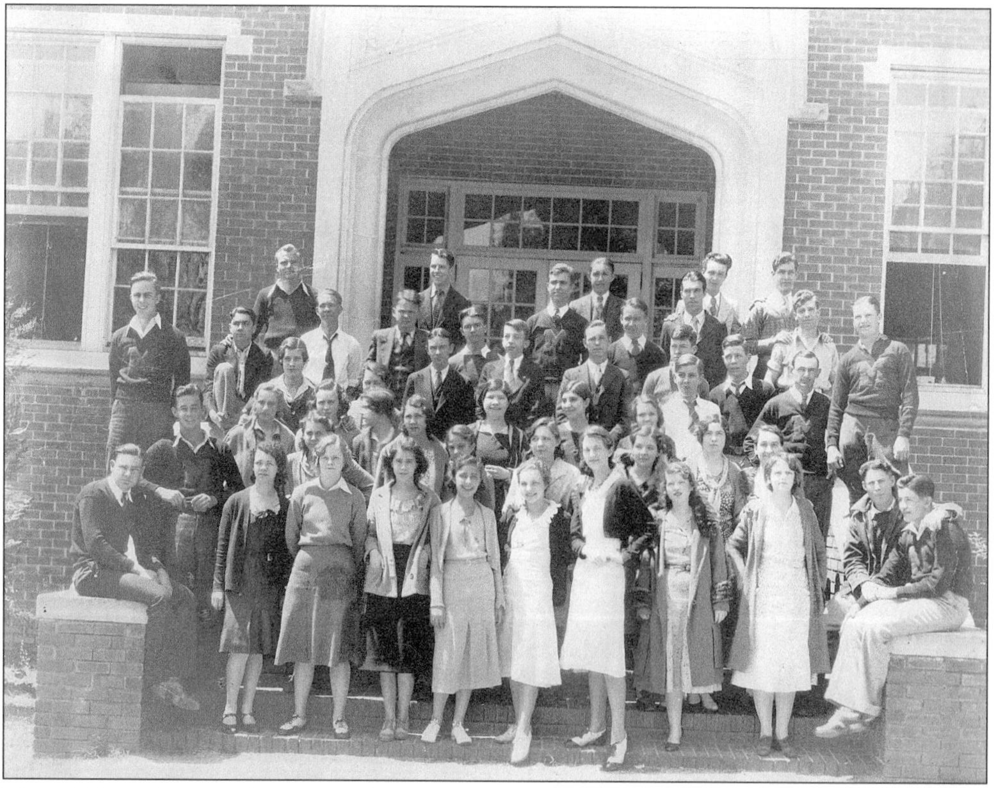

The 1934 graduation class poses (with shoes on) in front of Marion High School. (Photo courtesy of Bernard Hubbard.)

The Marion Training School Commencement Invitation (right) heralds the graduates of the Class of 1928. Principal D.C. McDuffie and Superintendent T.C. Easterling congratulated and delivered diplomas to 21 proud graduates of the Marion Training School. (Photo courtesy of Dr. James Blake.)

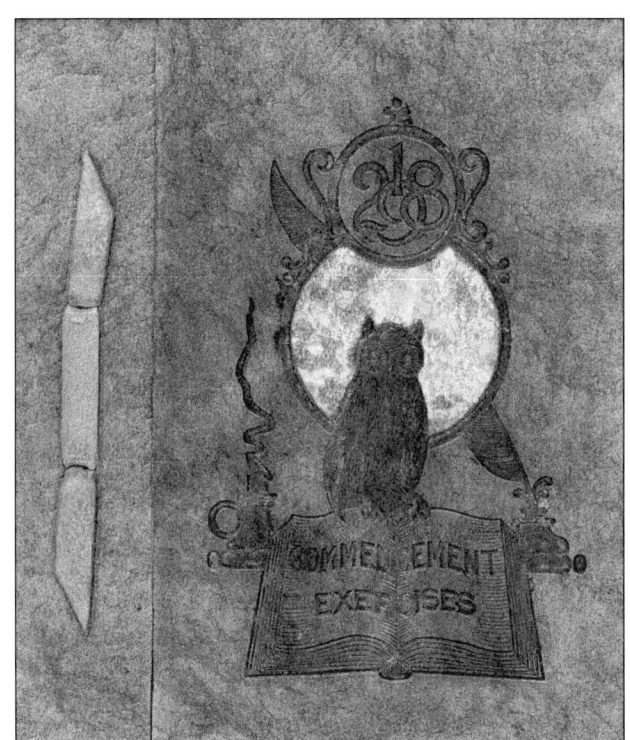

𝕿𝖍𝖊 𝕾𝖊𝖓𝖎𝖔𝖗 𝕮𝖑𝖆𝖘𝖘 𝖔𝖋

𝕿𝖍𝖊 𝕸𝖆𝖗𝖎𝖔𝖓 𝕮𝖔𝖚𝖓𝖙𝖞

𝕿𝖗𝖆𝖎𝖓𝖎𝖓𝖌 𝕾𝖈𝖍𝖔𝖔𝖑

𝖗𝖊𝖖𝖚𝖊𝖘𝖙𝖘 𝖞𝖔𝖚𝖗 𝖕𝖗𝖊𝖘𝖊𝖓𝖈𝖊 𝖆𝖙 𝖙𝖍𝖊

𝕮𝖔𝖒𝖒𝖊𝖓𝖈𝖊𝖒𝖊𝖓𝖙 𝕰𝖝𝖊𝖗𝖈𝖎𝖘𝖊𝖘

𝕱𝖗𝖎𝖉𝖆𝖞 𝖊𝖛𝖊𝖓𝖎𝖓𝖌, 𝕸𝖆𝖞 𝖊𝖑𝖊𝖛𝖊𝖓𝖙𝖍

𝖆𝖙 𝖊𝖎𝖌𝖍𝖙 𝖔'𝖈𝖑𝖔𝖈𝖐

𝕾𝖈𝖍𝖔𝖔𝖑 𝕬𝖚𝖉𝖎𝖙𝖔𝖗𝖎𝖚𝖒

CLASS MOTTO:
We finish to begin

CLASS COLORS: CLASS FLOWER:
Silver and Old Rose   Carnation

CLASS ROLL:
Lucy Black
William Freeman Braddy
Laura Mae Cannon
Lillie Altuise Coleman
Claudia Louise Donelley
Mildred Thelma Frierson
Roberta Eugenia Gregg
Bernice Beulah Hagins
Katherine Johnson
Lurena Johnson
Marion Augustus McCall
Lillian Mae Nichols
Ella Nora Robinson
Fleetie Louise Scott
Charles Arcarles Smith
Clara Belle Sparrow
Ada Christine Thomas
Clara Belle Thompson
Frederick Woodrow Wilson
Lanneau White
Reatha Beatrice Woodberry

Principal, D. C. McDuffie
Superintendent, T. C. Easterling

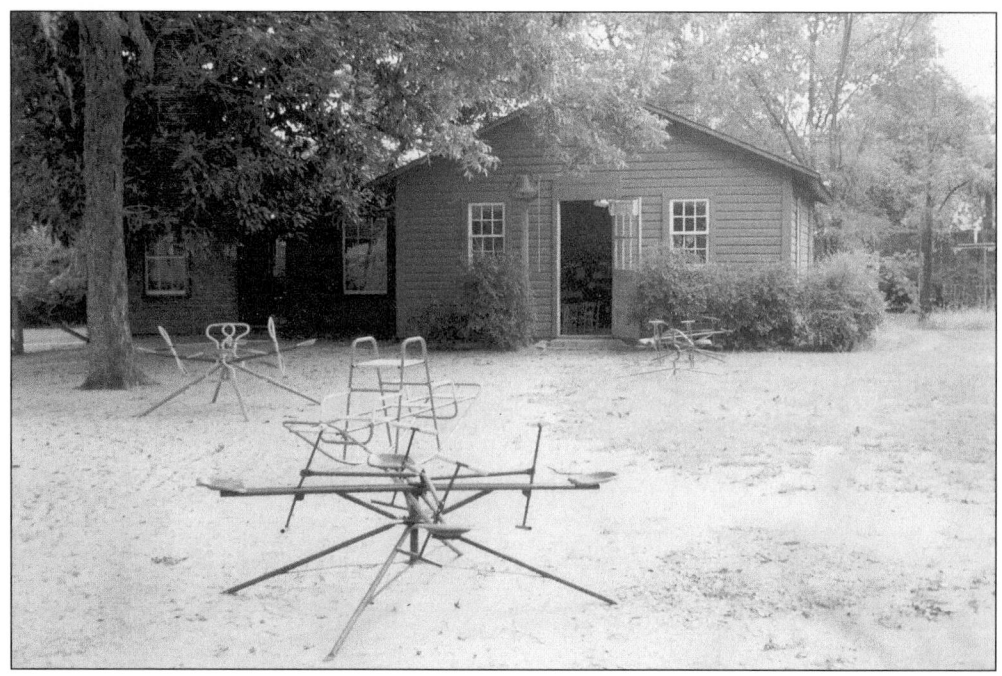

All the children have gone home from the Little Red School House on Railroad Avenue, where Mrs. Maggie Evans had a busy day teaching kindergarten. Mrs. Evans operated a kindergarten from 1948 until 1971. (Photo courtesy of Margaret E. Wood.)

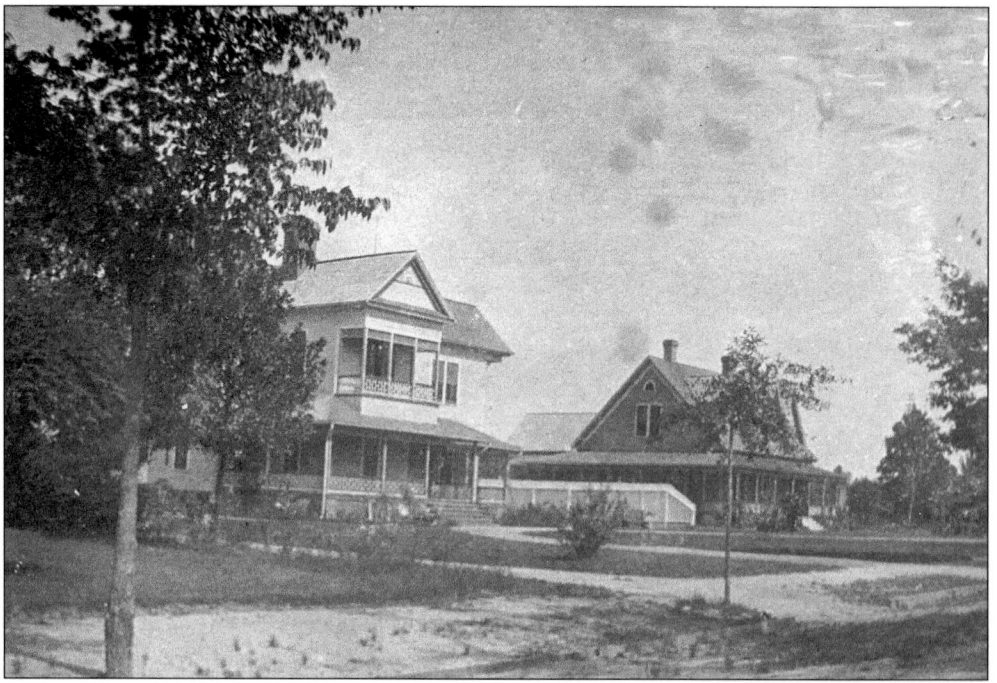

These two large Victorian homes on Willcox, built c. 1898 and c. 1900s (left to right), belonged to Mr. James Johnson and Mrs. Walter Stackhouse, respectively. (Photo courtesy of Suzanne Gasque McIntyre.)

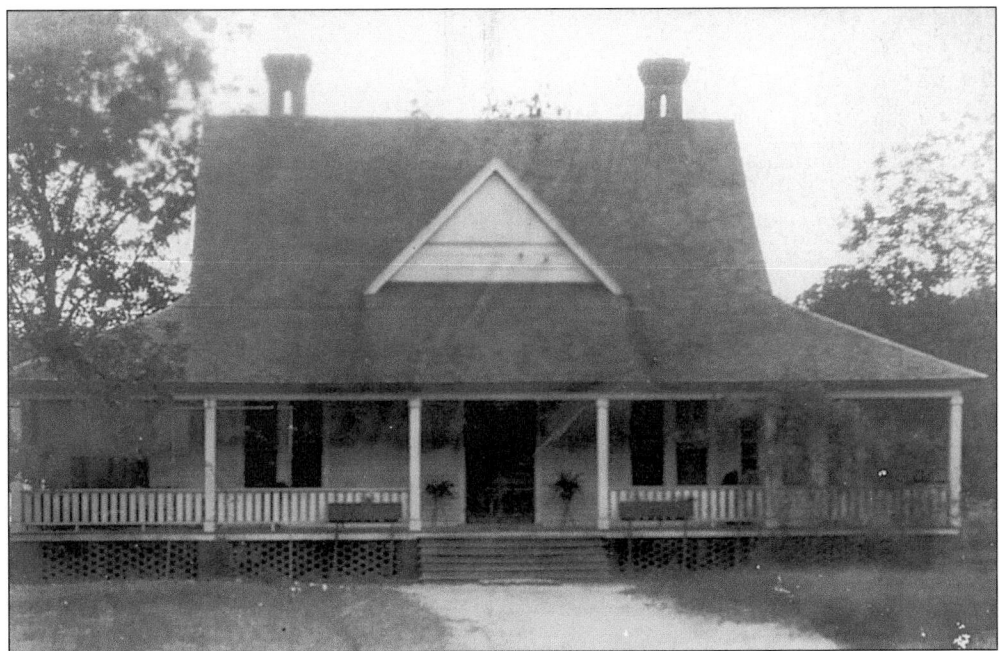

This home at 307 Willcox Avenue was built in 1889 by John Willcox and was later sold to David Albert Layton. (Photo courtesy of Margaret E. Wood.)

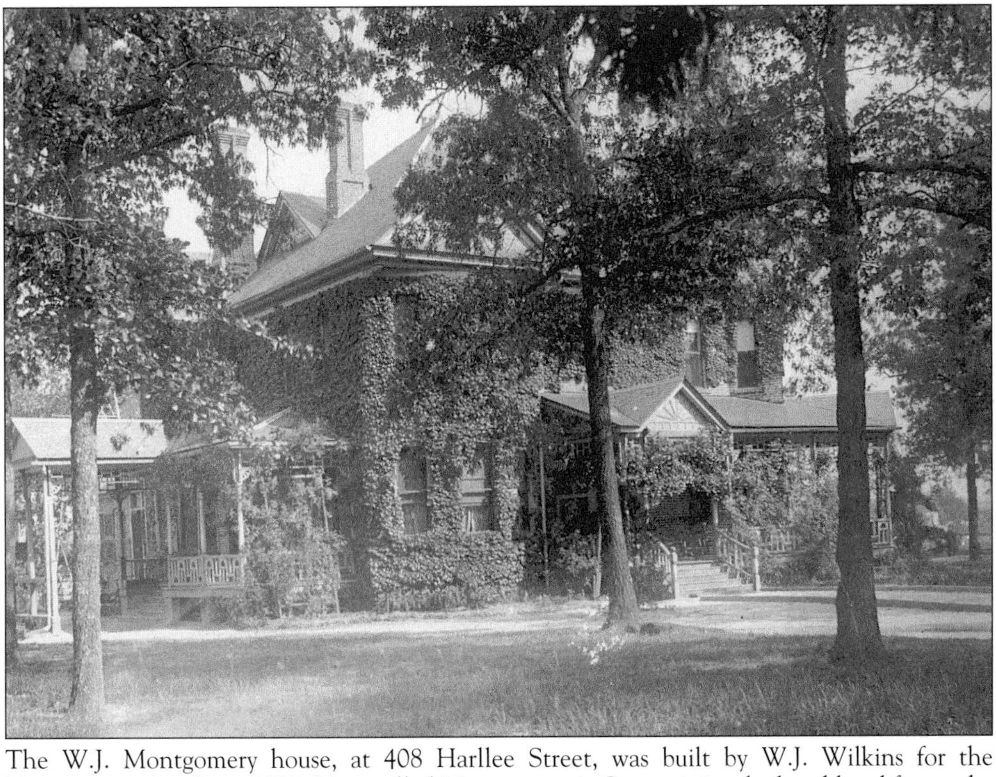

The W.J. Montgomery house, at 408 Harllee Street, was built by W.J. Wilkins for the Montgomery family in 1893. Now called Montgomery's Grove, it is a bed and breakfast and a beautiful example of Eastlake architecture. (Photo courtesy of Rick and Coreen Roberts.)

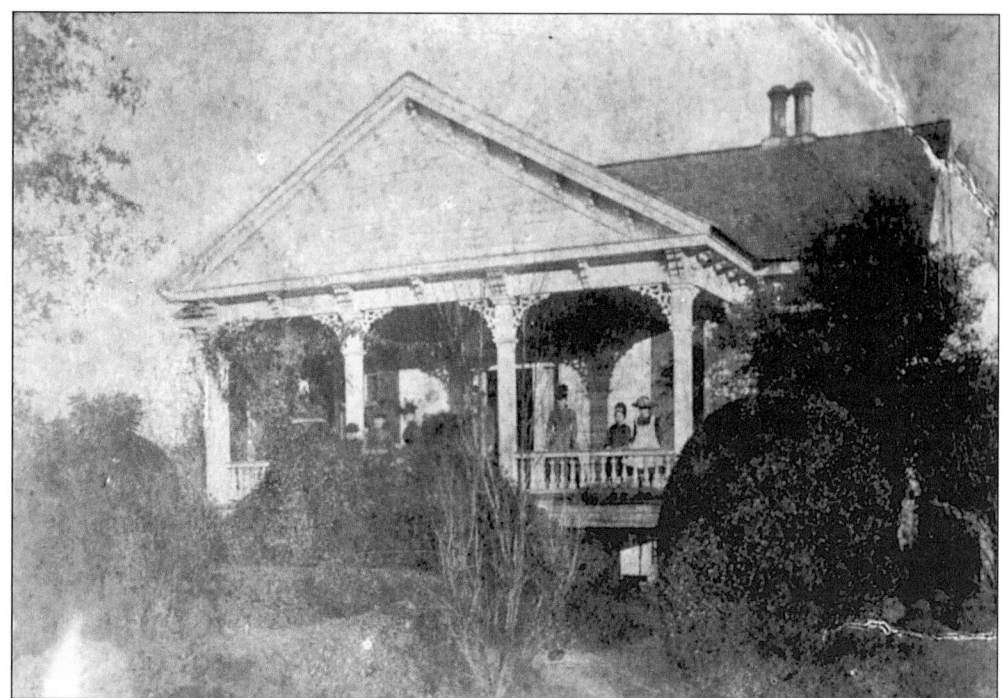

This home at 100 East Court Street, built in 1829 by Mary Hillen, was purchased by Captain Archibald and Sophia Howard McIntyre in 1830. J. Preston Davis purchased the house in 1880. Judge and Mrs. L.D. Lide bought it in 1922 and remodeled it in bungalow style. (Photo courtesy of Maxcy Foxworth.)

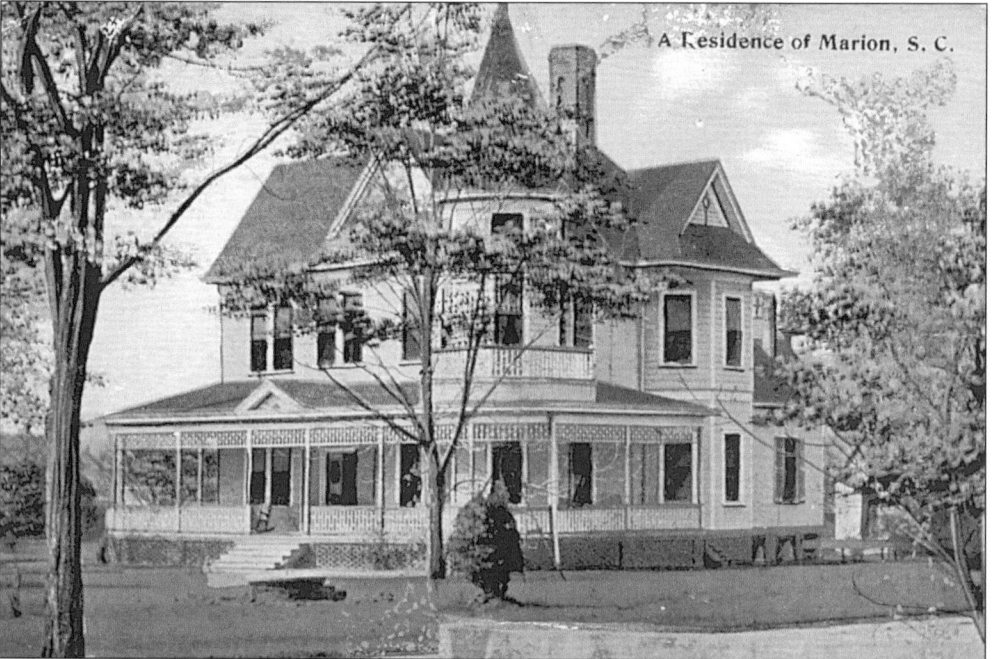

The E.T. Willcox house at 311 Willcox Avenue was built in 1893 and is a fine example of the Elizabethan style of Victorian architecture. (Photo courtesy of James and Nita Neely.)

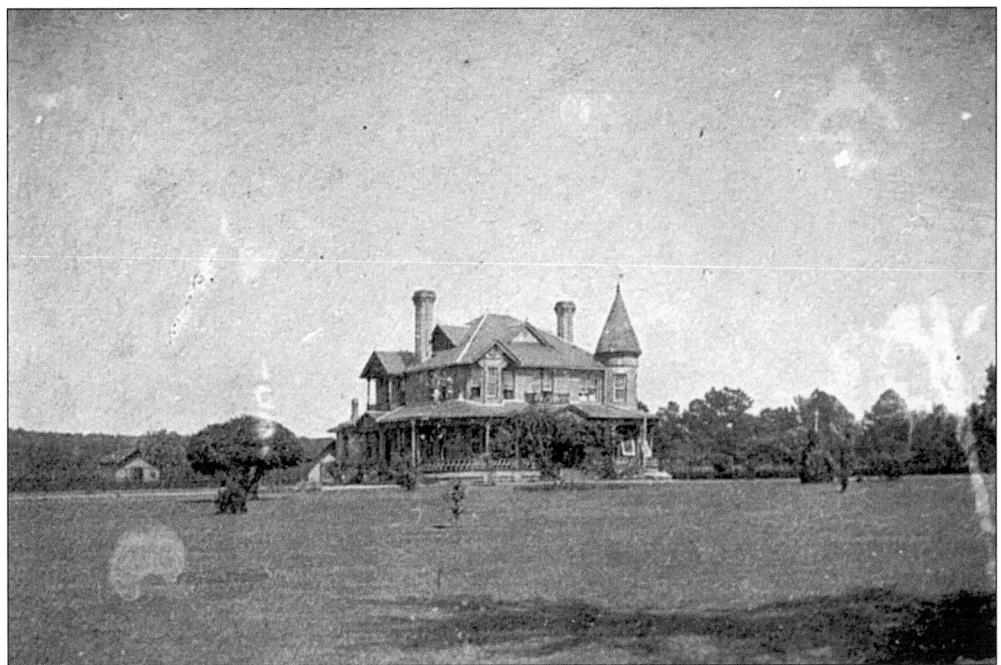

The Jesse Gray Holliday house on Willcox Avenue was built in 1895 and was said to have been the prettiest place on the railway between Wilmington and Columbia. It is presently Smith-Collins Funeral Home. (Photo courtesy of Suzanne Gasque McIntyre.)

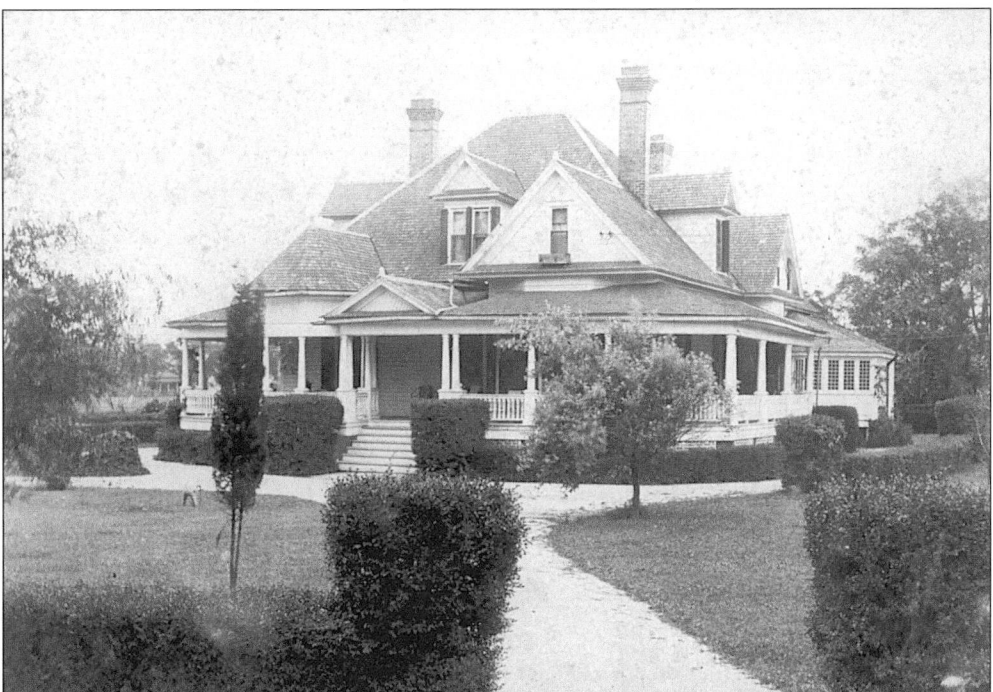

This impressive structure, also known as the Josie Dubose home, was the home of I.T. Wood at the corner of Willcox and Railroad Avenue before it burned. (Photo courtesy of Margaret E. Wood.)

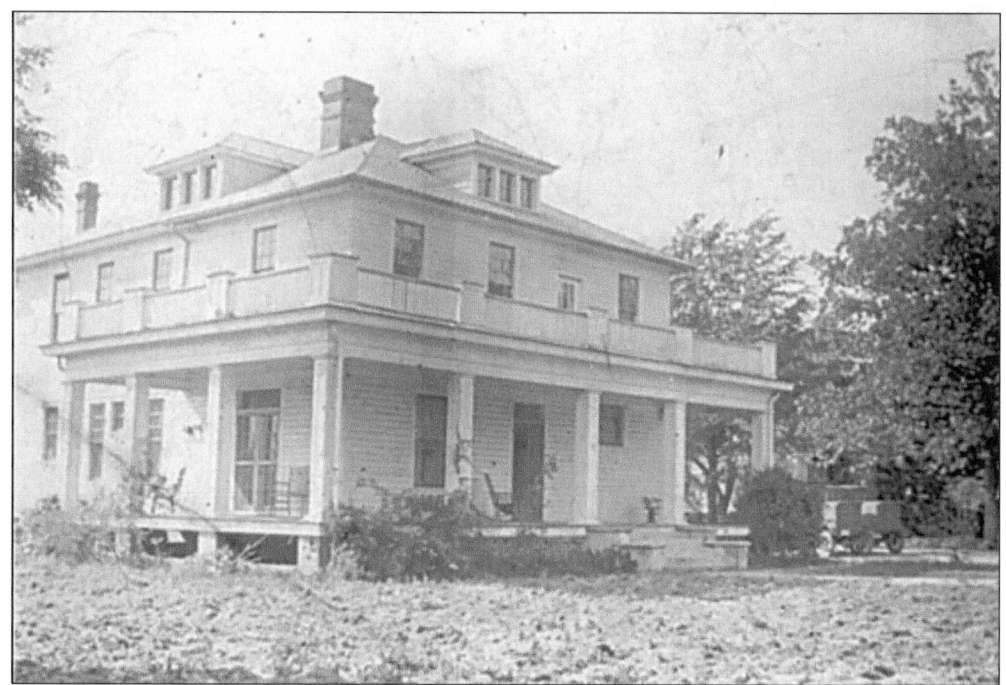

This is the home of Mr. and Mrs. Ben Mullins Jr. on North Main Street. The house has been in the family since it was built in 1913. (Photo courtesy of Ben and Beth Mullins.)

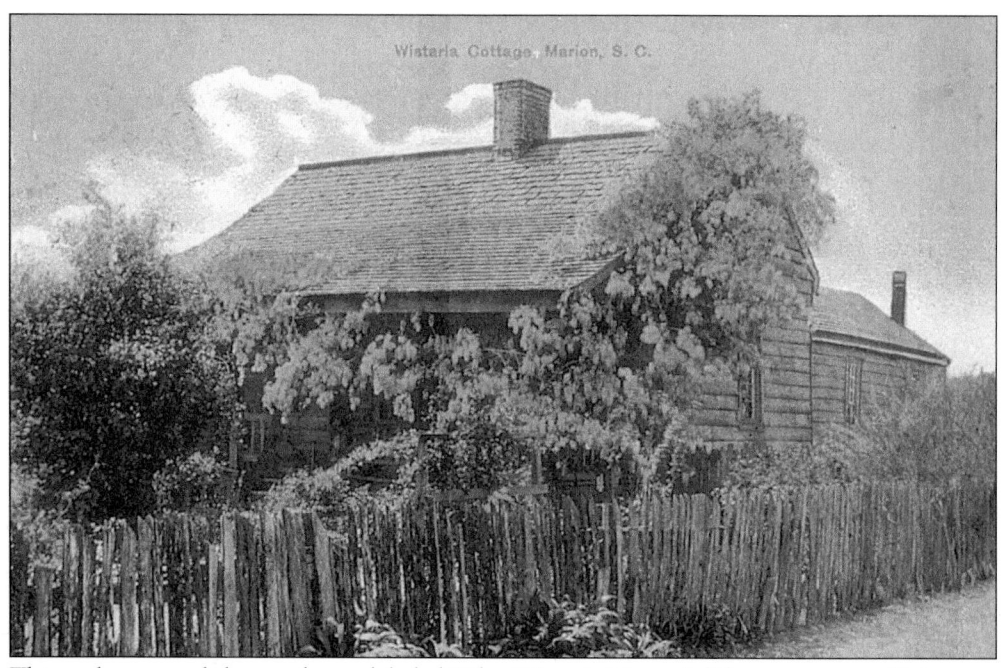

This early postcard shows a house labeled "The Wisteria House." (Photo courtesy of Margaret E. Wood.)

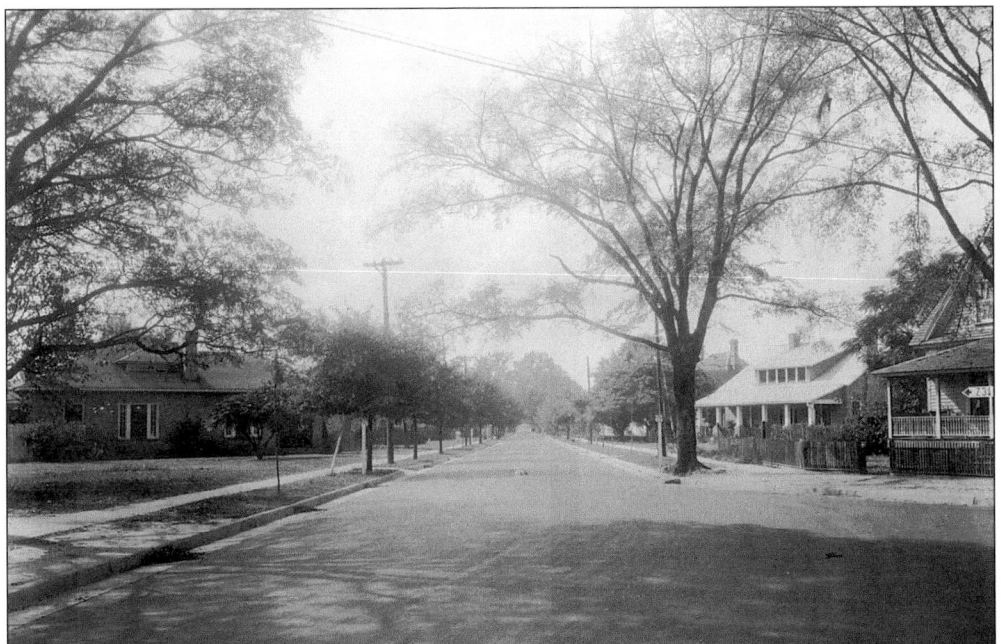

Looking southwest down Dunlop Street from Godbold is the home of the late Mr. and Mrs. Duncan McIntyre on the left. On the right is the home of the late Mr. and Mrs. Wesley Gregg and the home of the late Mr. and Mrs. Ernest Gresham. (Photo courtesy of Ginny McIntyre.)

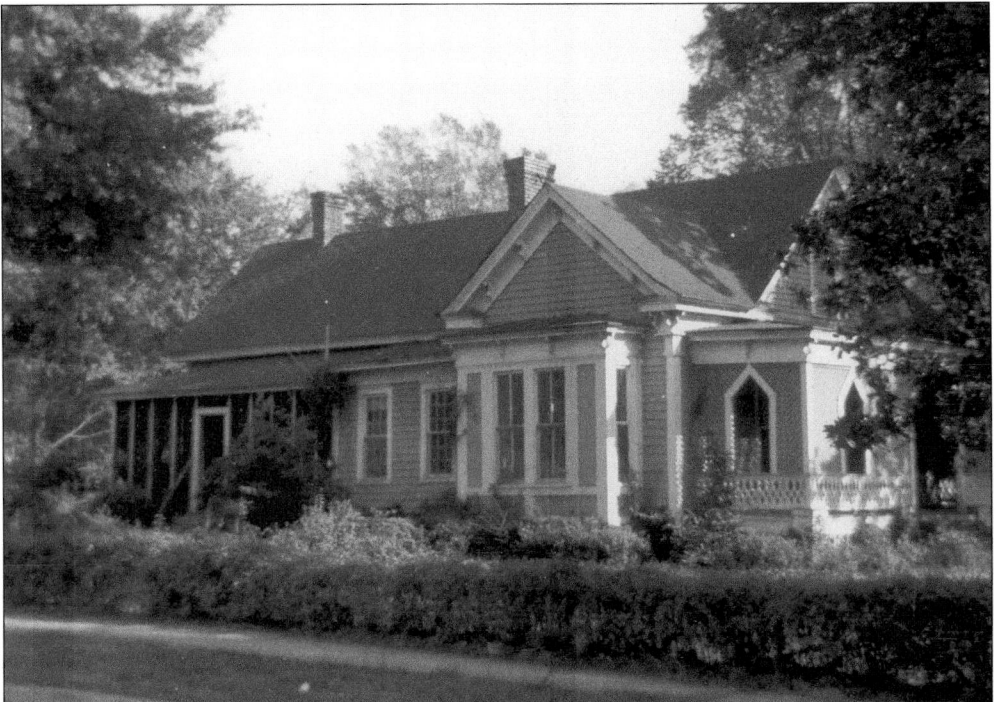

Dr. James Cade Mullins came to Marion from Fayetteville, North Carolina, in the mid-1800s and extensively remodeled this older house on South Main Street where the post office is now located. (Photo courtesy of Maxcy Foxworth.)

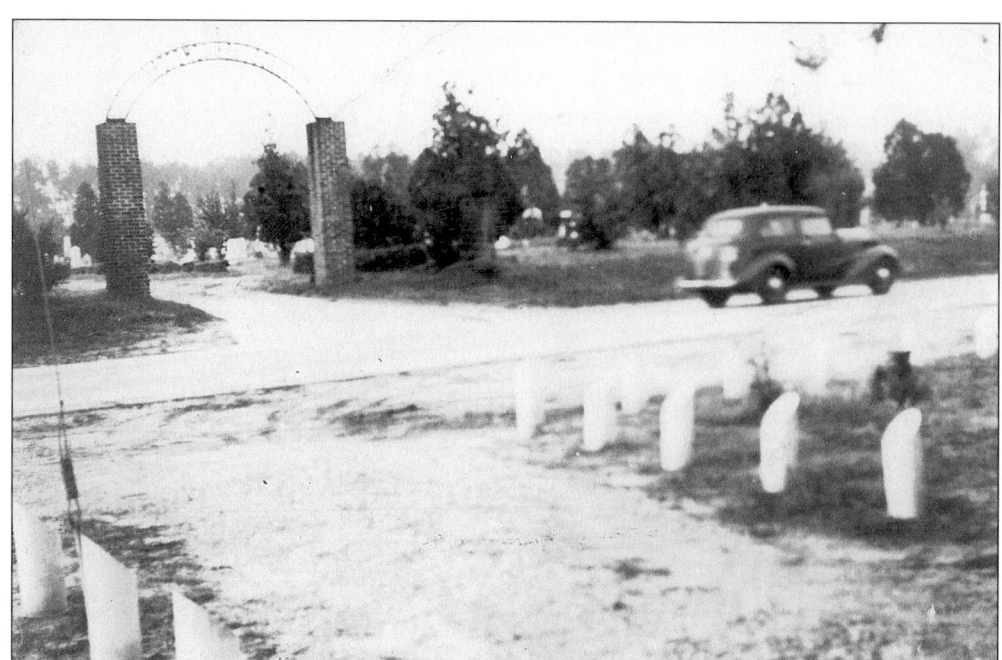

This early photograph is of the entrance to Rose Hill Cemetery. (Photo courtesy of Mitzi Winesett.)

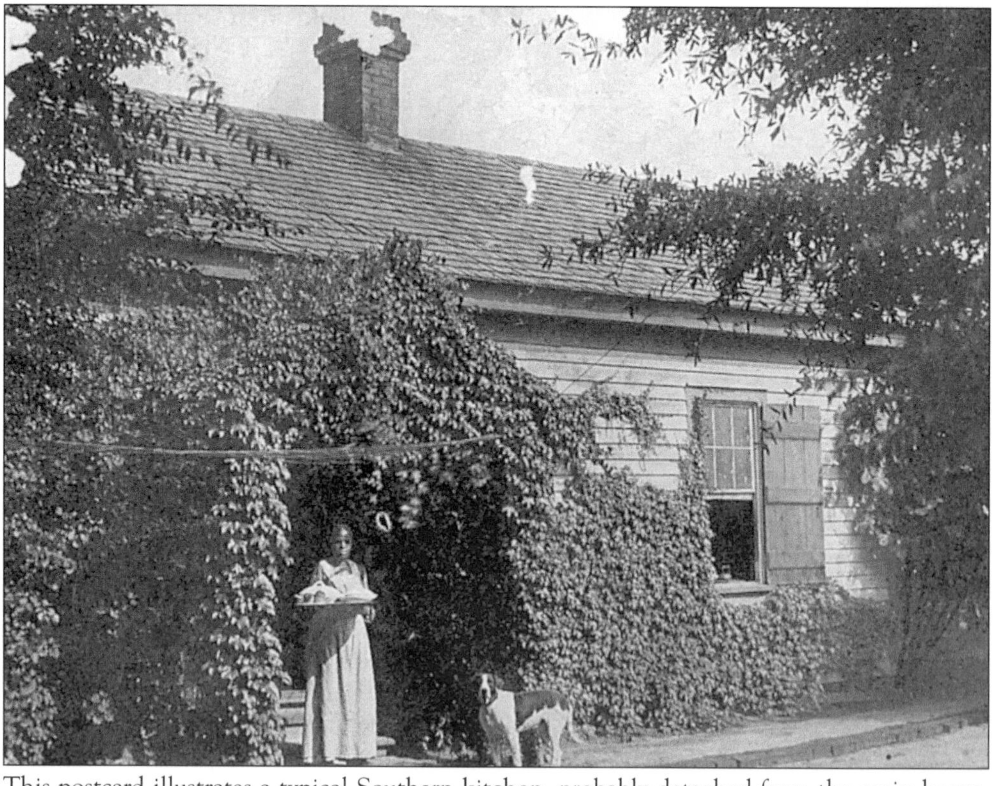

This postcard illustrates a typical Southern kitchen, probably detached from the main house. (Photo courtesy of Charlie Levy.)

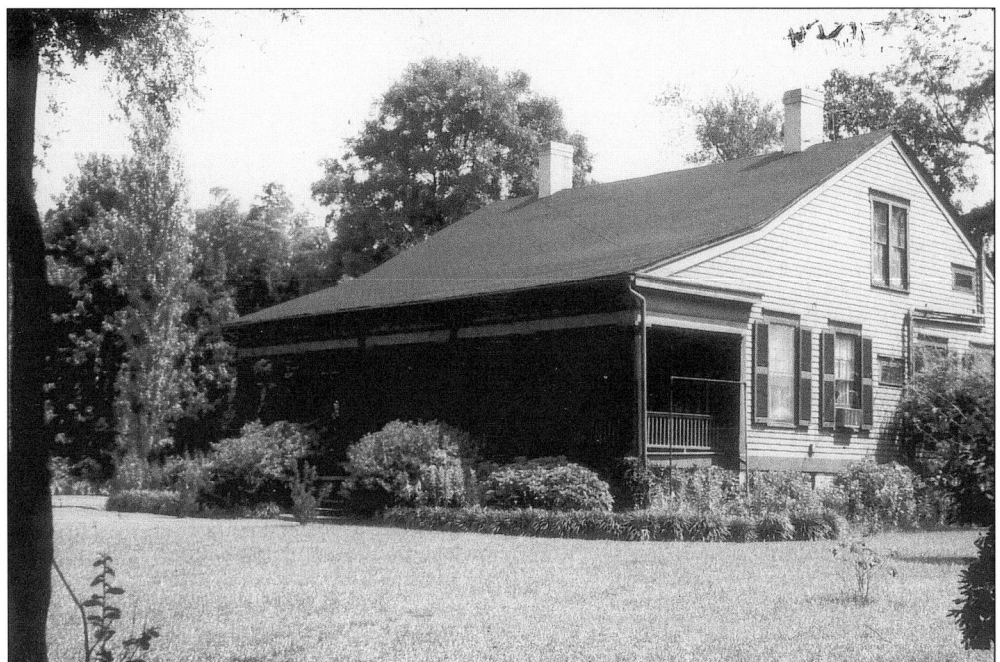

The Young-Johnson house on East Godbold Street was built by Major Johnson Blakely Young in the 1850s and was later the home of Colonel Monroe Johnson of the Rainbow Division. The Colonel's wife, Helen Barnwell Johnson, planted a poppy garden behind the house with seed from Flanders Field. (Photo courtesy of Maxcy Foxworth.)

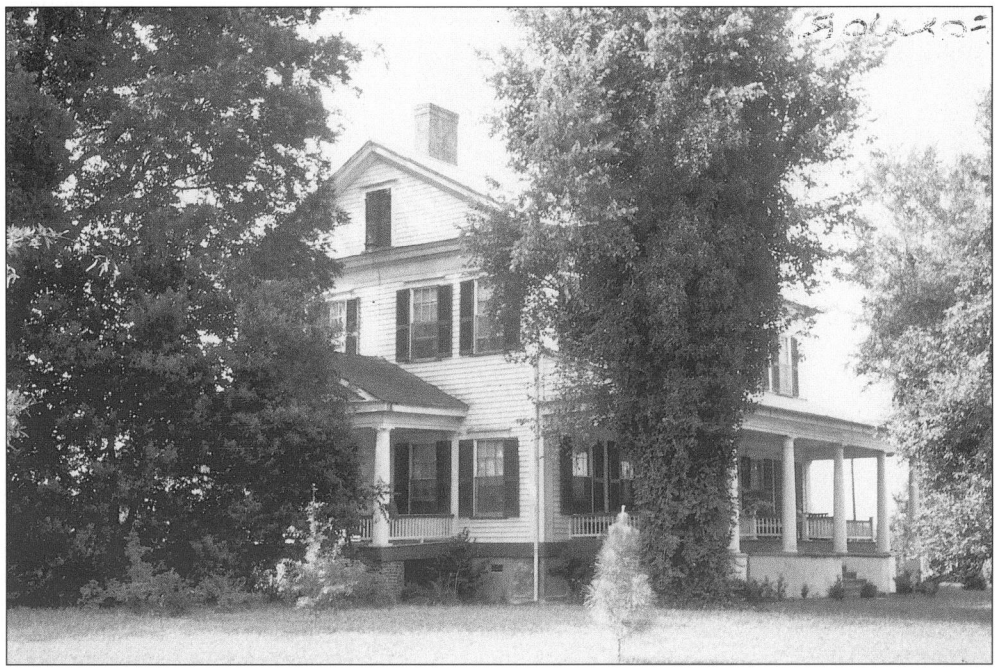

Oak Hall, just north of Marion, was built c. 1850 by William James Dickson for General William Evans. In front stood the Asbury oak, beneath which Methodism was begun in the Pee Dee by Bishop Francis Asbury. (Photo courtesy of Maxcy Foxworth.)

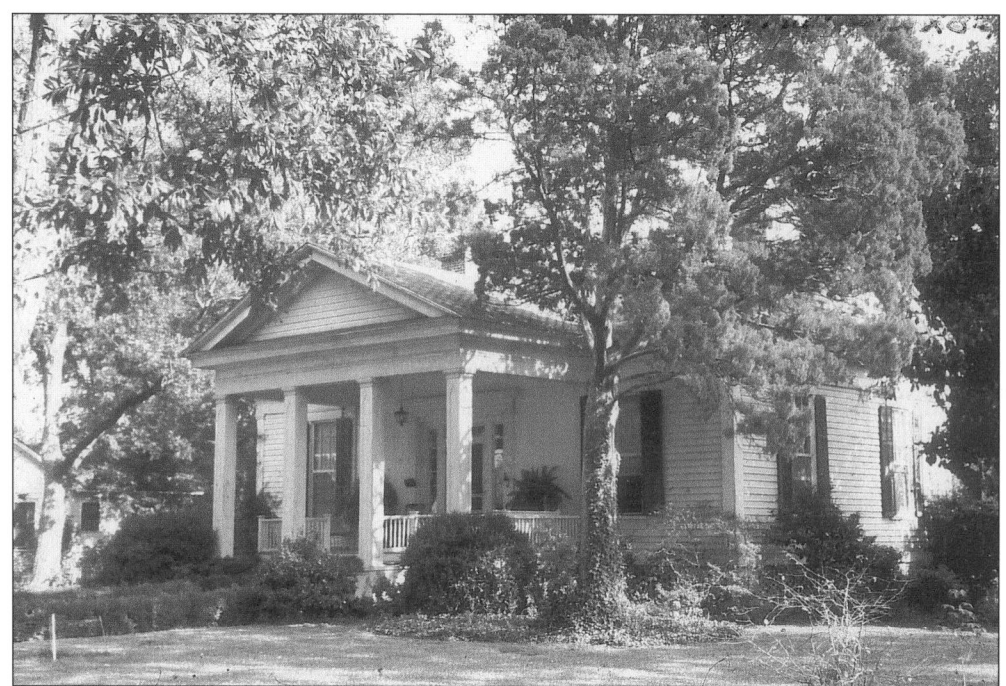

The Witherspoon house on Baptist Street was built in 1853 by William A. McCall and sold in 1867 for use as the Methodist district parsonage. (Photo courtesy of Maxcy Foxworth.)

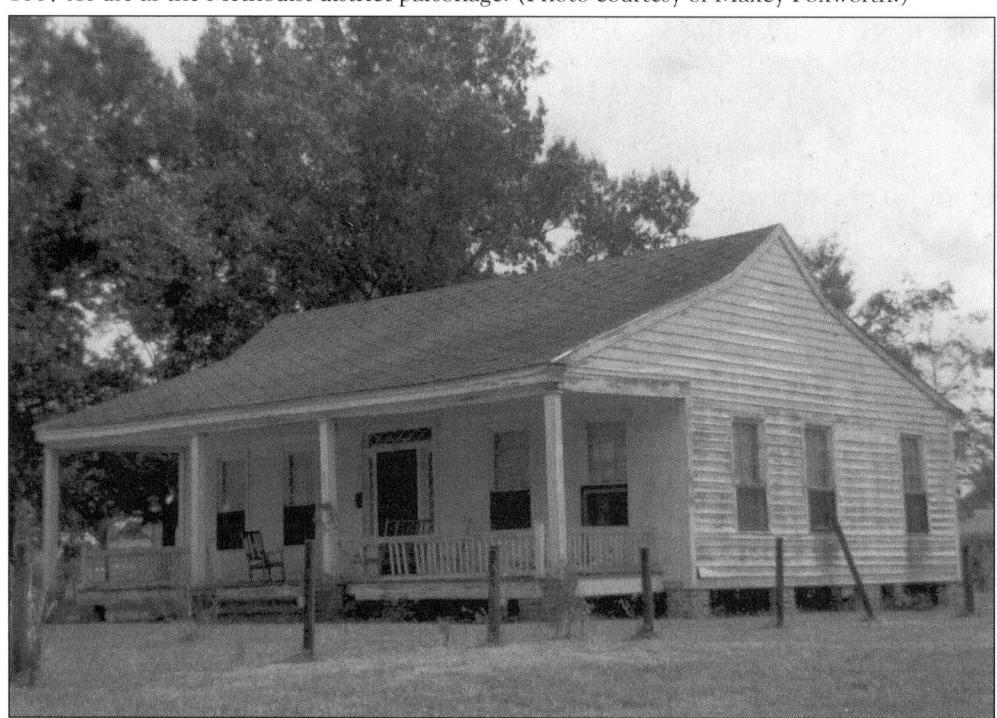

The Gregg house was constructed in 1850 by J.F. Finger for Eleanor Laurens Wayne, wife of Wesley Washington Gregg. Located on Main Street, the house was moved for the construction of the Mark I Motel c. 1960. (Photo courtesy of Maxcy Foxworth.)

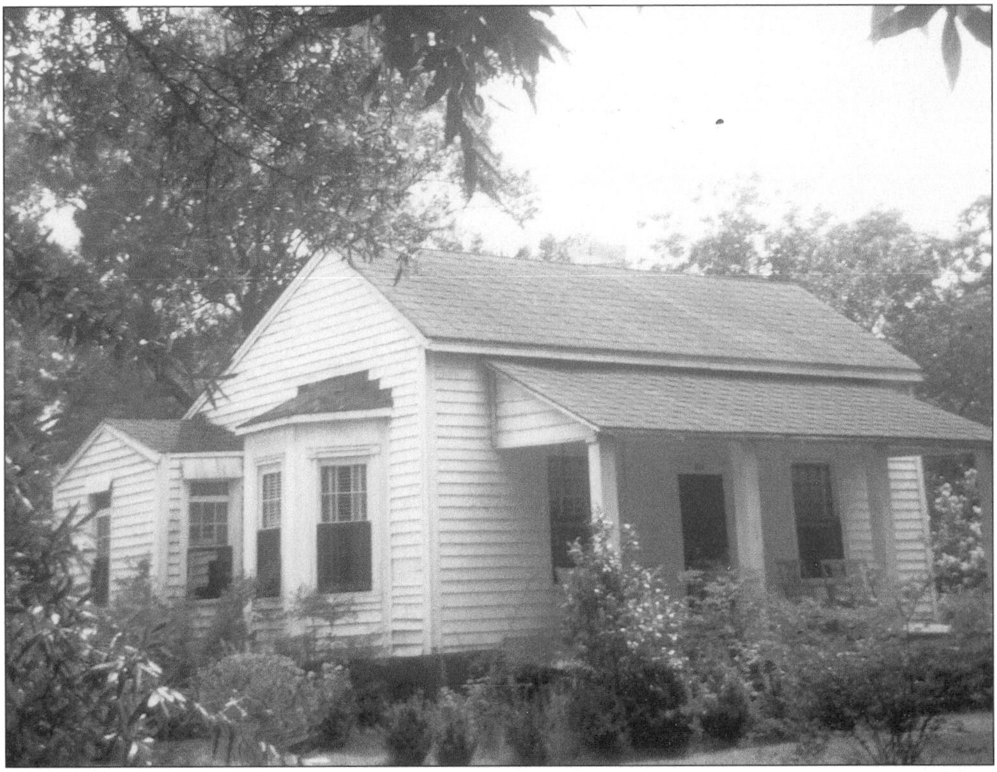

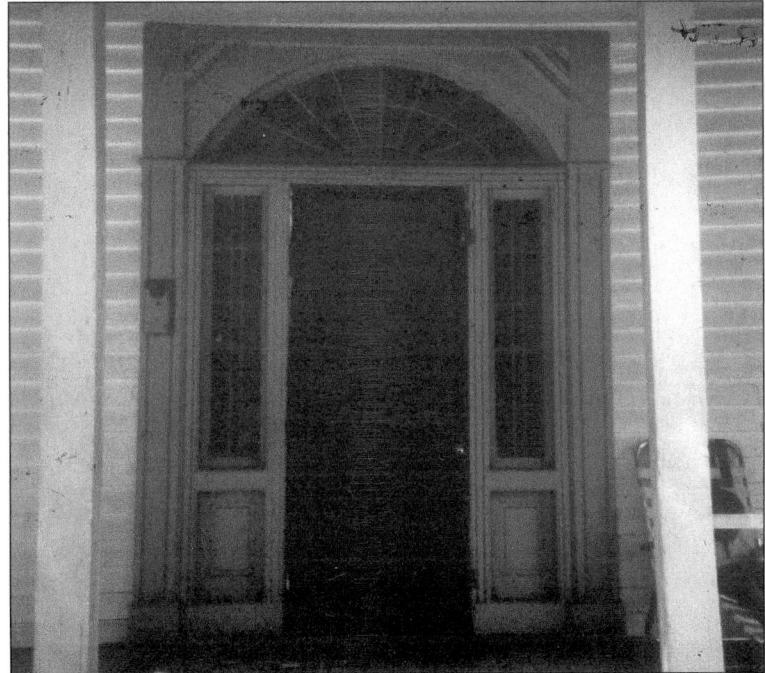

This 1840s house stood on East Bond Street and was formerly used as a district parsonage at different times by both the Baptists and the Methodists. It later burned. (Photo courtesy of Maxcy Foxworth.)

Built in the 1840s on the northwest corner of Bond and Pine Streets, this house featured an elegant fanlight doorway. This house was demolished in the early 1970s. (Photo courtesy of Maxcy Foxworth.)

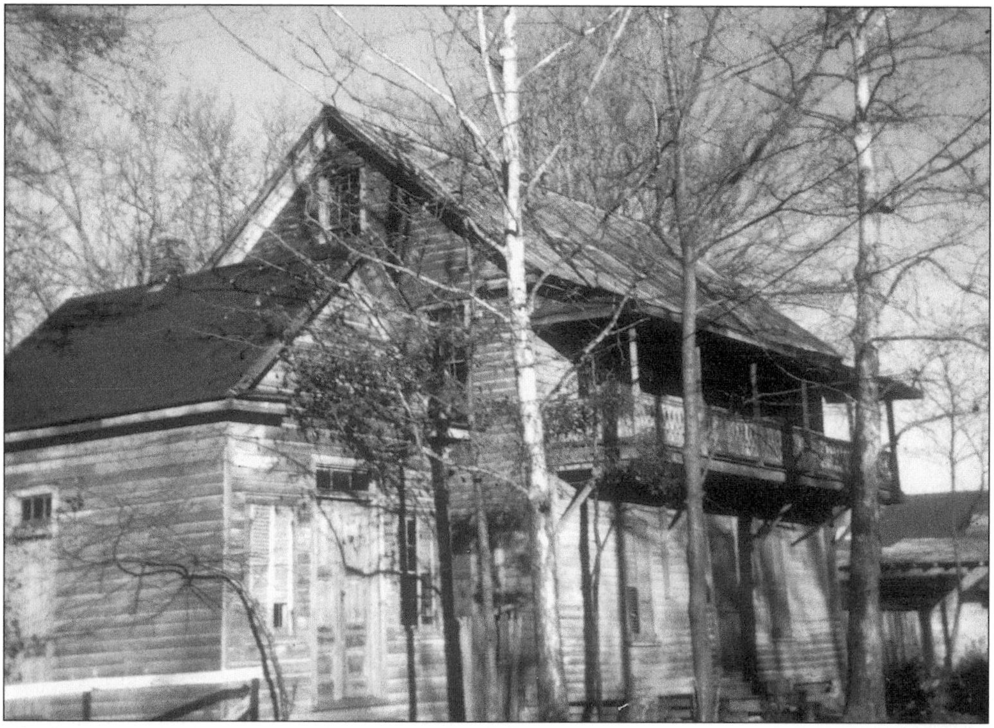

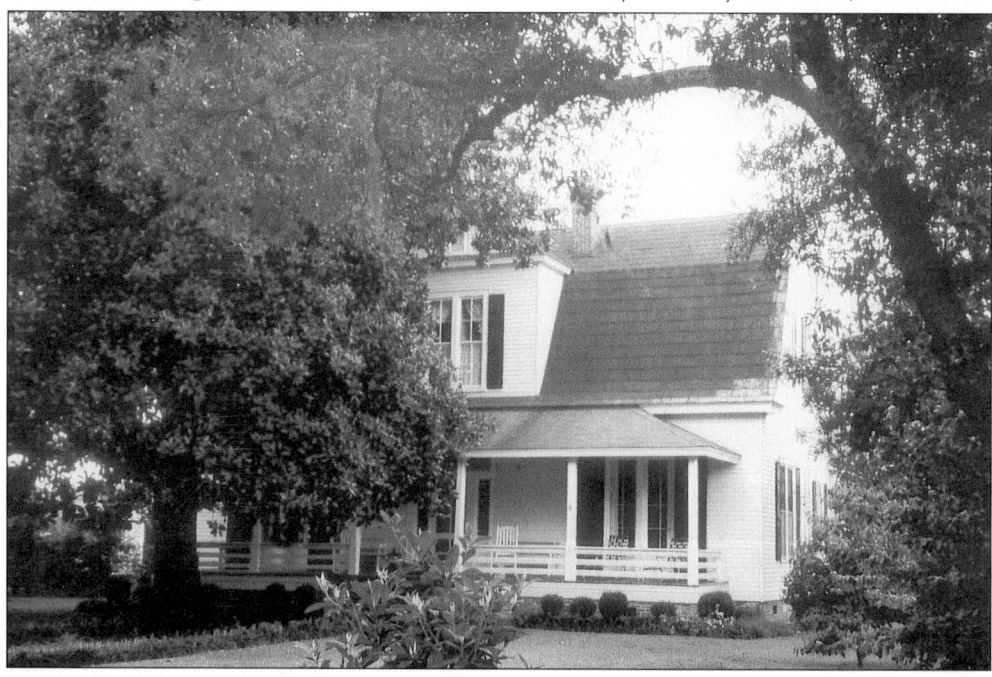

This picturesque pair of buildings, owned by Plum and Gertrude Johnson, stood on Manning Street before being demolished about 1970. (Photo courtesy of Maxcy Foxworth.)

Bluefield on North Main Street, photographed in the mid-1960s, was formerly the home of the Blue family, whose children included Rear Admiral Victor Blue, U.S. Surgeon General Rupert Blue, Kate Lilly Blue, and Henriet Blue. (Photo courtesy of Maxcy Foxworth.)

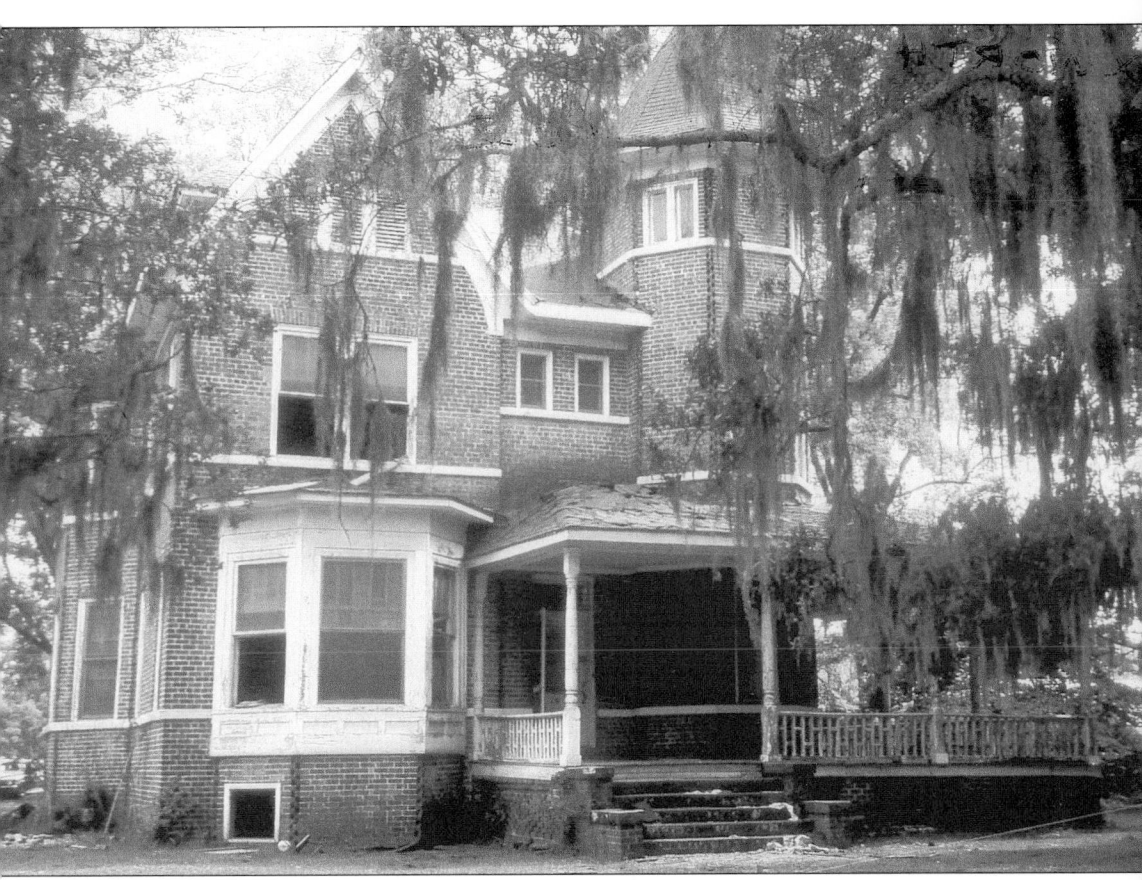

This wonderful Queen Anne–style home, with a magnificent staircase, stained-glass, and interior shutters, was built in 1901 on East Godbold Street by Thomas Monroe and later was the home of the Dr. Douglas McIntyre family. This photograph was taken as it was being demolished. (Photo courtesy of Maxcy Foxworth.)

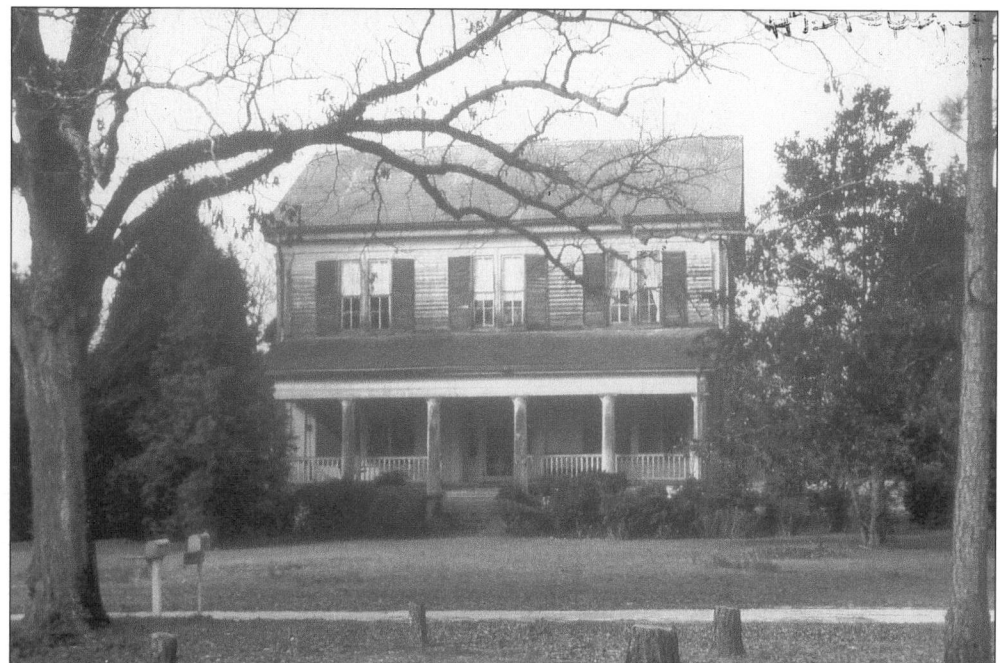

The Richardson-Godbold house near Centenary was built by Philander Curtis for William Fladger Richardson in the late 1850s and was inherited by his daughter, Augusta, wife of James Godbold. It is noted for the spectacular trompe l'oeil and the mahogany and maple woodgraining on the interior woodwork. (Photo courtesy of Maxcy Foxworth.)

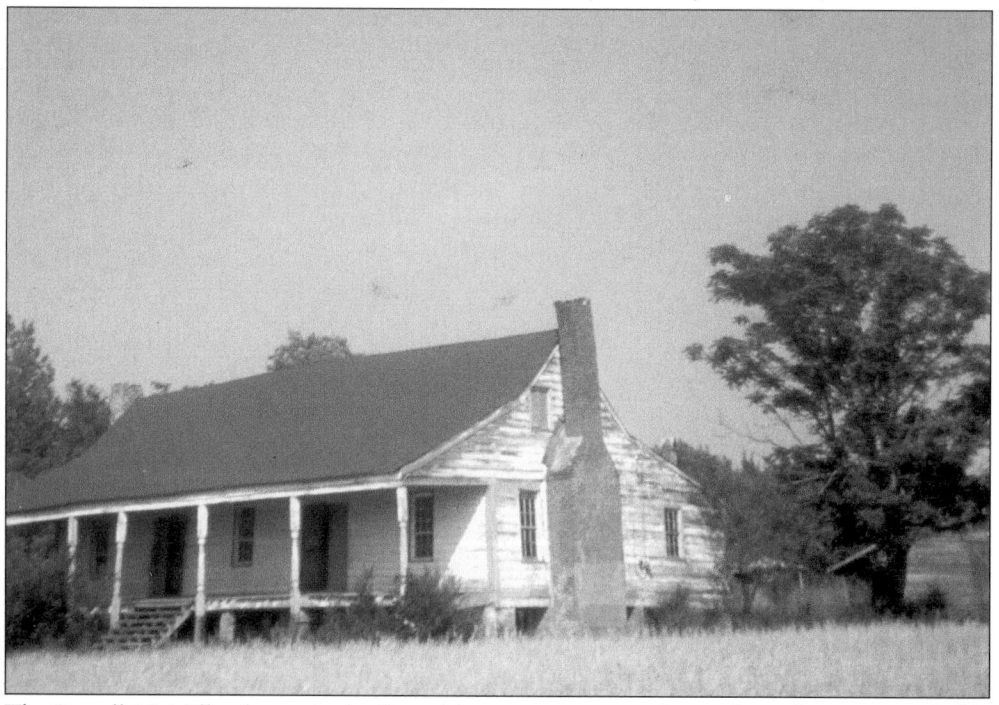

The Rowell-McMillan house in the Friendship community, with two front doors, was probably built c. 1830s. (Photo courtesy of Maxcy Foxworth.)

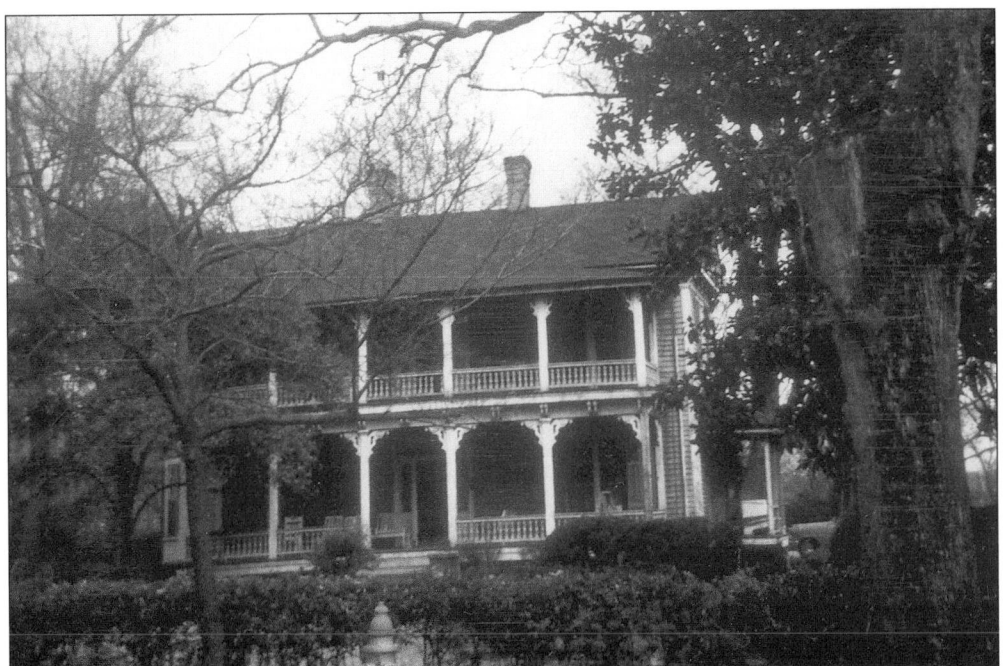

This lovely late-1800s house stood just north of the Episcopal Church of the Advent on South Main Street. The house burned c. 1970. It was formerly the home of the Francis Covington family, whose daughter Hallie was a missionary to Korea from 1917 to 1941. (Photo courtesy of Maxcy Foxworth.)

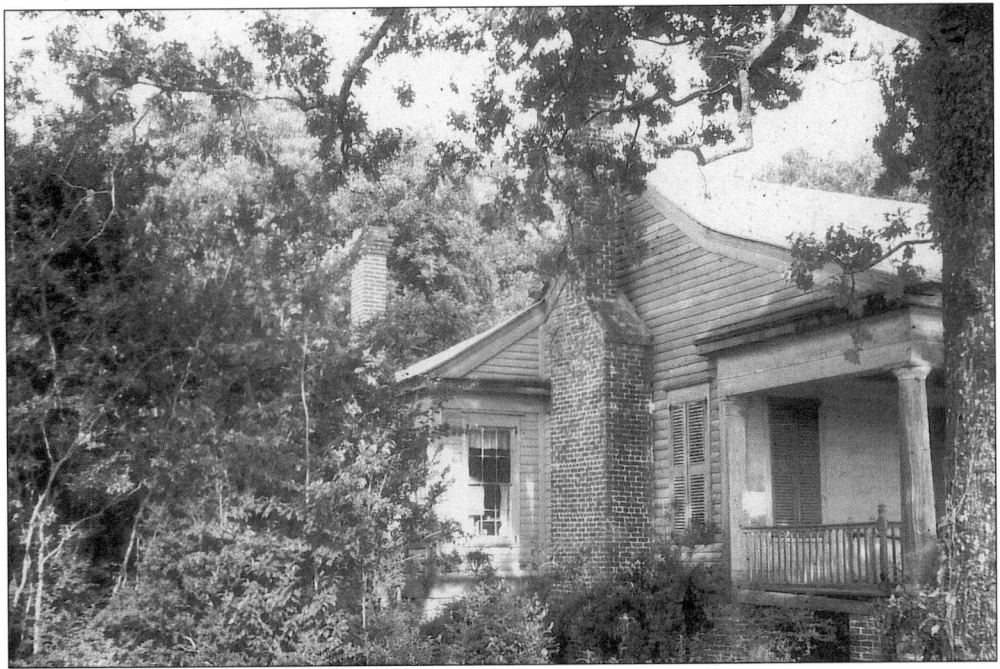

Durantia was built in the 1850s, probably by Philander Curtis, for Colonel W.W. Durant. It stood on South Main Street until being moved near Millers Church, which was near Mullins, to make way for the new Marion High School. (Photo courtesy of Maxcy Foxworth.)

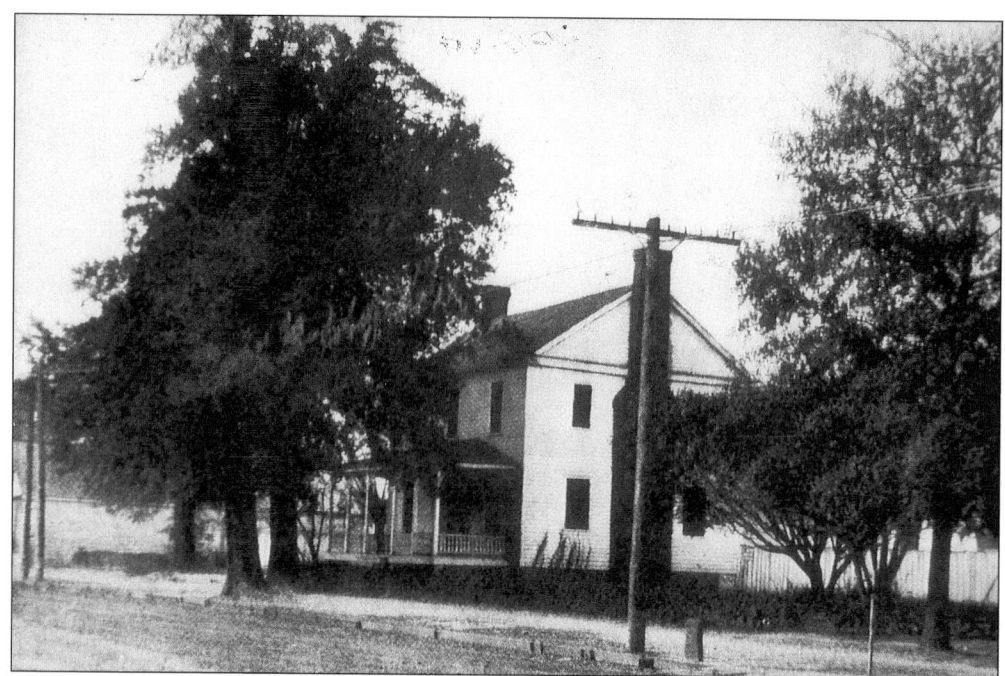

The original courthouse was built in 1800 and moved about 1823 to the lot where the Baptist church is located. It was remodeled as the residence of the Honorable Thomas Evans and his wife, Jane Beverly Daniel. (Photo courtesy of Maxcy Foxworth.)

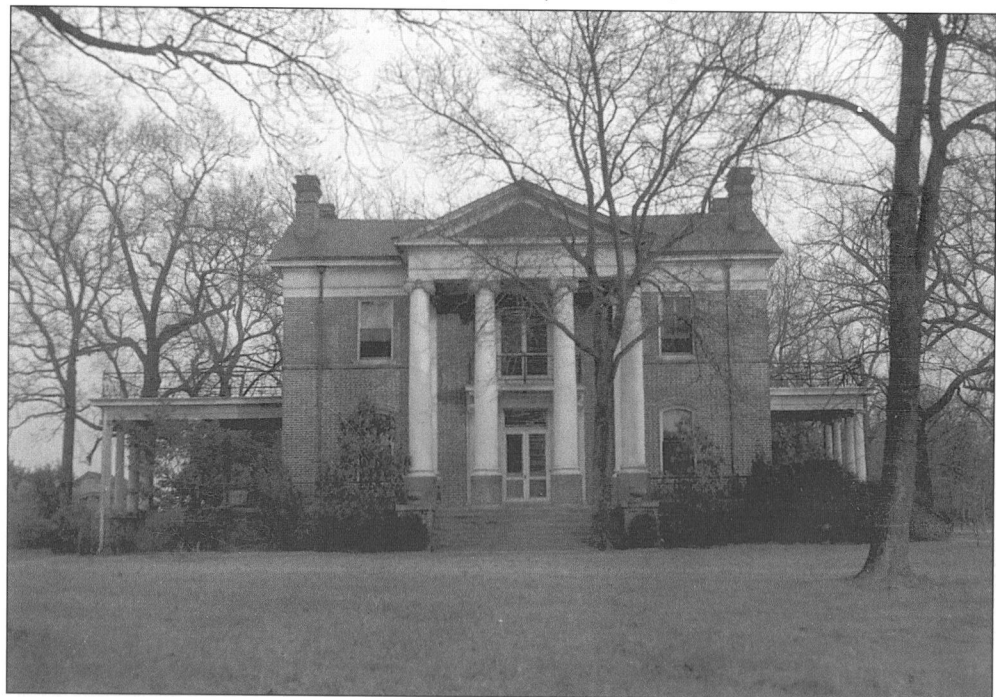

The Stackhouse-Rose house was built about 1895 by Will Stackhouse, director of the Seaboard Railroad. It was later the home of the McKoy Rose family. Currently, the home is a bed and breakfast. (Photo courtesy of Mitzi Winesett.)

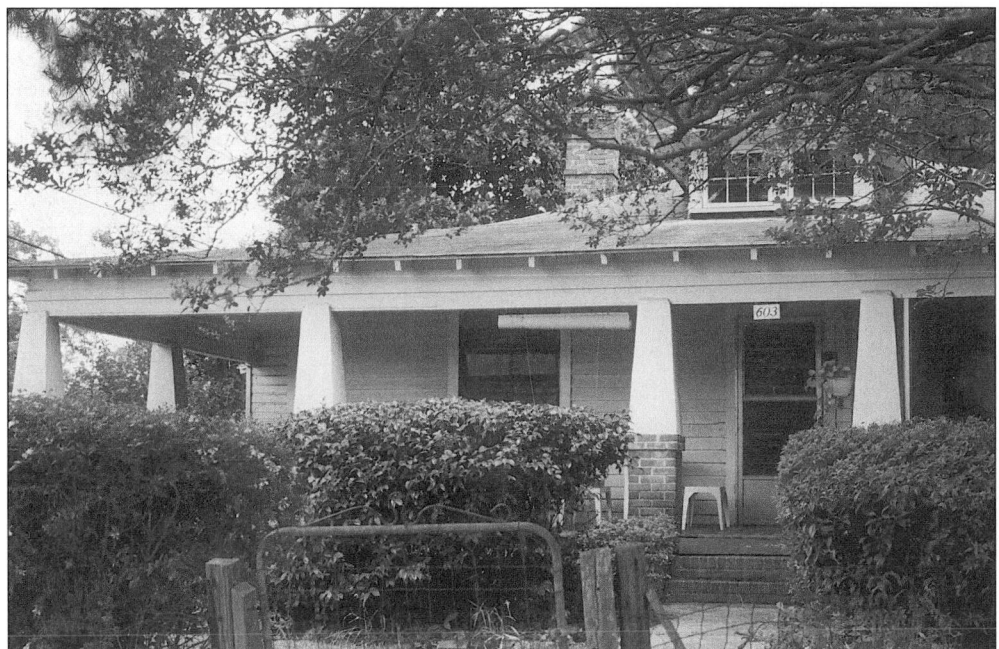

This cozy dwelling on Eutaw Street was built in 1921 by William "Bill" Braddy and Arabella Hunter Braddy. Mr. Braddy was a cabdriver in Marion. His fellow cabdrivers were Sam Woodbury, David Conner, and Henry Lester. Mrs. Braddy taught in Marion and Horry Counties for 17 years before becoming a full-time homemaker at the request of her husband. She was the founder of the Lily of the Valley Eastern Star and was the first Worthy Matron. The home has remained in the Braddy family since it was built. (Photo by Laney Baumrind.)

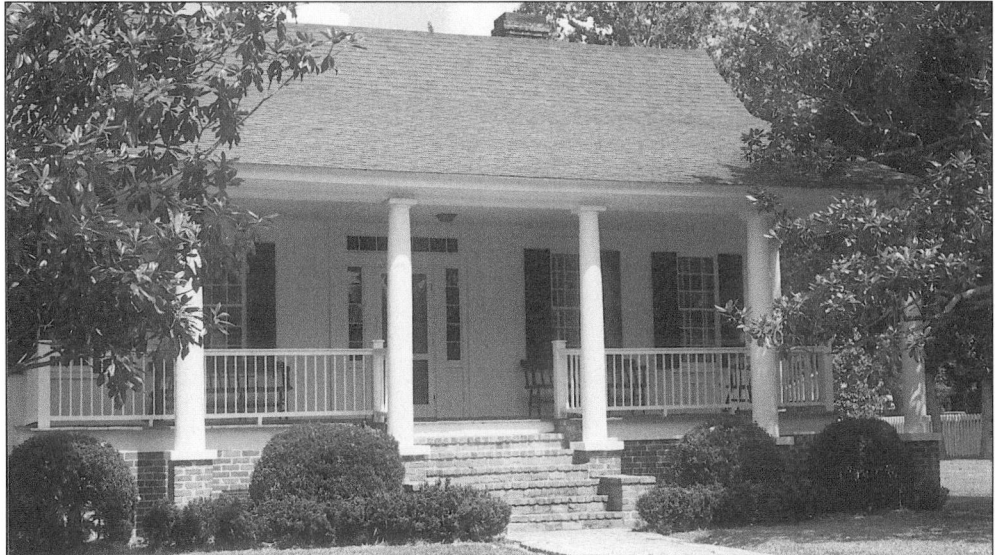

The McLendon house on 403 South Main Street was probably built by Duncan J. McDonald in the late 1840s. A Greek Revival cottage with freestanding Tuscan columns on brick piers, it has a recessed porch and a porch roof continuous with the main roof—an architectural feature found mainly in the northeastern part of South Carolina, mostly from Marion to Camden. (Photo by Laney Baumrind.)

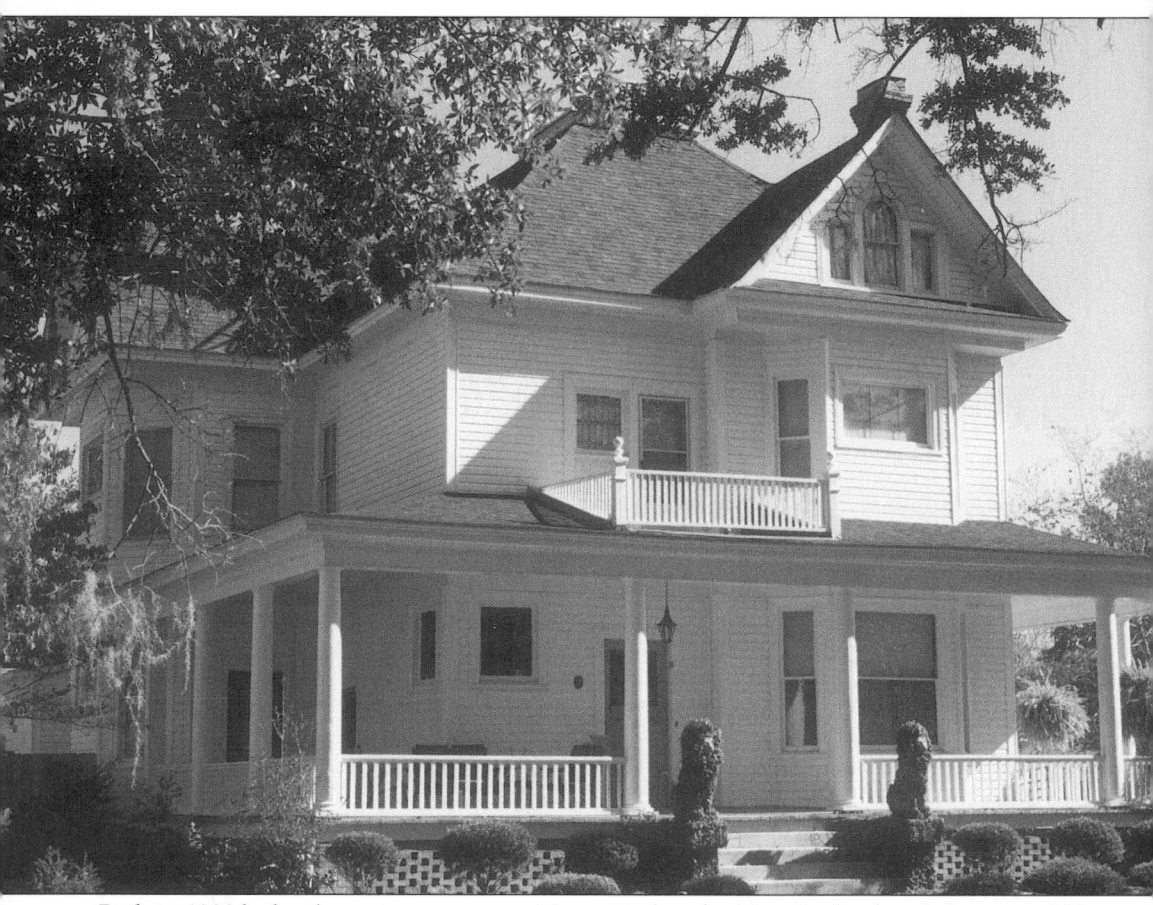

Built in 1900 by local prominent attorney Henry Buck is this New England–style home on 200 Willcox Avenue. The house was built complete with a widow's walk on top to please the attorney's grandfather, who came to South Carolina from Maine. (Photo by Laney Baumrind.)

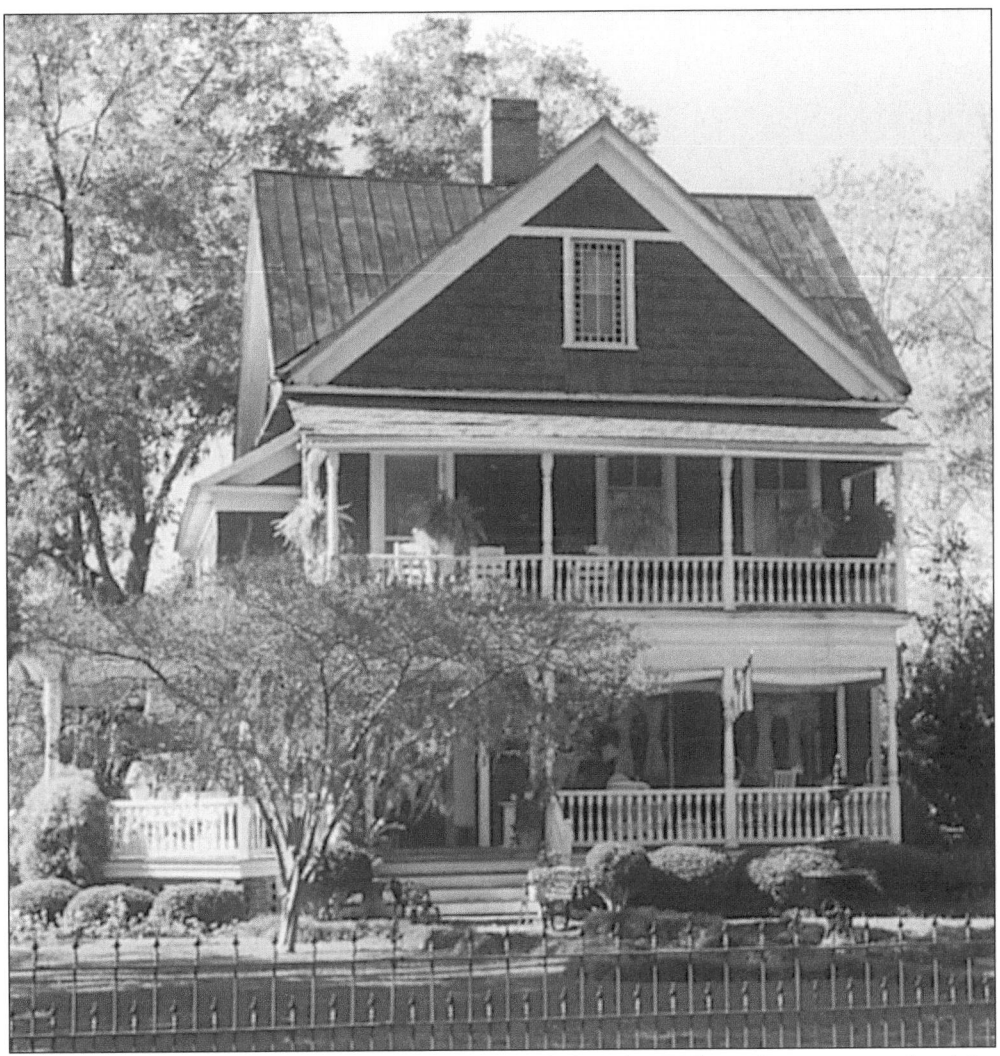

Erected in 1886, this home at 301 Willcox was built by John Willcox. It is an example of the Victorian style with an offset kitchen that is primitive in every aspect. (Photo by Laney Baumrind.)

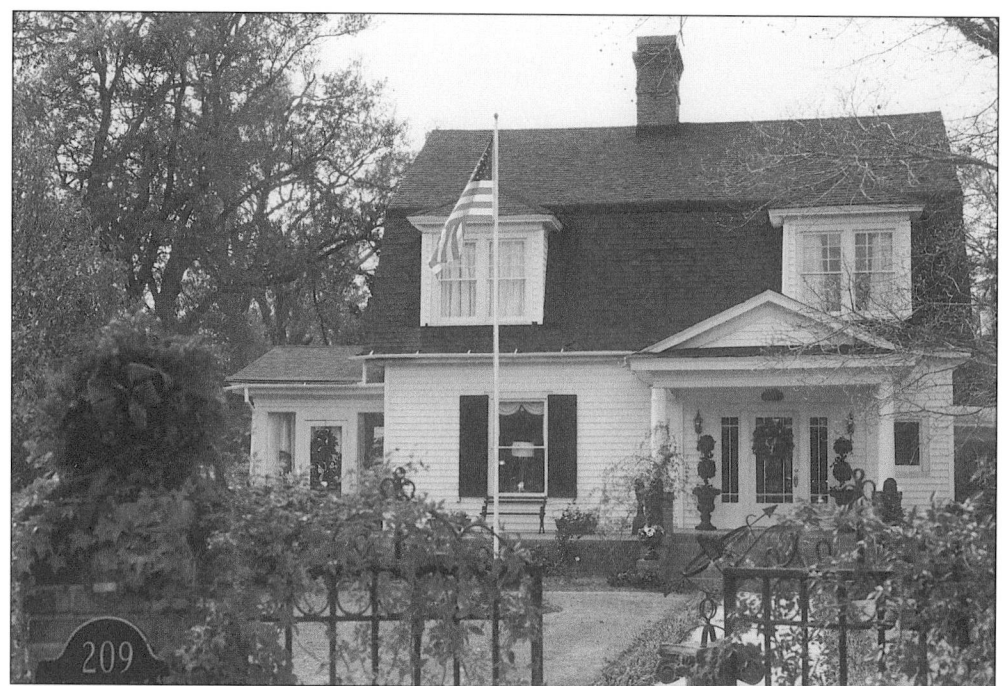

The "old Gasque house," as it is often referred to, was built in 1904 by Frances Pratt, who came to Marion from Scranton, Pennsylvania. (Photo by Laney Baumrind.)

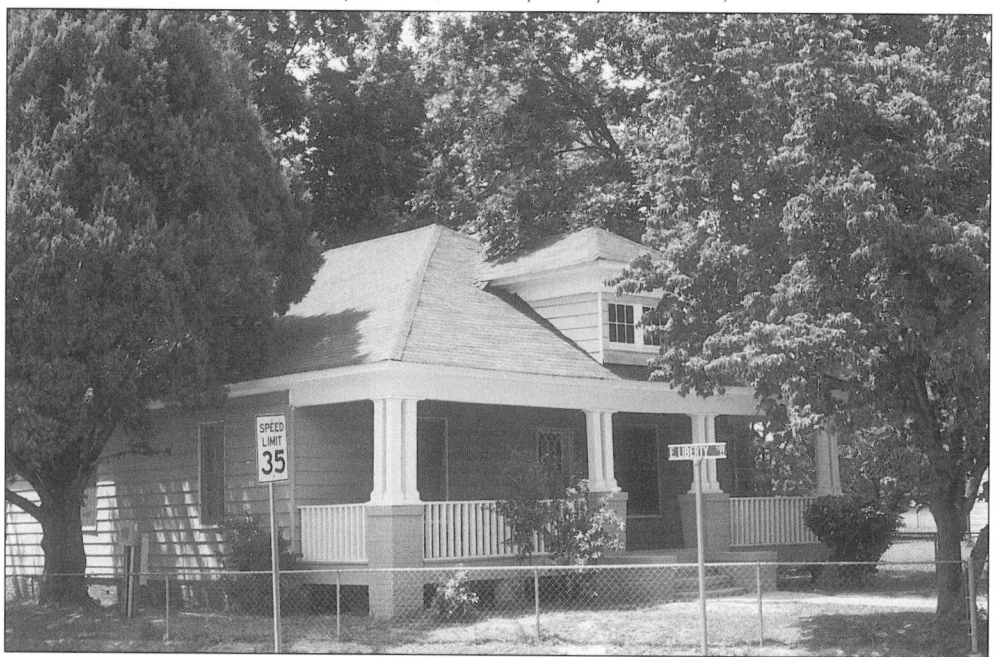

As a child, Mrs. Dorothy Bartelle went often to the home of Mr. and Mrs. Arthur Frazier, located on the corner of Liberty and Gregg Streets. The Fraziers welcomed children to their home and were known as "Miss Lee" and "Mr. Arthur." Miss Lee was a Hamilton before her marriage, and her sisters were Maude, Zorah, and Mamie Hamilton, who were known for their upholstery skills. (Photo by Laney Baumrind.)

Two

ALL DRESSED UP WITH PLACES TO GO

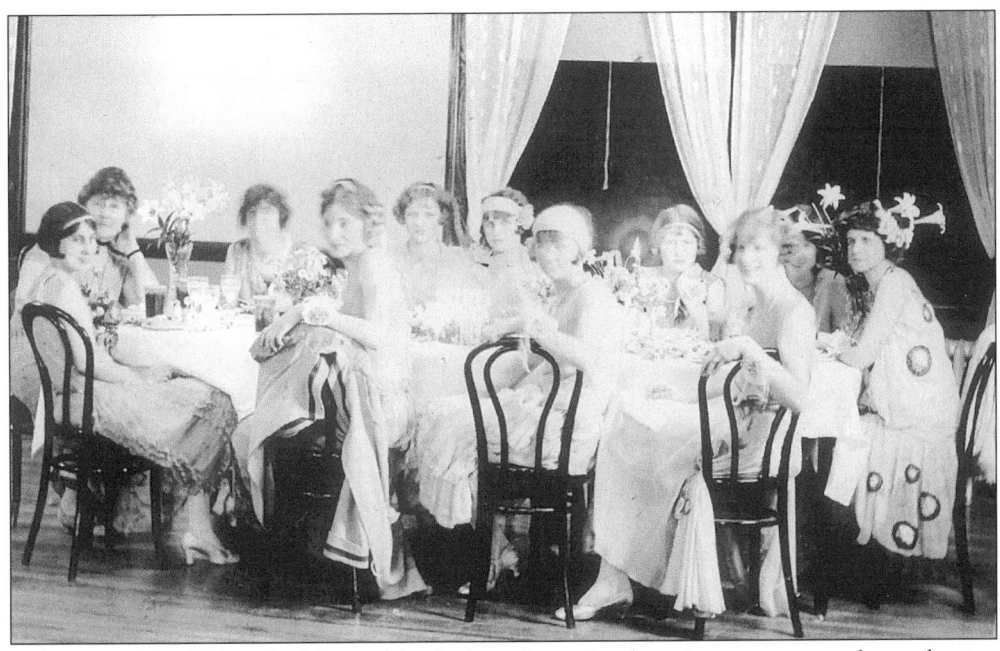

Taken May 20, 1925, at the Marion Hotel, these dressed up beauties were among the graduating class of Marion High School.Mrs. Nellie C. Ellerbe, hostess, heads the table at the far left. The graduates clockwise around the table are:Reubie Holliday, Hattie Bell Bethea, Caribel Mace, Sara Miles Smith, Mrs. O. K. LaRoque, Lenora Monroe Martin, Jennie Lou Stackhouse, Editha Willcox, Margaret McLucas, and Elizabeth McIntyre.Photo courtesy of Elizabeth McIntyre

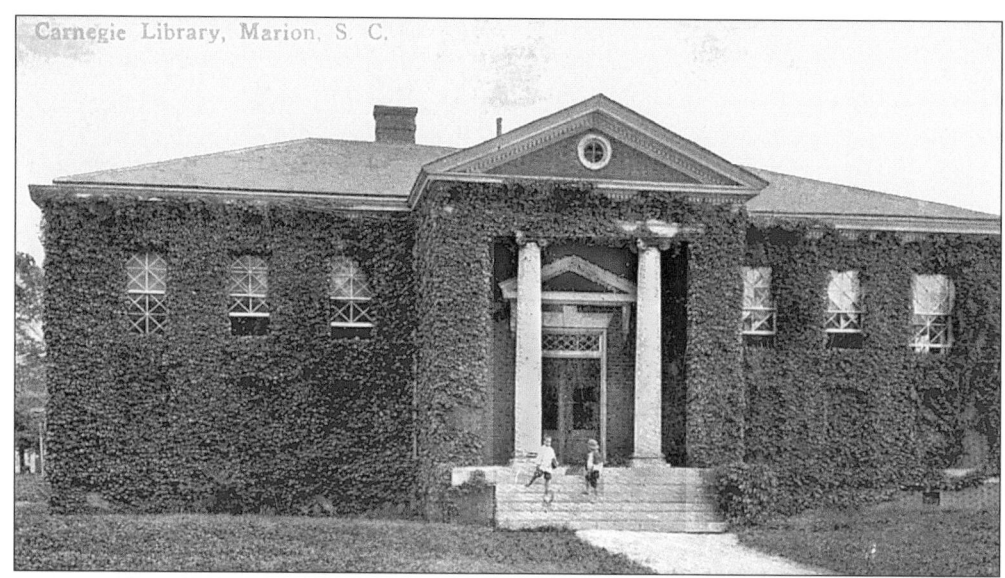

An important place to go was, and remains, the Carnegie Library. The present site was contributed by 120 citizens for its first permanent home. A rectangular building of red brick with matching mortar wash and the Greek Revival influence is shown in recessed portico with Ionic columns. It has "Union Jack" windows. The cornerstone of the present building was laid in 1905, and the library opened in 1906. In 1975, additional space was added to the main floor, and work rooms were built at the lower level. (Photo courtesy of James and Nita Neely.)

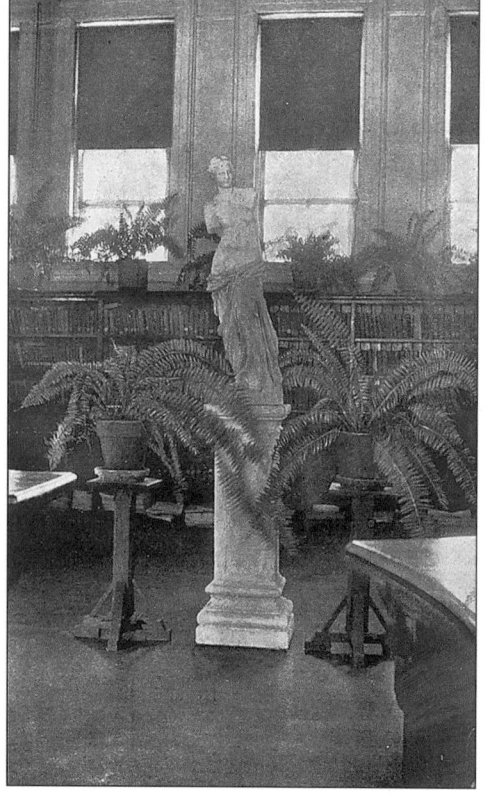

Ferns and a Neoclassical statue dressed up the interior of the Marion Public Library. (Photo courtesy of Valerie Baumrind Bonatis.)

All dressed up are Henry L. Jackson and his first wife, Mary Elizabeth. Mr. and Mrs. Jackson were the owners of Henry L. Jackson Funeral Home. (Photo courtesy of Poiette McGill.)

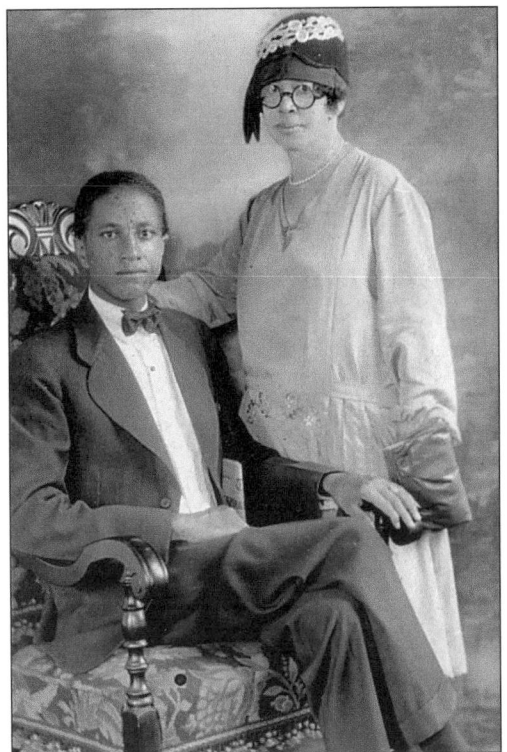

The dressed-up daughters of Henry L. Jackson, with places to go, are Sylvia E., Jacqueline A., and Cynthia A. Jackson. The Jackson daughters assisted their father in the funeral business in the city for many years. (Photo courtesy of Poiette McGill.)

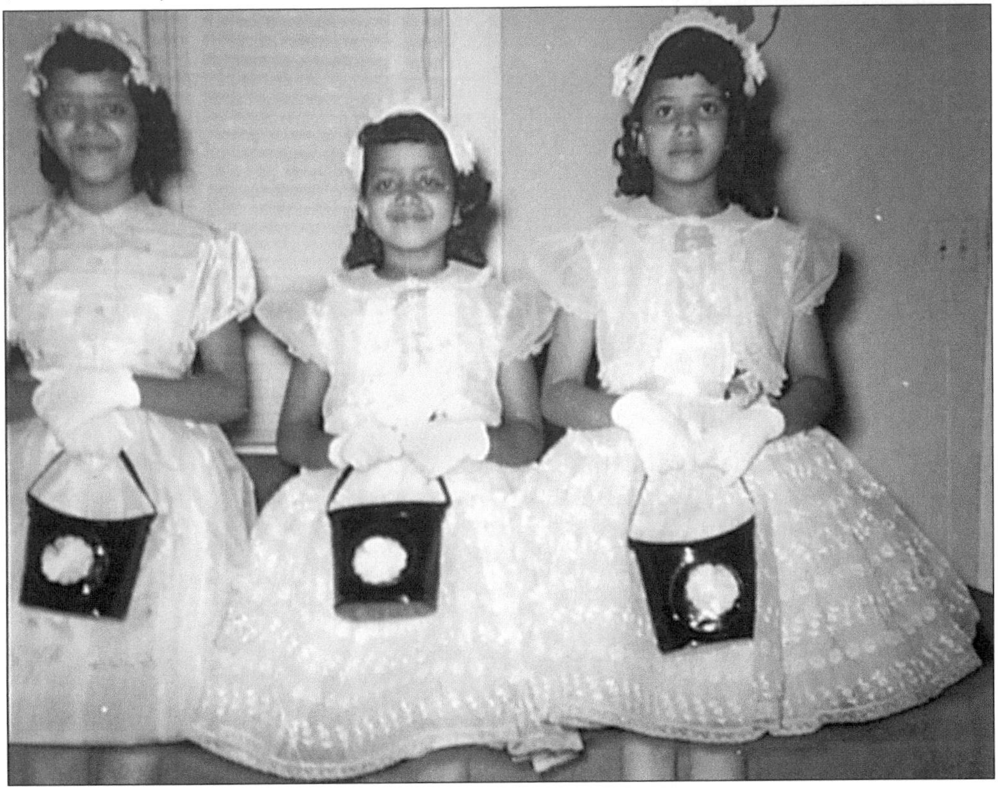

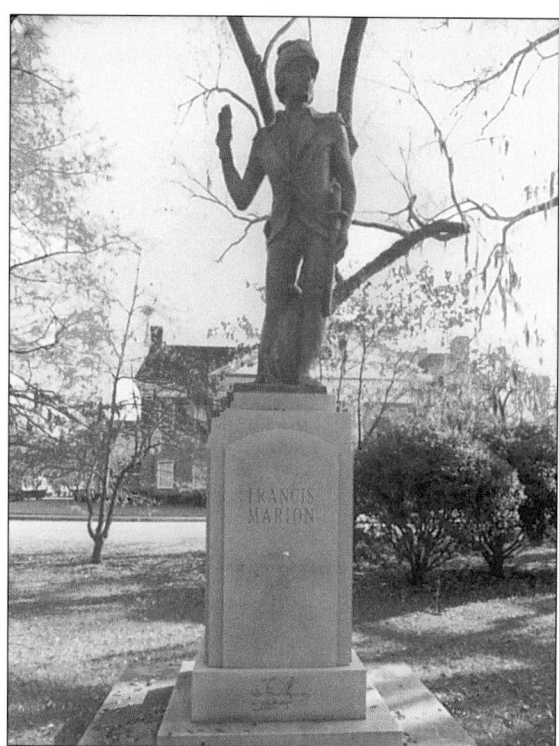

One place all residents and visitors should go is to the statue of General Francis Marion. The statue was unveiled on April 9, 1976, as part of the county's bicentennial celebration. (Photo courtesy of Libby Stanley.)

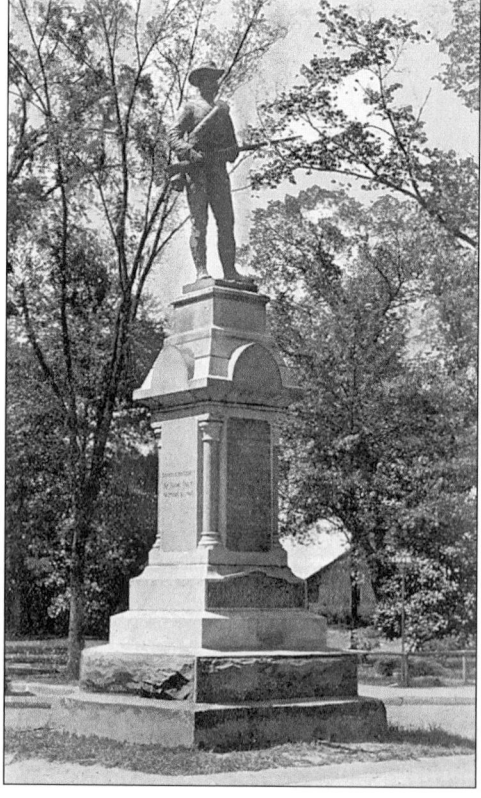

The Confederate Monument was unveiled on October 21, 1903. On top of a granite shaft stands a larger-than-life–size bronze replica of a Confederate soldier, his musket at rest. The statue, originally placed in the middle of the intersection of Main and Godbold Streets, was moved to the southeast Town Square in the 1950s. (Photo courtesy of Valerie Baumrind Bonatis.)

48

Being the clerk of court for Marion County, a member of the South Carolina House of Representatives, and a medical doctor, Dr. David Franklin Miles had many places to go. (Photo courtesy of Libby Stanley.)

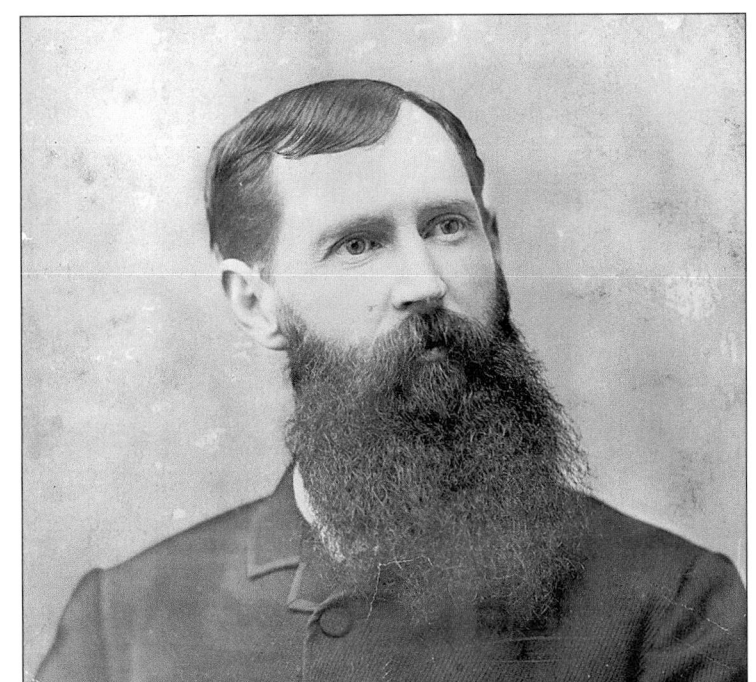

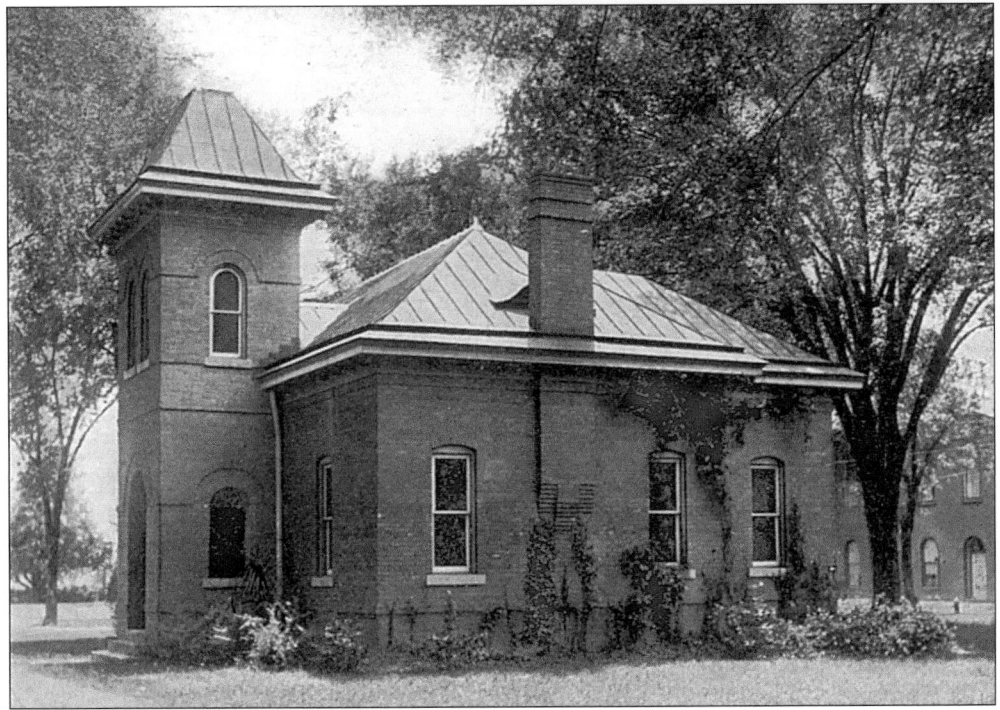

Dr. D.F. Miles was a striking figure entering the Hall of Records building. Completed in 1903, it is located on the site of the 1823 Court House. The architectural style is adapted from late Romanesque revival, which influenced the design of many public buildings of that period. Offices of Clerk of Court and Judge of Probate were located here until 1979. (Photo courtesy of Valerie Baumrind Bonatis.)

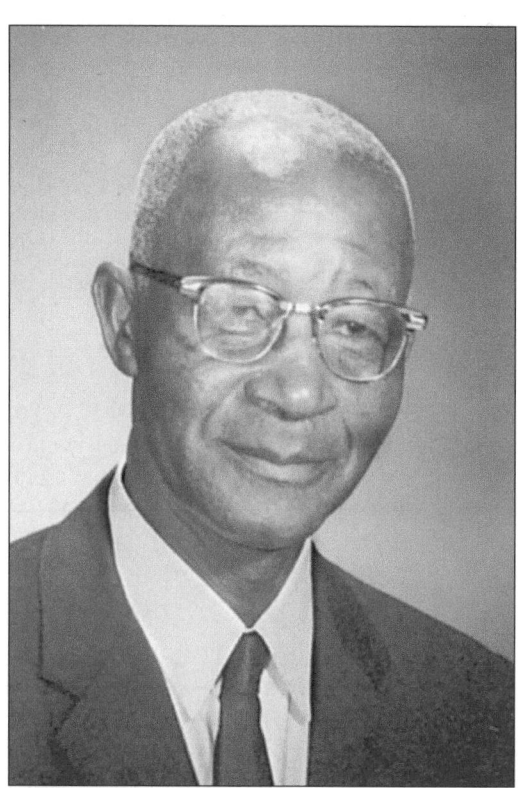

Mr. Milbia Johnakin, a classic role model, was always ready for his students. Mr. Johnakin came to Marion in 1931 to accept a job as principal and remained in that position until 1966. Johnakin High School was named in his honor. (Photo courtesy of Dr. James Blake.)

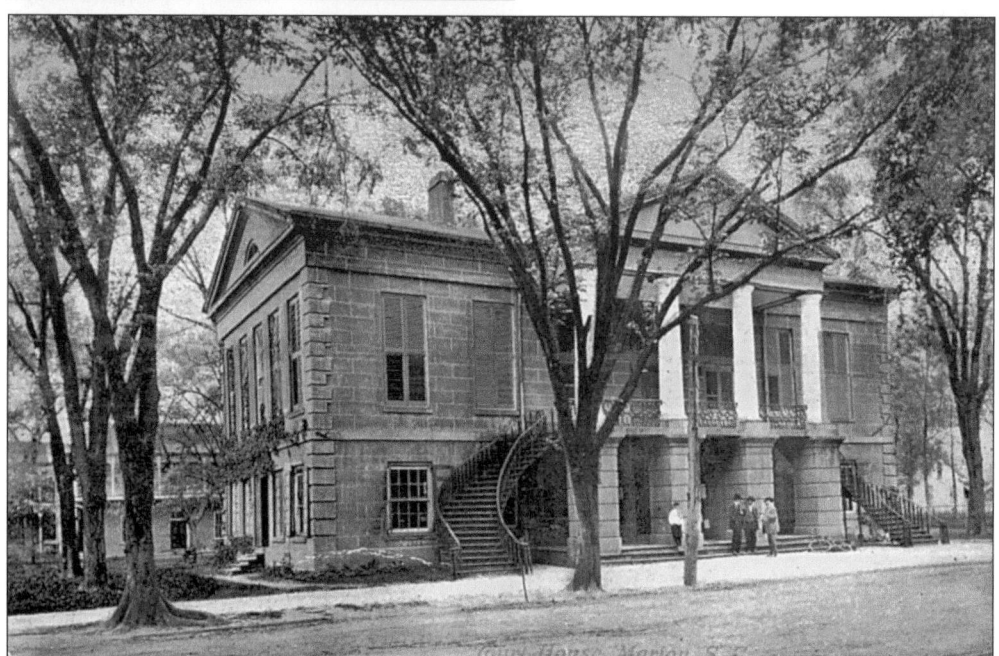

One of the places Professor Johnakin might have taken his students was the Marion County Court House. The present courthouse was completed in 1853 and continues to be a working courthouse today. The architect was Peter H. Hammarskold, who was also the first architect for the State House of South Carolina. (Photo courtesy of James and Nita Neely.)

While traveling, noted vocalist Sarah Jane "Sallie" Foxworth Gasque was invited to sing with Madame Shuman-Heink in New York and with the Sousa Band on a riverboat. "Sallie" was the second wife of E.H. Gasque. (Photo courtesy of Maxcy Foxworth.)

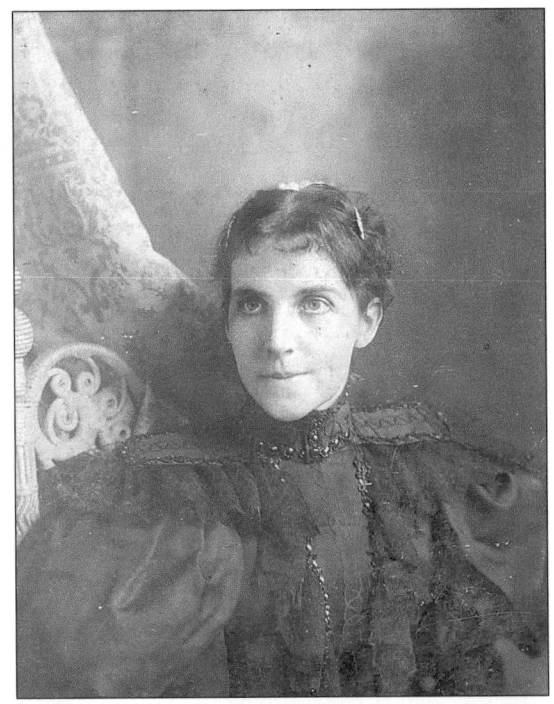

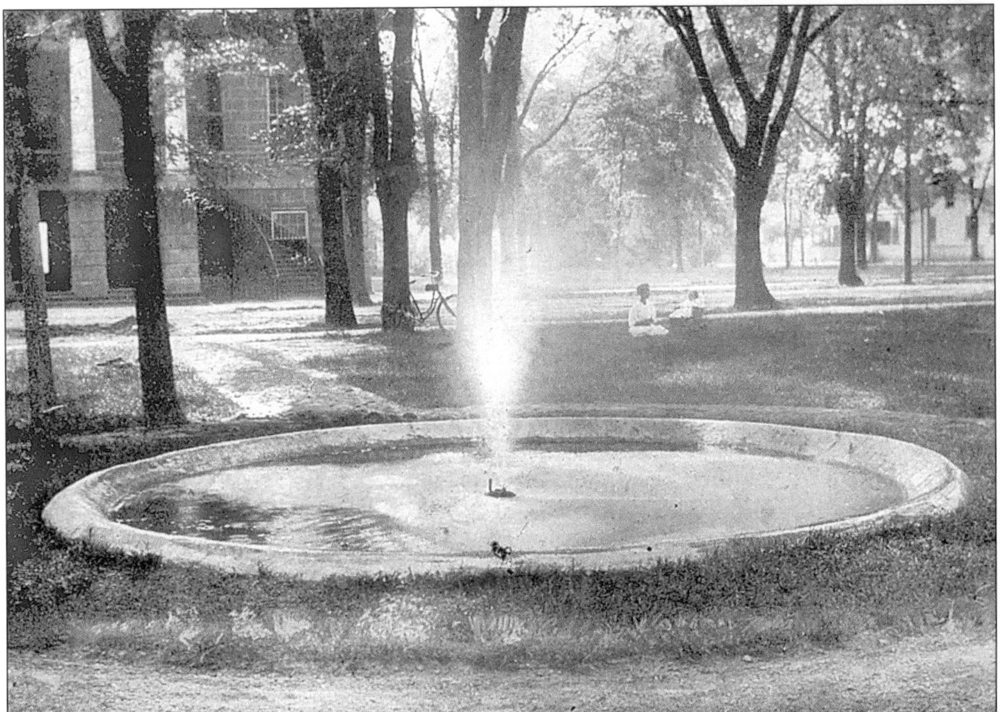

Many dressed-up folks would go to the E.H. Gasque Fountain on the Town Square. Mr. Gasque is said to have been the first president of the Marion Civic Improvement League and encouraged the beautification of the Public Square. (Photo courtesy of Valerie Baumrind Bonatis.)

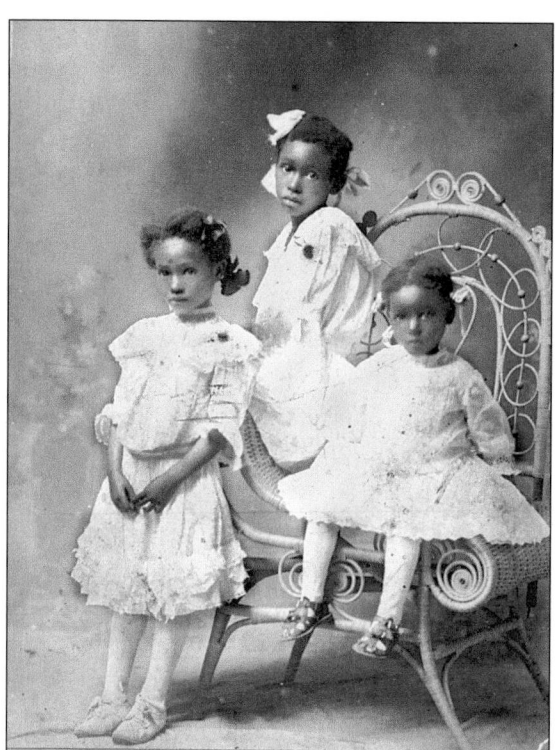

Perhaps these three little Davis girls did not want to stop playing and get all dressed up to have their photograph made. (Photo courtesy of Charlie Levy.)

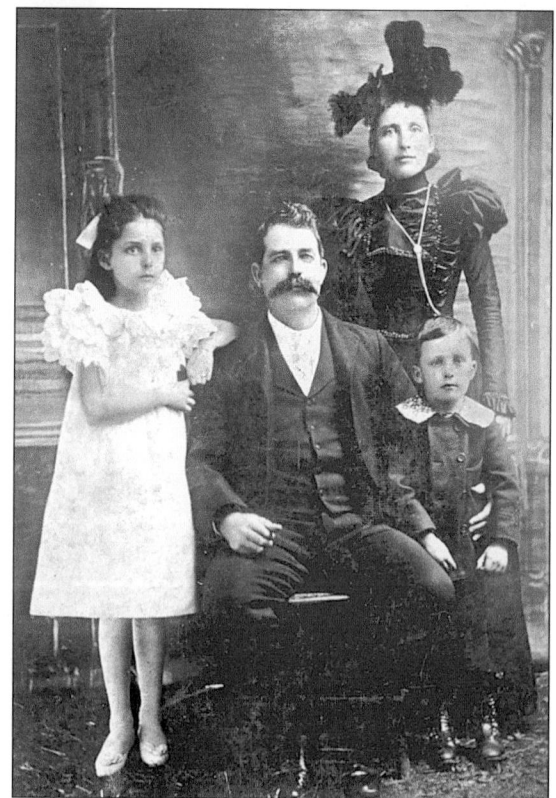

D.A. Layton gets his family posed for this portrait. Left to right are Margaret Layton Evans, D.A. Layton, Mary Elizabeth Berry Layton, and D.A. Layton Jr. (Photo courtesy of Margaret E. Wood.)

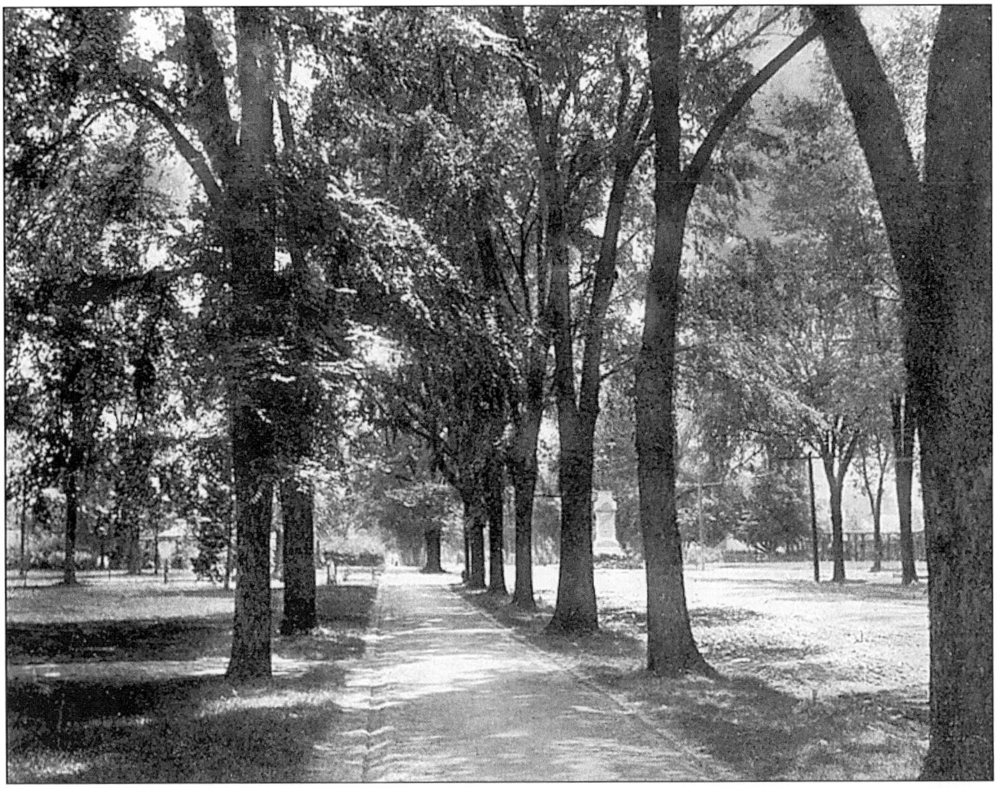

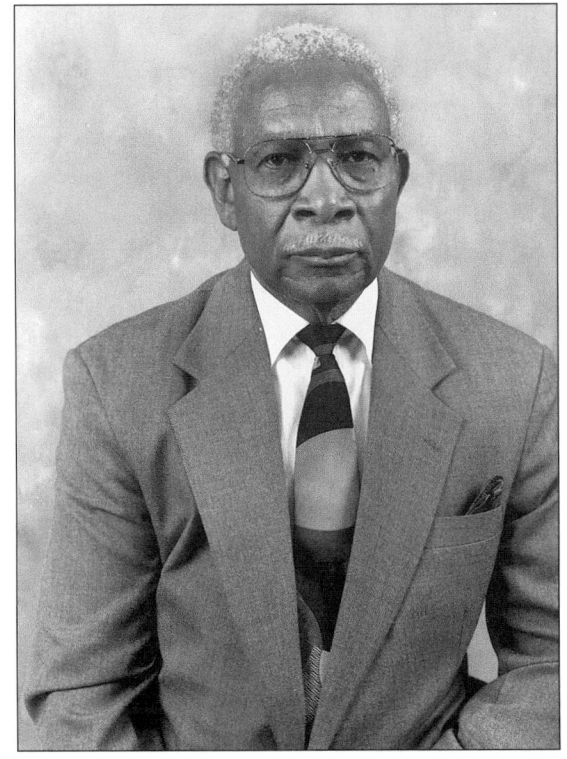

After reluctantly getting all dressed up, it is hoped the Davis and Layton children would go to walk under the canopy of trees at the Public Square. (Photo courtesy of Valerie Baumrind Bonatis.)

Dr. James A. Blake Sr. was the valedictorian of the Marion County Training School Class of 1947. He was a high school mathematics teacher, associate principal, and later assistant superintendent of Marion School District One. Among his many accomplishments was his appointment as the first black member of the South Carolina State Board of Education, of which he later became chairman. (Photo courtesy of Mrs. James Blake.)

53

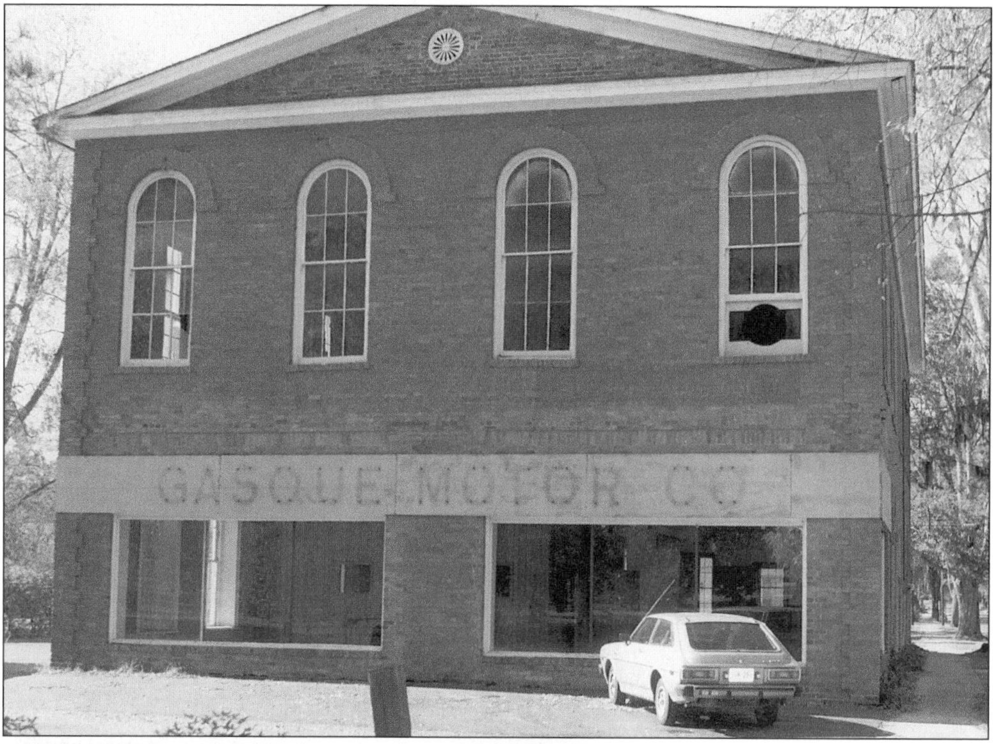

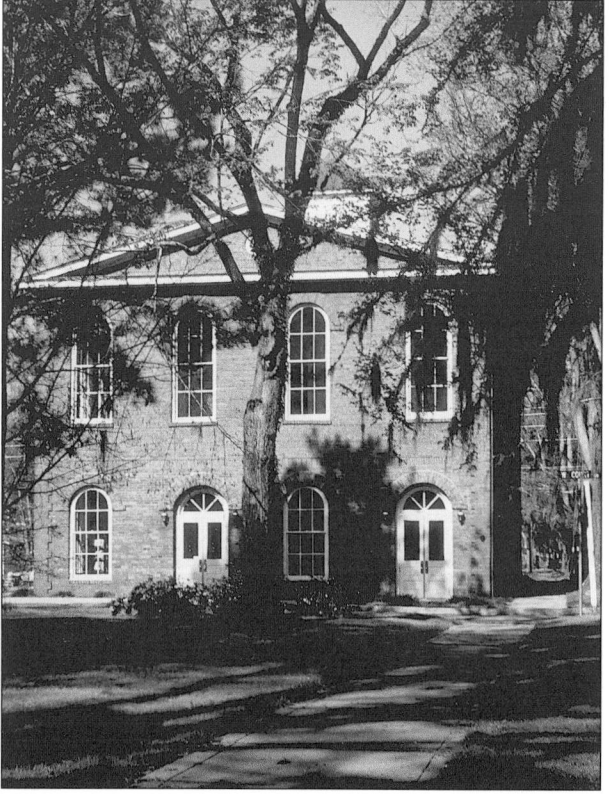

This photograph shows where the Gasque family sold Plymouths as the Gasque Motor Company. Prior to serving as a family business, the building was the Town Hall and Opera House. The first floor housed the town courtroom, the town jail, and the fire department; the second floor was used for graduation exercises, public speaking, and theatrical productions. (Photo courtesy of the Marion Chamber of Commerce.)

Thanks to a lot of hard work by some dedicated citizens of Marion, the Town Hall and Opera House once again became a gathering place for cultural events in Marion and home to the Marion Chamber of Commerce in 1983. (Photo courtesy of the Marion Chamber of Commerce.)

Rear Admiral Victor Blue (1865–1928) spent his boyhood at Bluefield, the family home, in Marion. He commanded the *Yorktown* in 1910 and the *Texas* from 1916 until 1918. (Photo courtesy of Ben and Beth Mullins.)

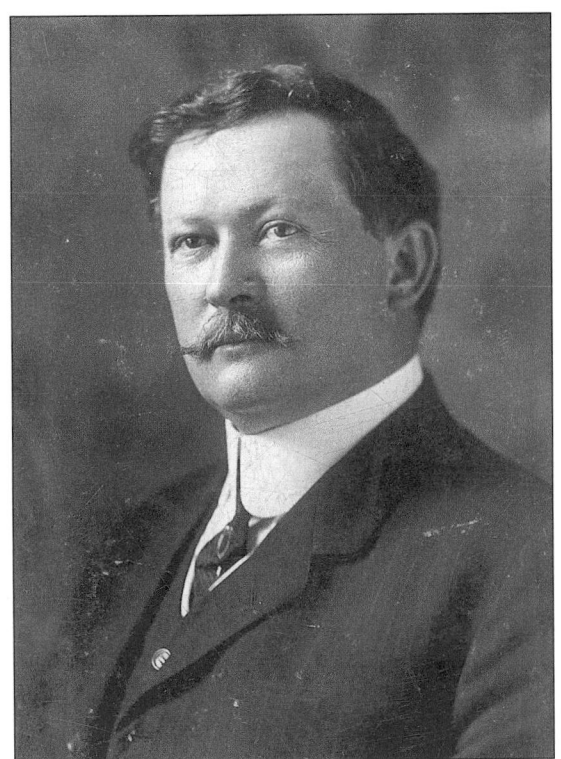

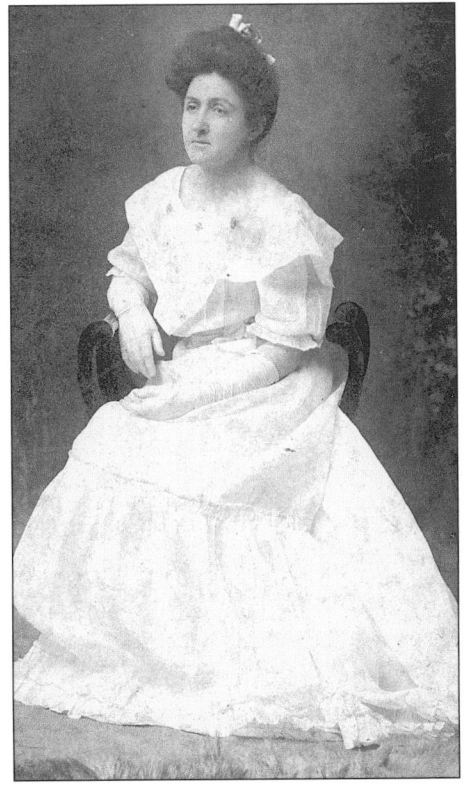

Kate Lily Blue (1869–1954) was the daughter of Colonel John Gilchrist Blue and Annie M. Evans and the sister of Rear Admiral Victor Blue and U.S. Surgeon General Rupert Blue. Kate Lily Blue was a charter member of the Marion Daughters of the American Revolution (DAR) and a state historian. A prolific author, she contributed to the literary world through books and articles to the *Marion Star*, *The State*, and many other daily newspapers throughout the state. (Photo courtesy of Ginny McIntyre.)

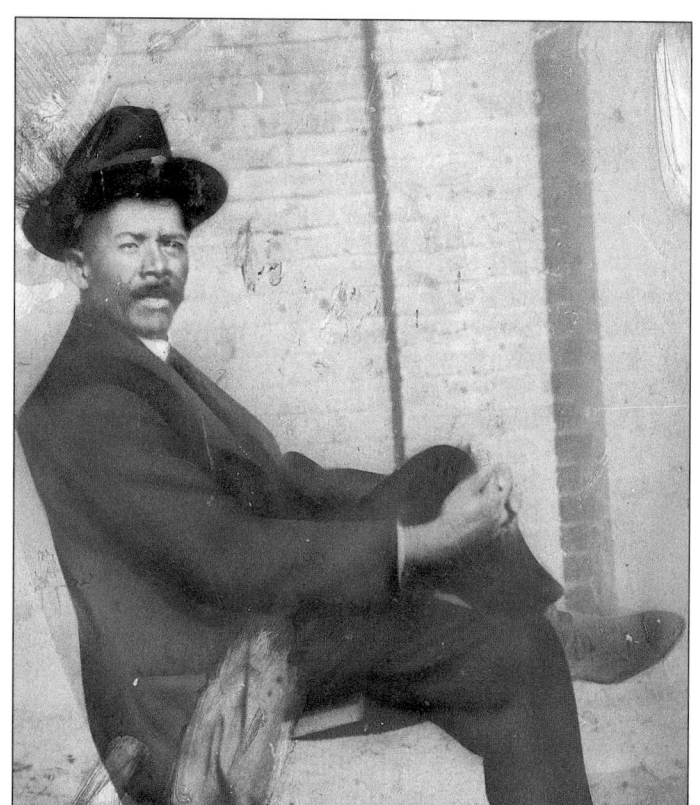

Reverend Elley Lawson Nelson, father of Mrs. Alma Finklea, was the local minister at Wise Chapel A.M.E. Church. Reverend Elley Nelson and wife, Mamie Etta Smith Parson Nelson, had a large family. They instilled in this family "belief in God, Family, and Education." (Photo courtesy of Alma Amelia Nelson Finklea.)

Attired in the tennis garb of the day are the tennis clubs as shown in the 1913 Marion High School annual, the *Swamp Fox*. (Photo courtesy of Mary B. Smith and Rusty Ammons.)

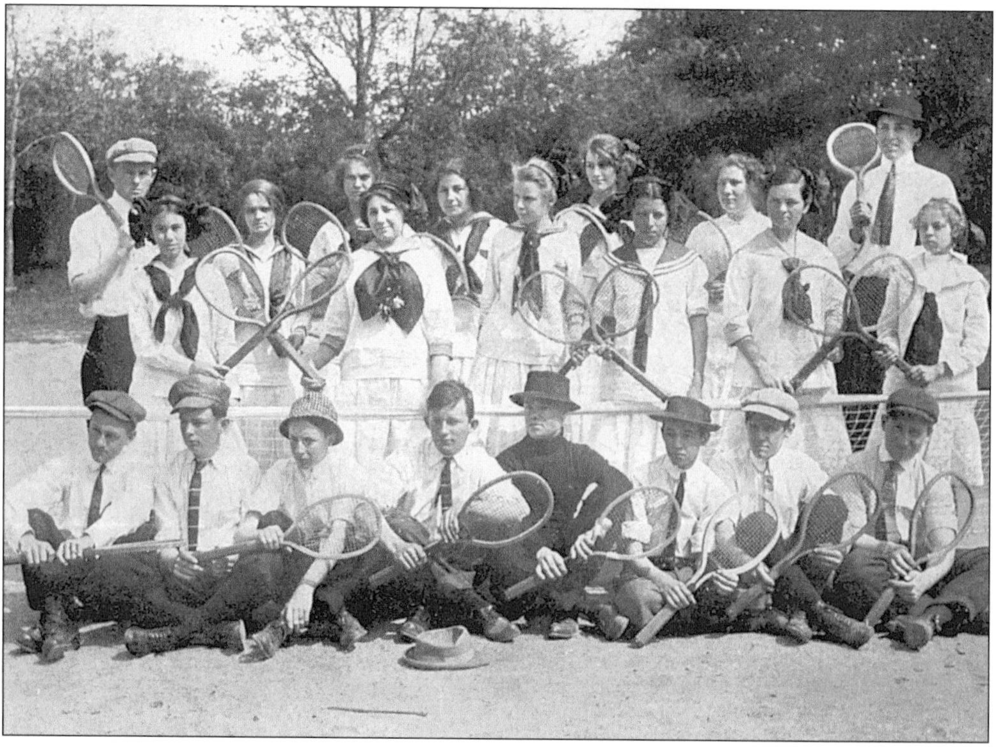

Three
DOIN' BUSINESS

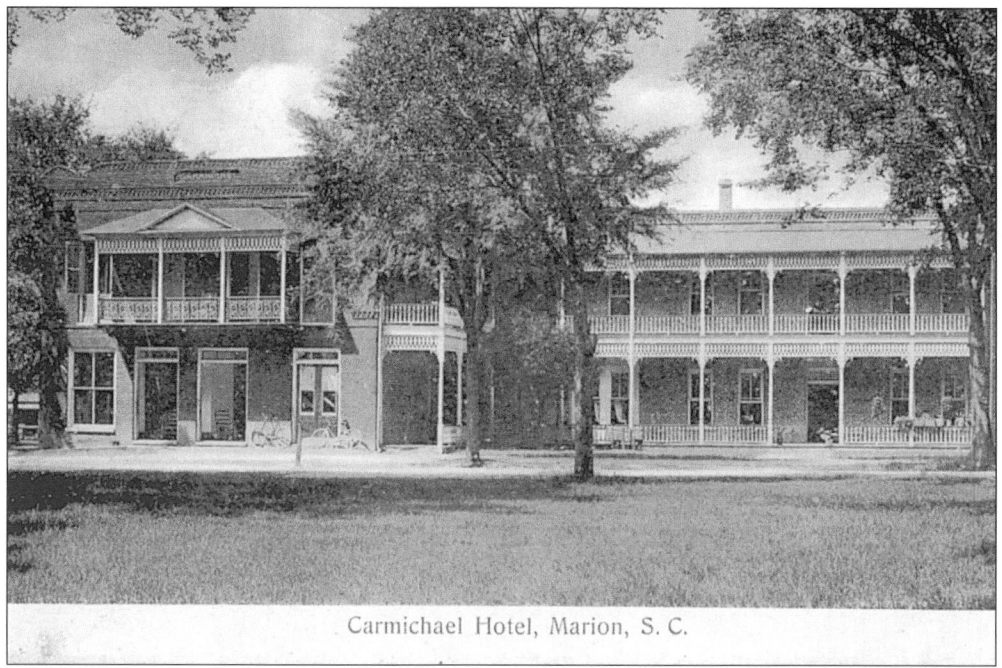

Carmichael Hotel, Marion, S. C.

The Carmichael Hotel on West Court Street behind the courthouse was built around the turn of the century. (Photo courtesy of Margaret E. Wood.)

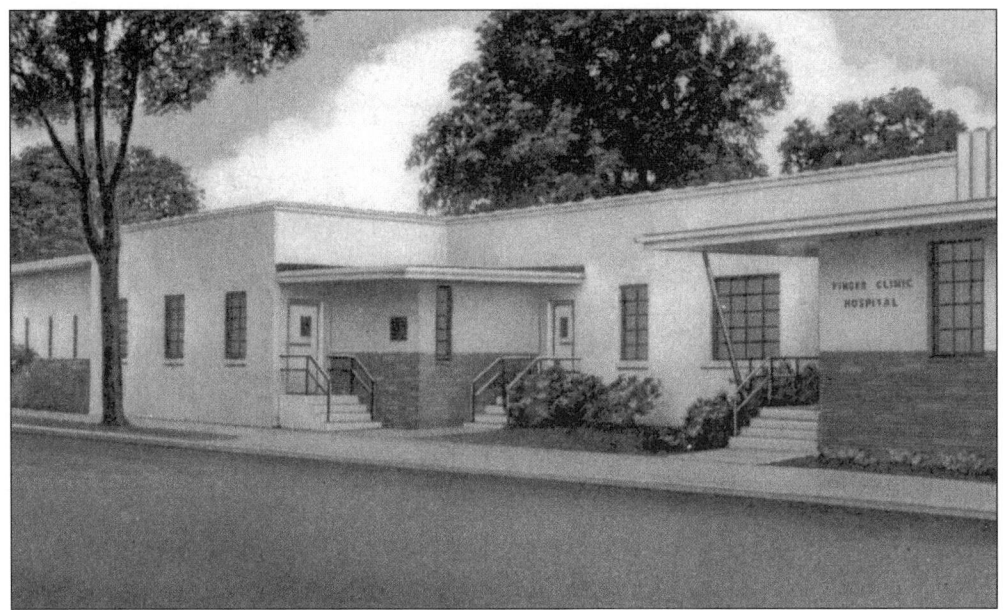

For decades, Finger Clinic on Harllee Street was served by many fine doctors, such as Dr. Elliott Finger. (Photo courtesy of Laney Baumrind.)

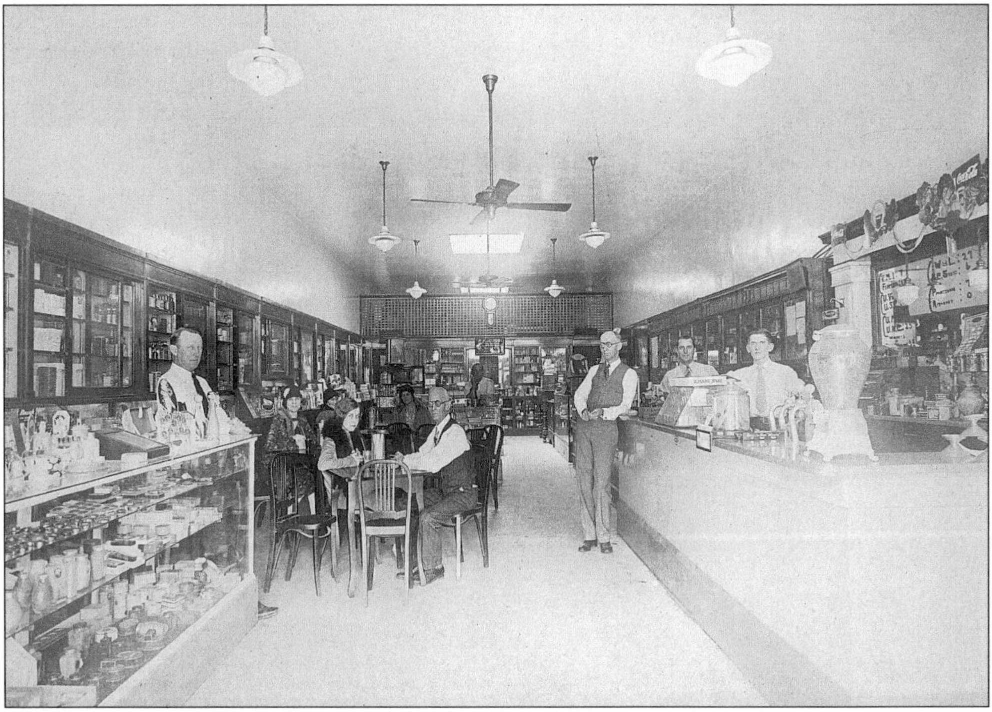

Dr. E.B. Bridgers and Joe Davis are pictured in the interior of Bridgers' Drug Store on Main Street in the 1930s. (Photo courtesy of Adele Hewitt.)

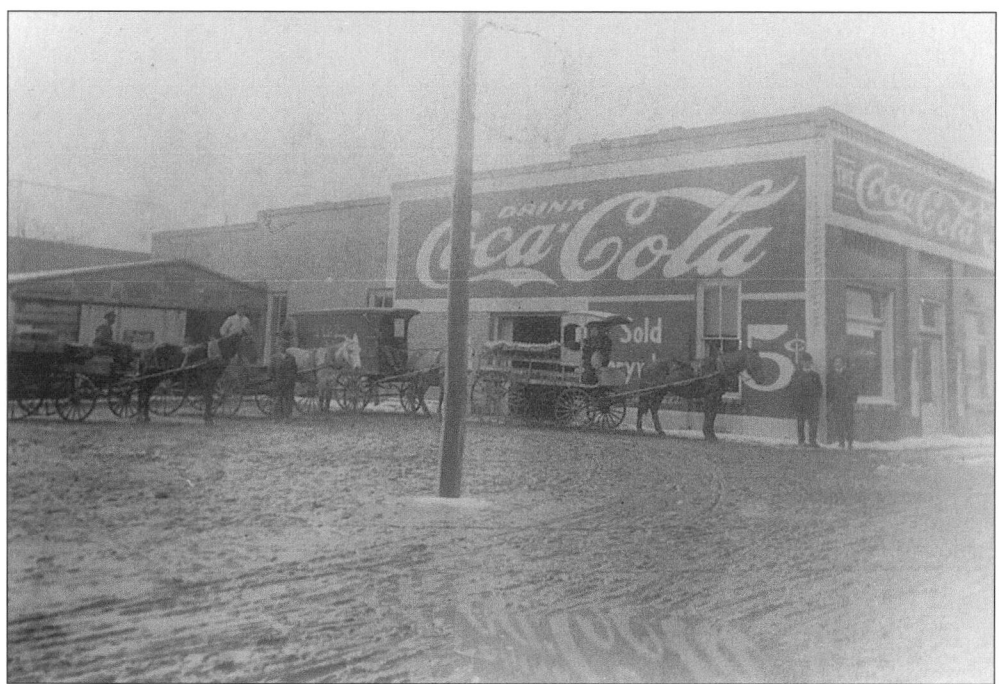

Pictured is the Coca-Cola Bottling Works during the winter of 1910, with horse-drawn delivery wagons parked in front. A rare, welcome snow reflects the Coca-Cola sign in the puddle formed by the melting snow. (Photo courtesy of Cindi Sloan.)

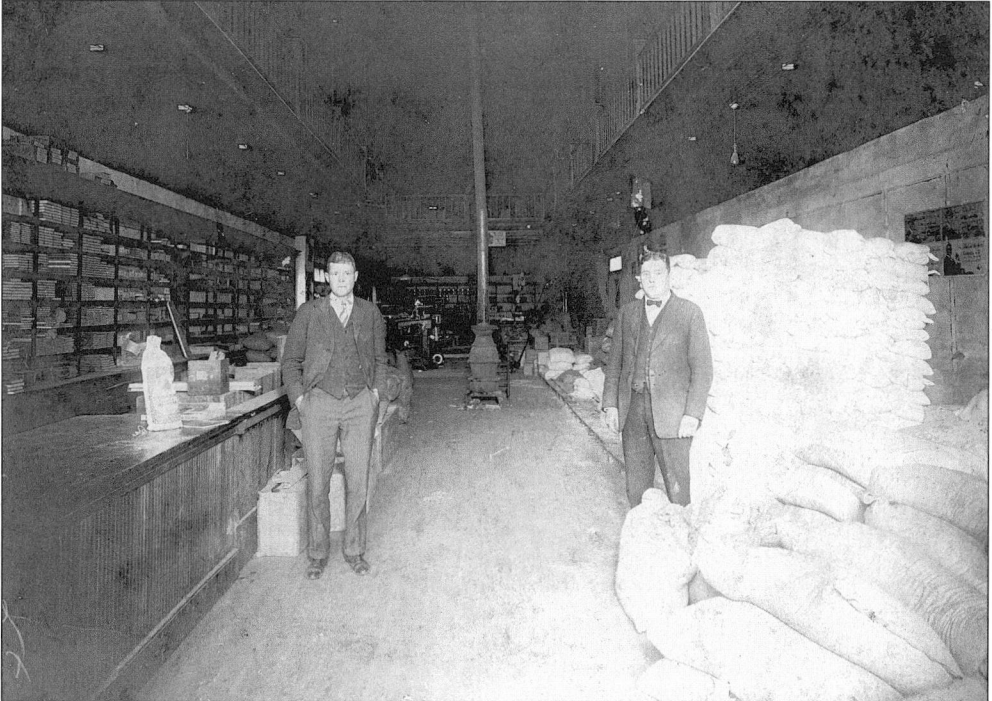

Pictured here inside Blackwell Brothers' Store are John and Frank Blackwell in 1924. (Photo courtesy of Jane Thompson.)

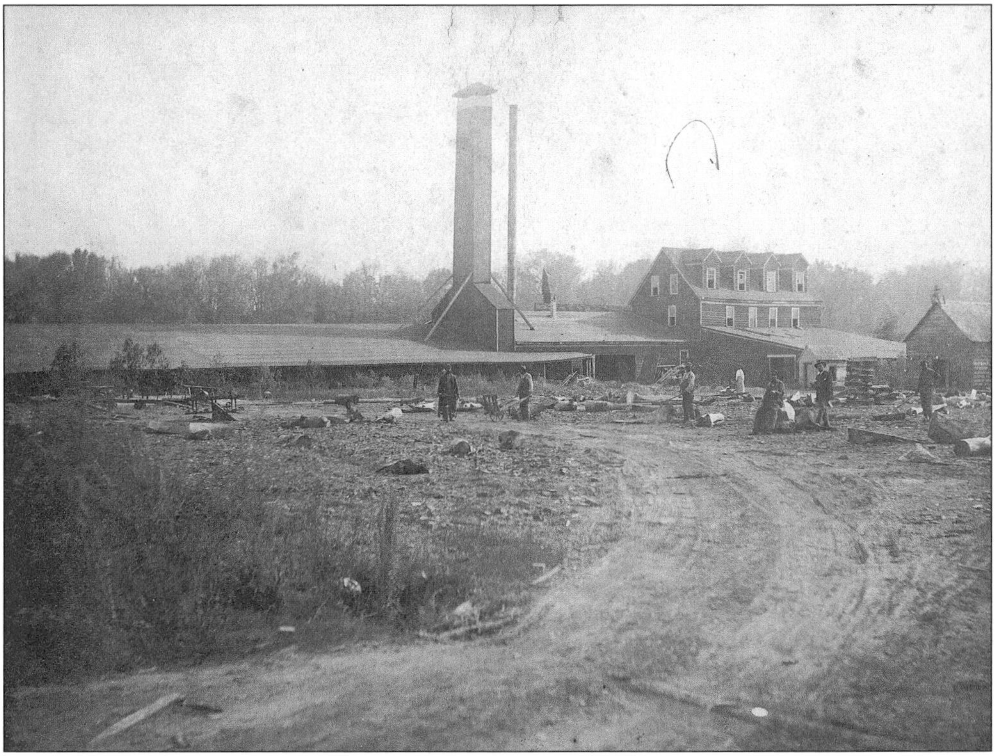

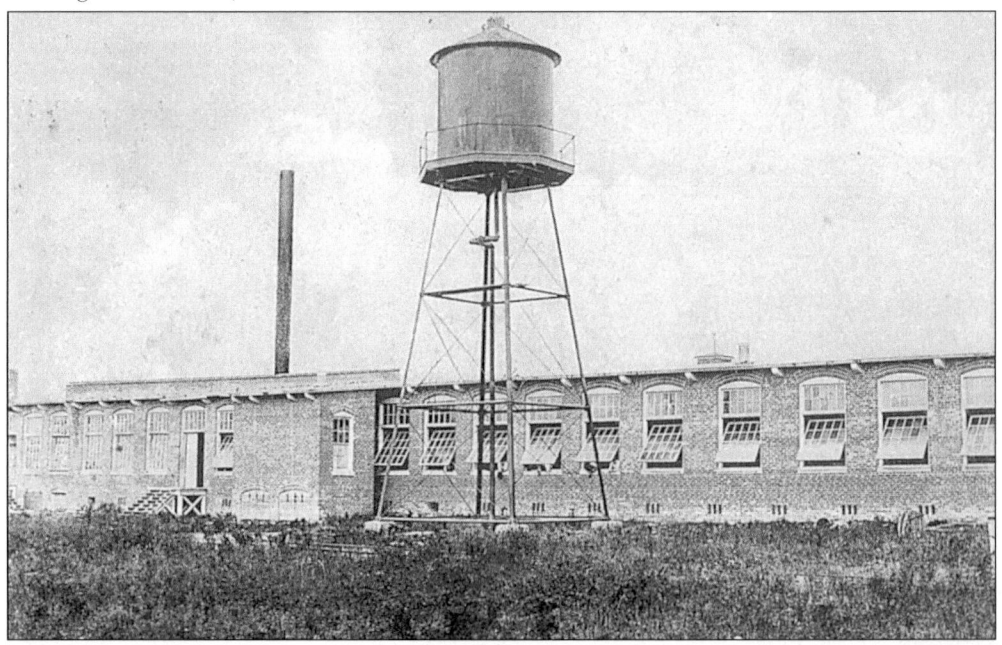

Layton Brick Works in West Marion was doing business during the early 1900s. (Photo courtesy of Margaret E. Wood.)

Located on Manning Street, Marion Cotton Mill, which made cotton thread, was owned by Mr. Will Stackhouse. In the 1940s, it was used by Marion Synthetics. (Photo courtesy of James and Nita Neely.)

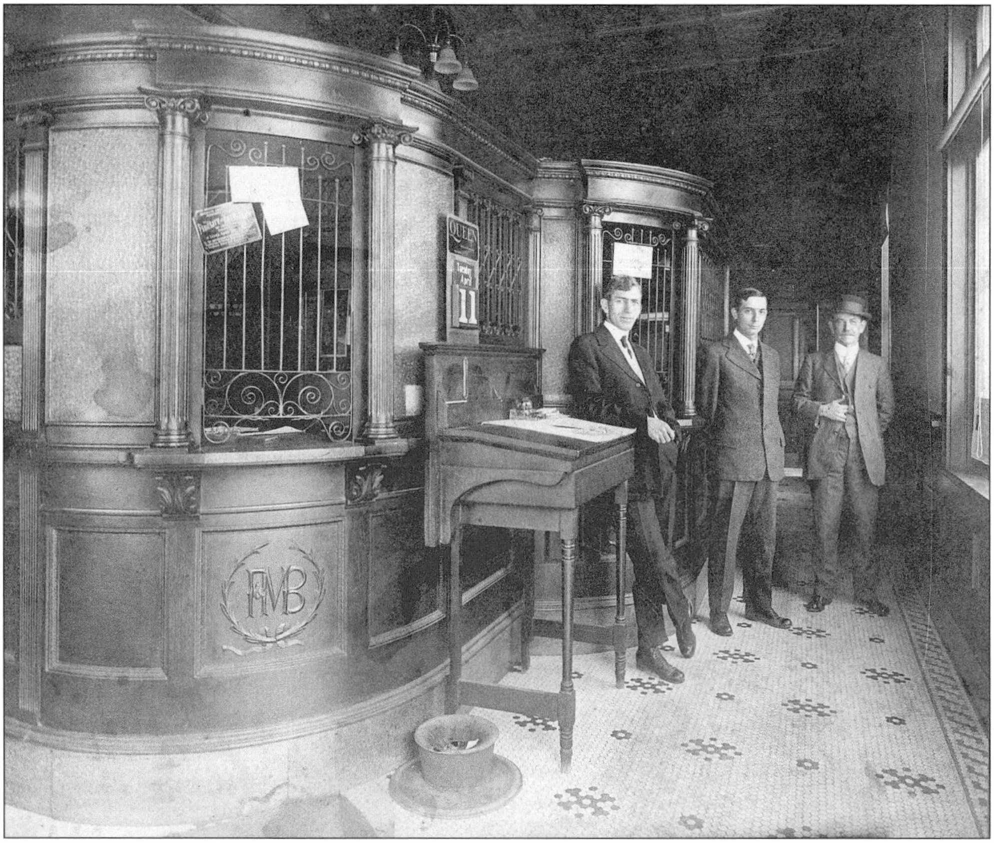

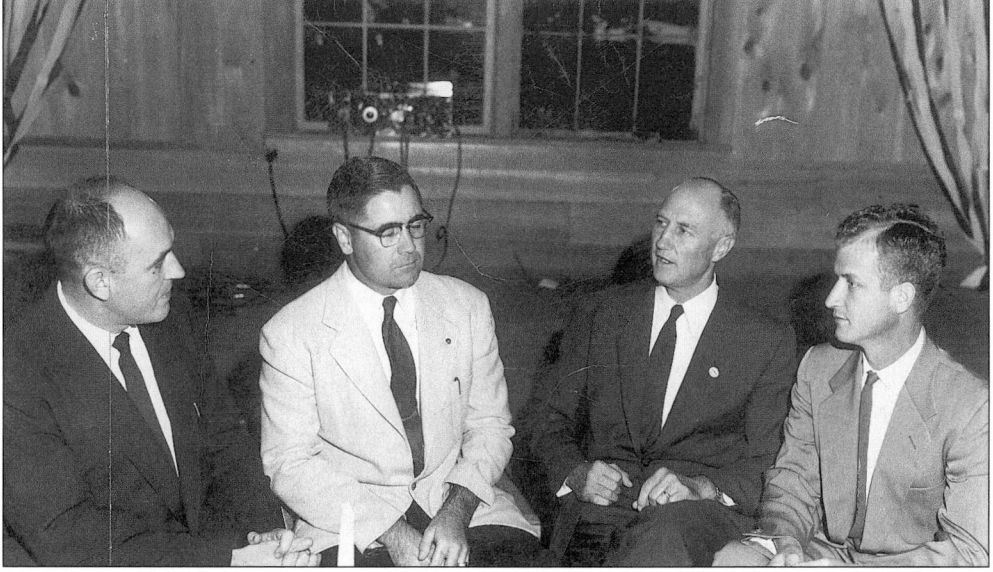

This photograph is of the interior of the Farmers and Merchant Bank, located at the corner of Main and Harllee Streets during the early 1900s. (Photo courtesy of Ginny McIntyre.)

Local and state business leaders James Dixon, Dick Lewis, Strom Thurmond, and Carroll Atkinson discuss the county's economy in the early 1960s. (Photo courtesy of Mary Lib Dixon.)

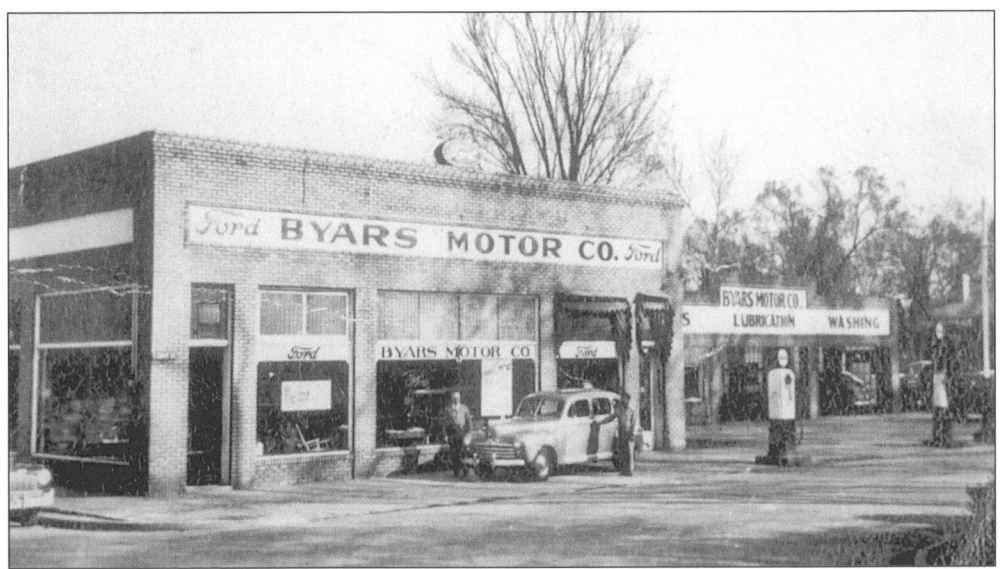

Byars Motor Company was located on Court Street facing the square. It was founded by the Byars family in 1918. (Photo courtesy of Lurline Stedman.)

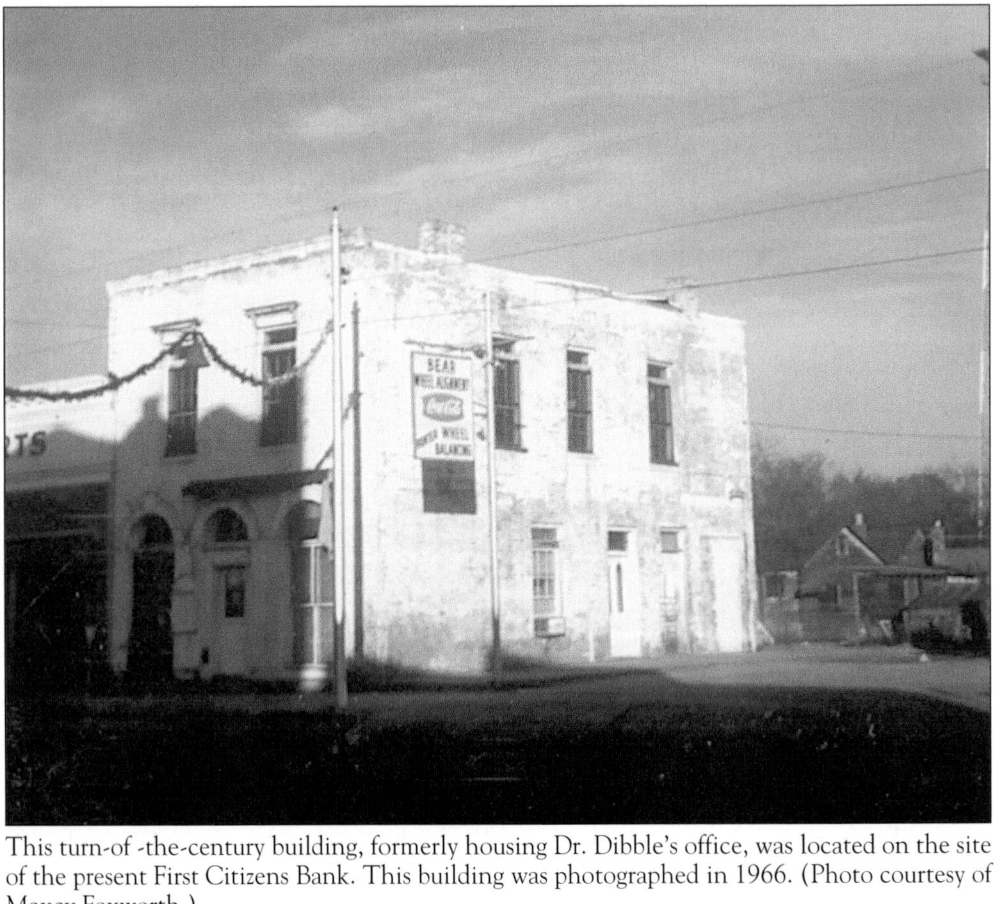

This turn-of-the-century building, formerly housing Dr. Dibble's office, was located on the site of the present First Citizens Bank. This building was photographed in 1966. (Photo courtesy of Maxcy Foxworth.)

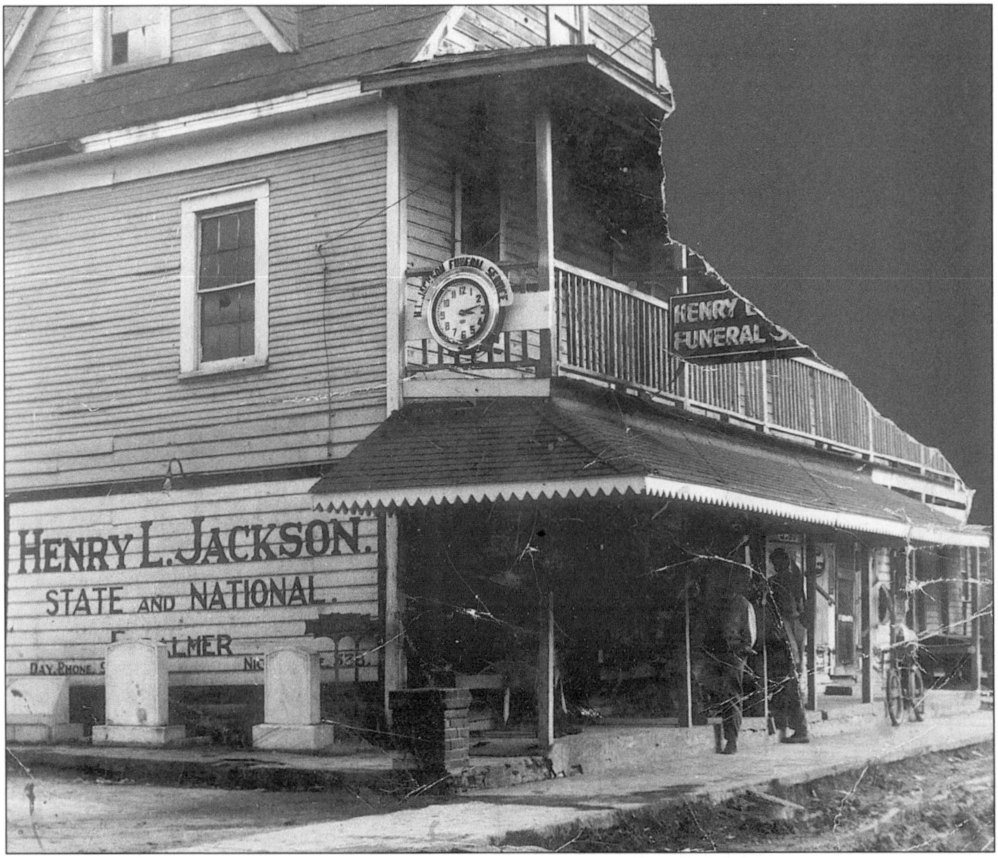

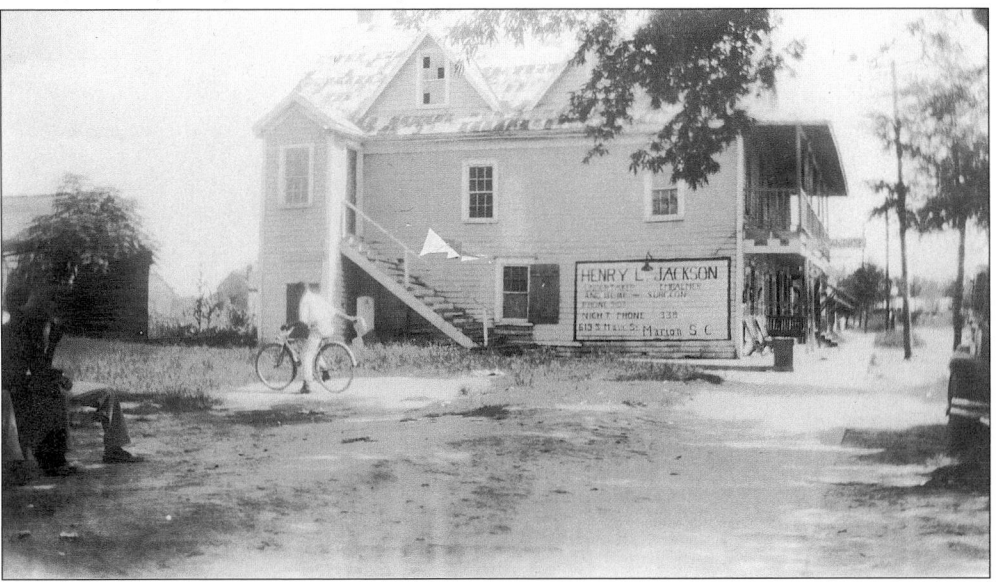

In 1928 Henry L. Jackson Funeral Service was located on South Main on the present site of IGA. (Photo by Pete Johnson; courtesy of Poiette McGill.)

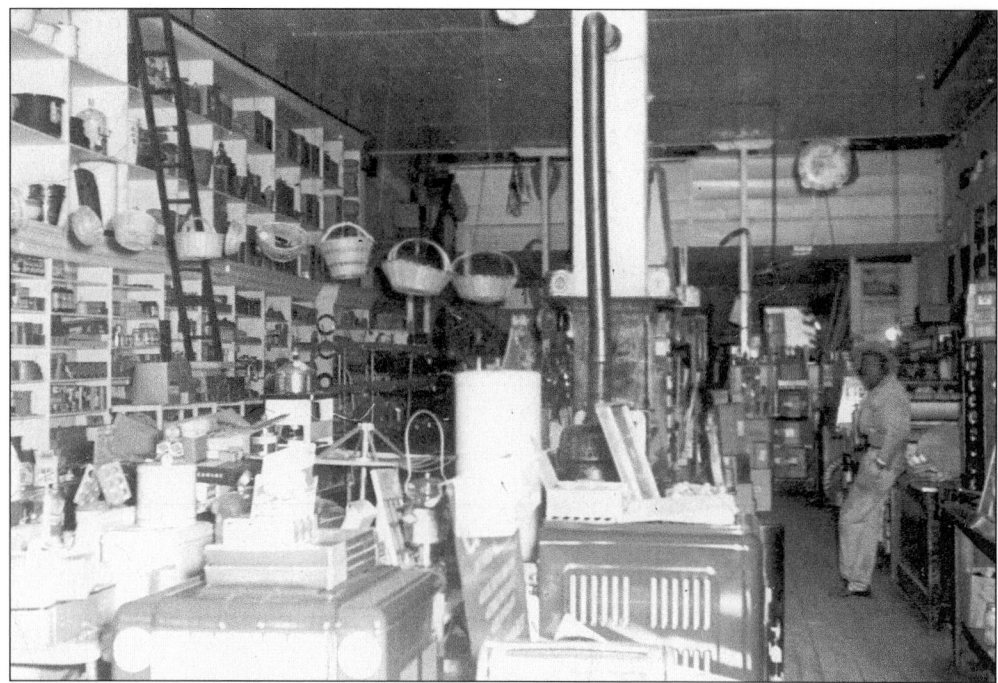

During the winters, customers of Planter's Hardware were welcomed by the warmth of the pot-bellied stove. (Photo courtesy of Lurline Stedman.)

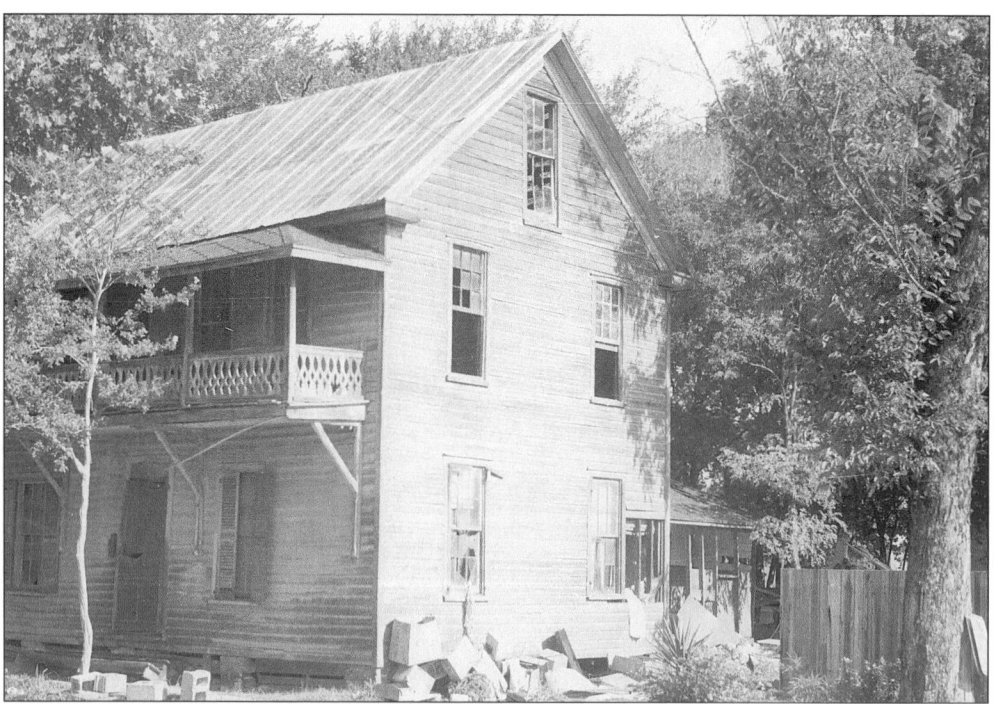

The boardinghouse on Manning Street, operated by Plum and Gertrude Johnson, was famous for its delicious ice cream. The family business was located east of the present Brown Insurance Agency. (Photo courtesy of Pat Z. Bethea.)

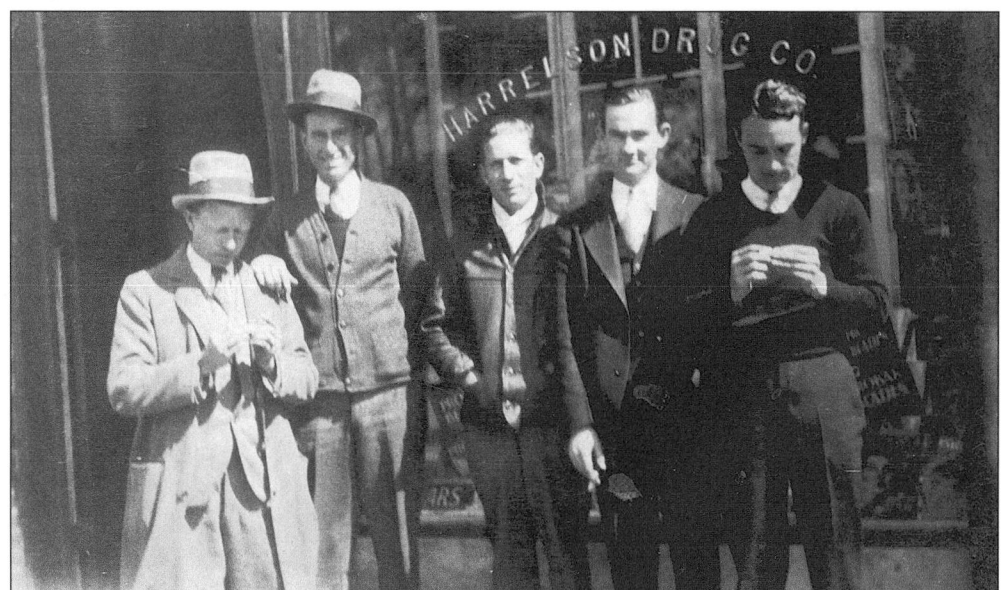

Standing left to right are Dixie Davis, Grady Wall, Walter Stackhouse, Hal Allison, and Junior Huteau in front of Harrelson Drug Co. in the early 1930s. (Photo courtesy of Dot D. McIntyre.)

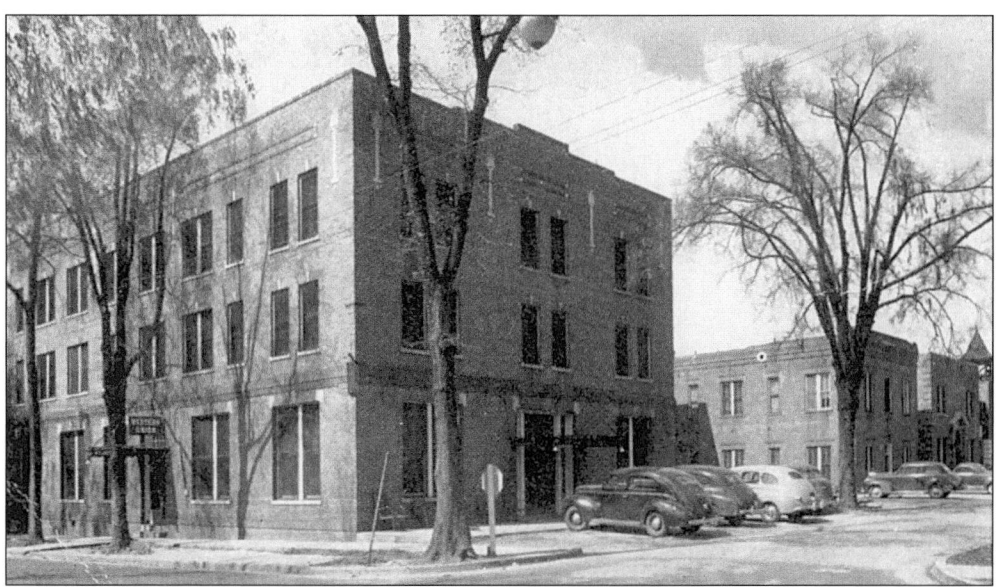

The Hotel Marion, on the corner of West Court Street and Godbold Street, was built about 1920. (Photo courtesy of Margaret E. Wood.)

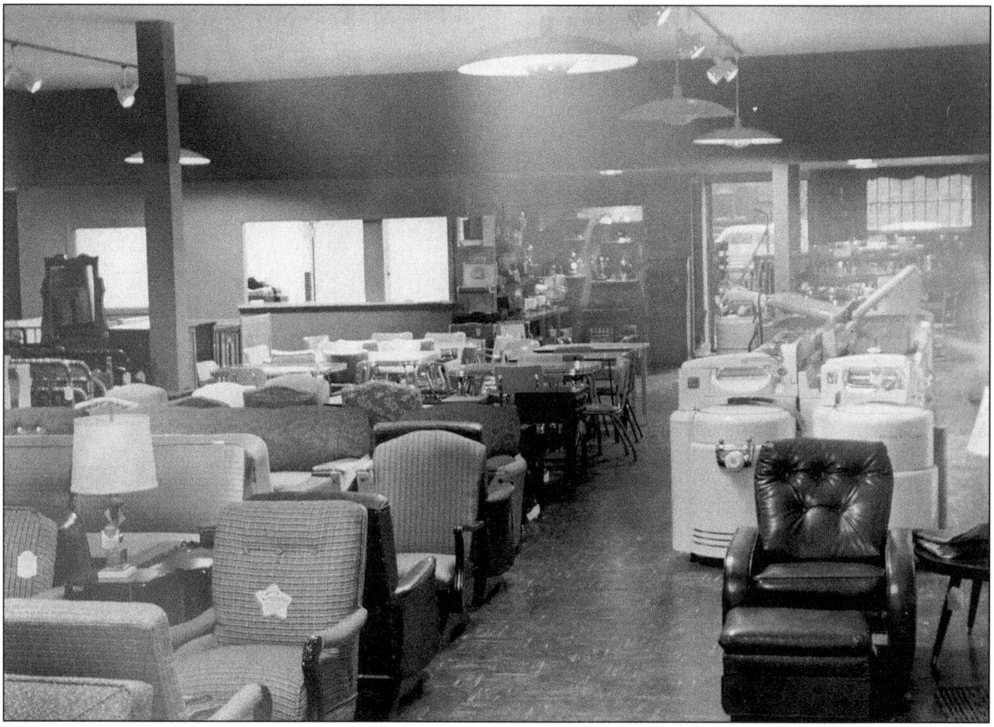

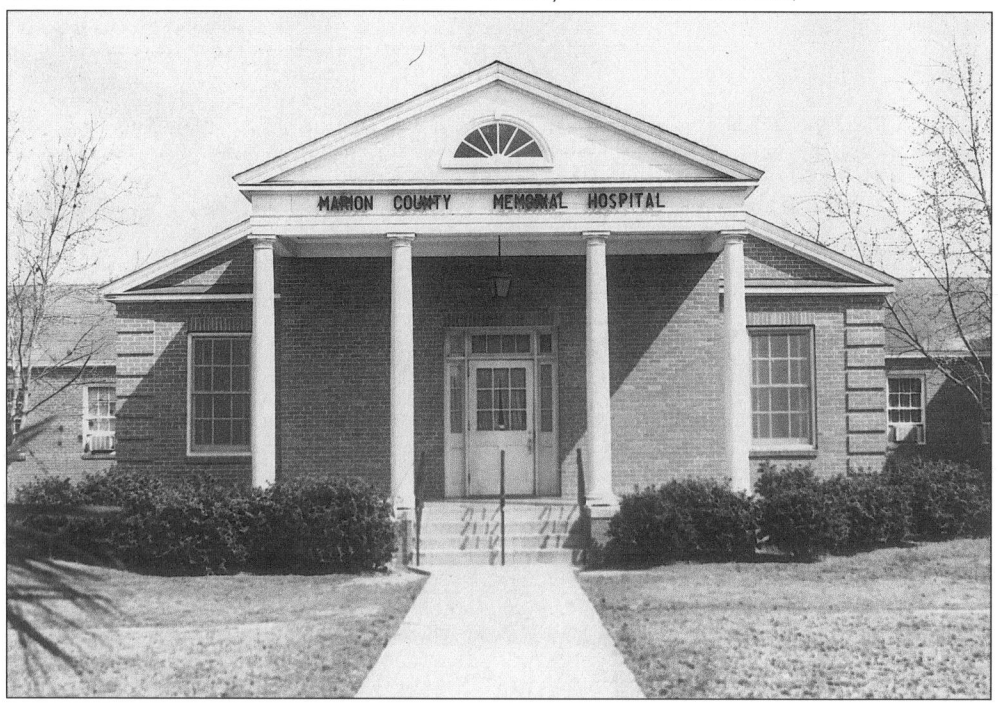

Ammons Furniture Store shows platform rockers, wringer washing machines, and chrome dinette sets for sale in the late 1950s. (Photo courtesy of Demont Ammons.)

Pictured here is Marion County Memorial Hospital, which was built in 1950. (Photo by Bob Mitchell Photography; courtesy of Marion County Medical Center.)

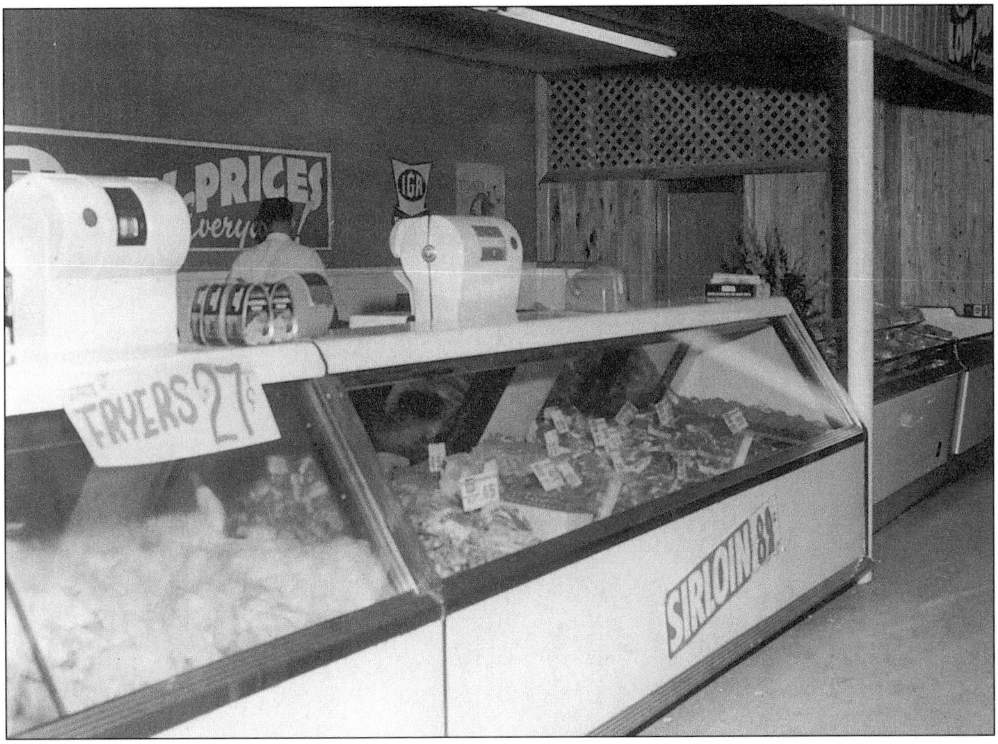

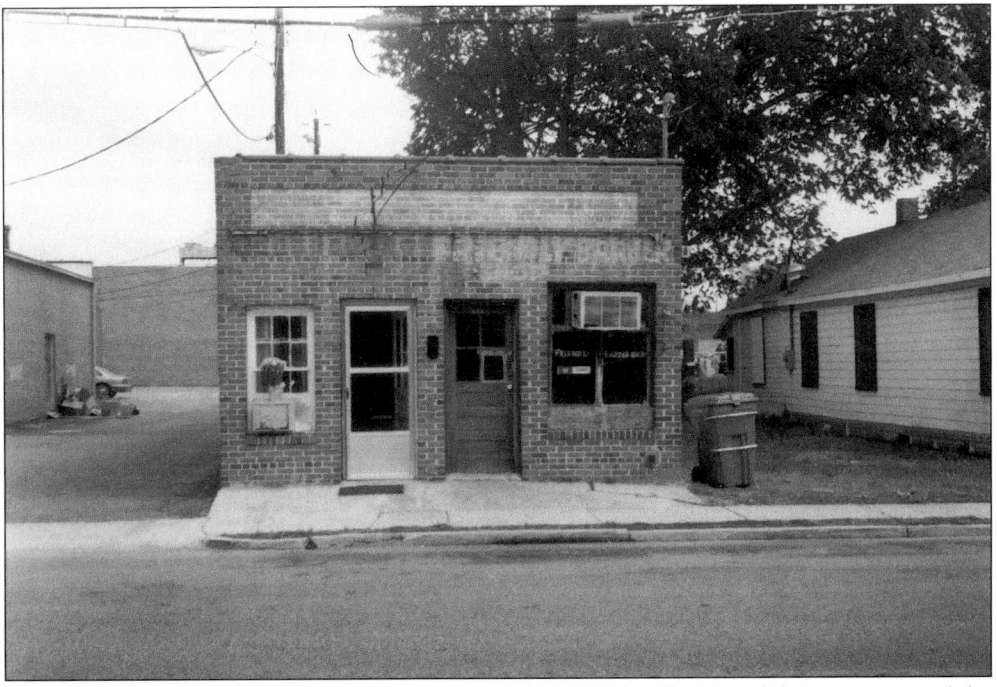

Ammons IGA Foodliner was doing business in 1962 with bargain meat prices. (Photo courtesy of Demont Ammons.)

Inez Fogan has operated this beauty shop on Arch Street for 50 years. (Photo courtesy of the Fogan family.)

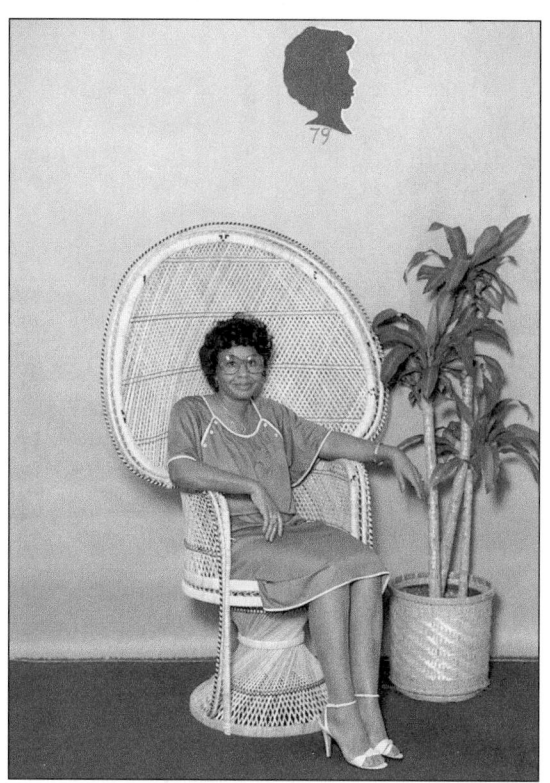

This photograph was taken while Mrs. Inez Fogan attended a cosmetology institute to keep her accreditation up to date. (Photo courtesy of the Fogan family.)

On the site where Zeman's now does business, a mule stable was located. In 1898, this business was owned by Mr. D.G. Atkinson. (Photo courtesy of F.T. Zeman.)

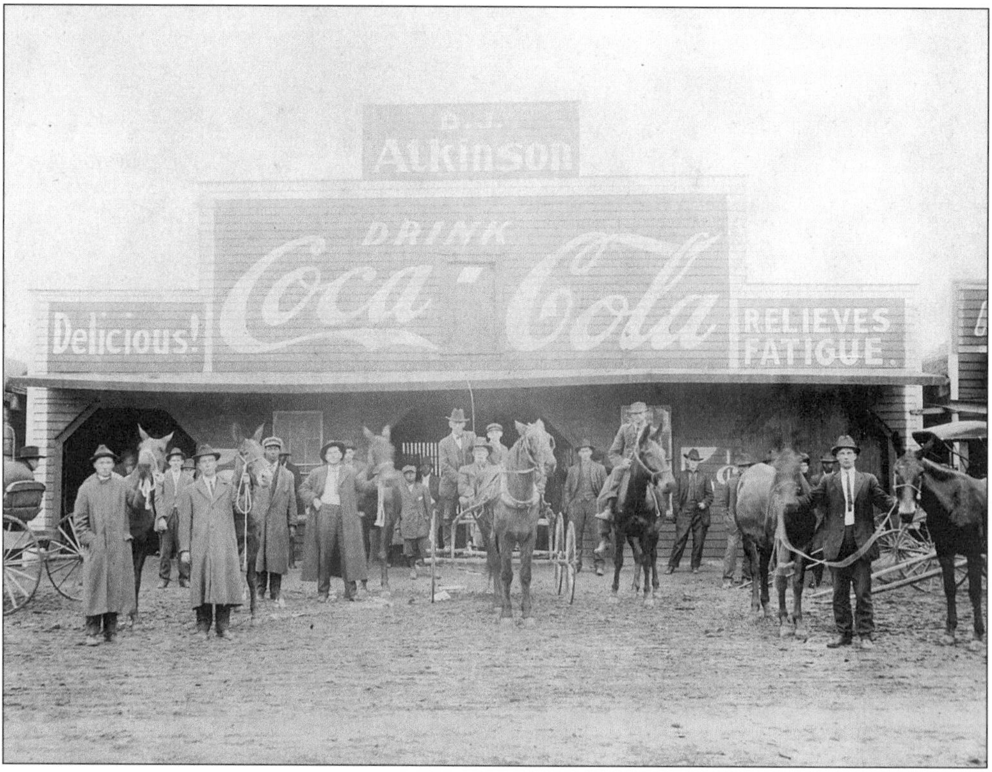

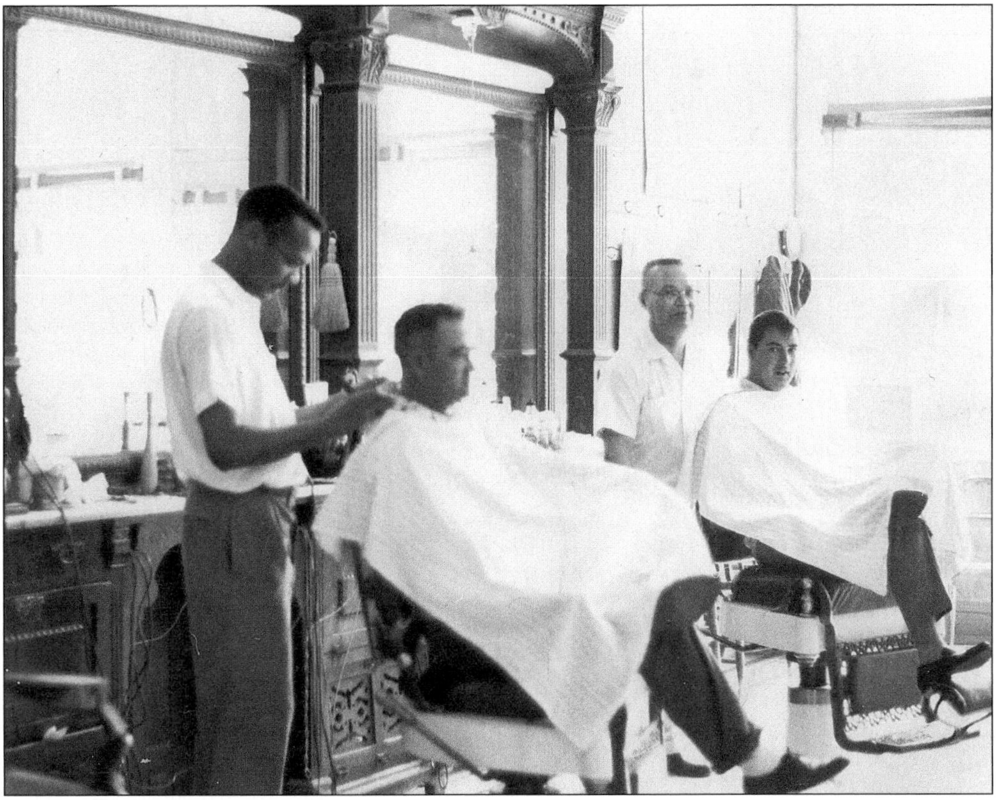

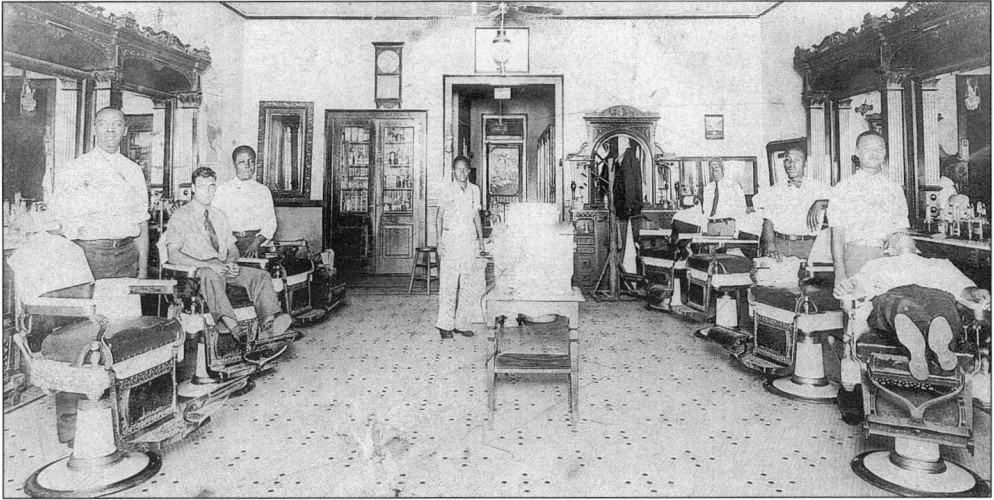

Richard Isaial Taylor, son of Reverend Thomas E. Taylor, is giving a customer "a shave and a haircut." Working beside him is his nephew Frank Brunson Patterson Jr. (Photo courtesy of Shirley Patterson.)

This photograph of the inside of Taylor's Barber Shop depicts the barbershop staff ready for business. On left, front to back, are William Brunson Patterson, unidentified customer, and unidentified barber; on right, front to back, are Richard Isaial Taylor (son of Reverend Thomas E. Taylor), Alford Ellerbe (brother of William Brunson Patterson), and Reverend Thomas E. Taylor (founder). (Photo courtesy of Shirley Patterson.)

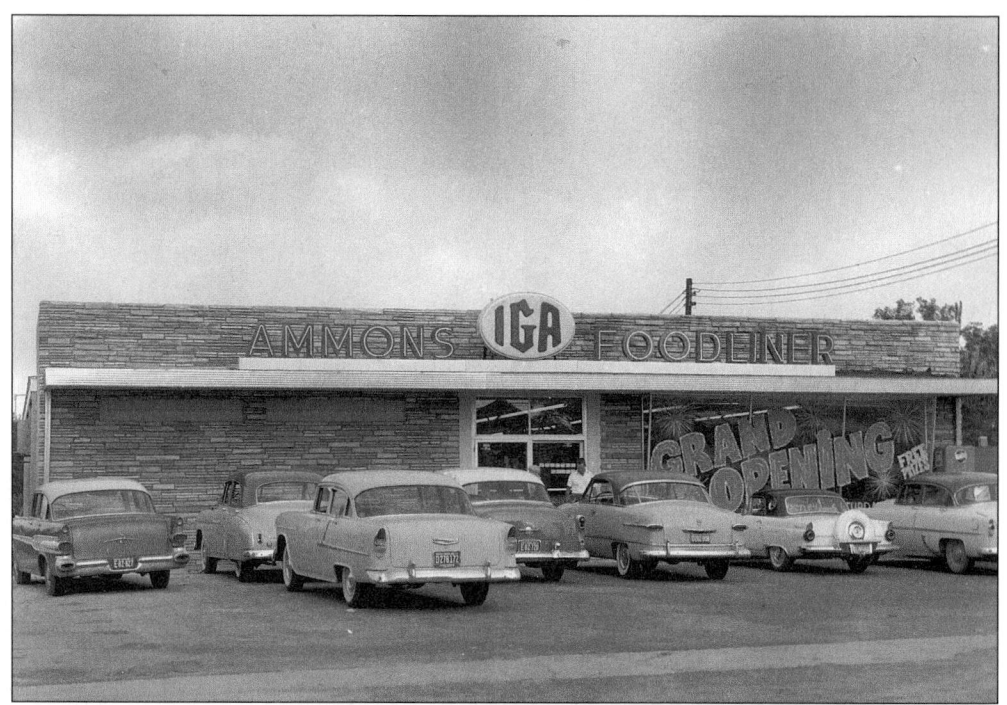

A variety of automobiles are parked at the 1962 grand reopening of Ammons IGA Foodliner, including Lem Winesett's Thunderbird. (Photo courtesy of Demont Ammons.)

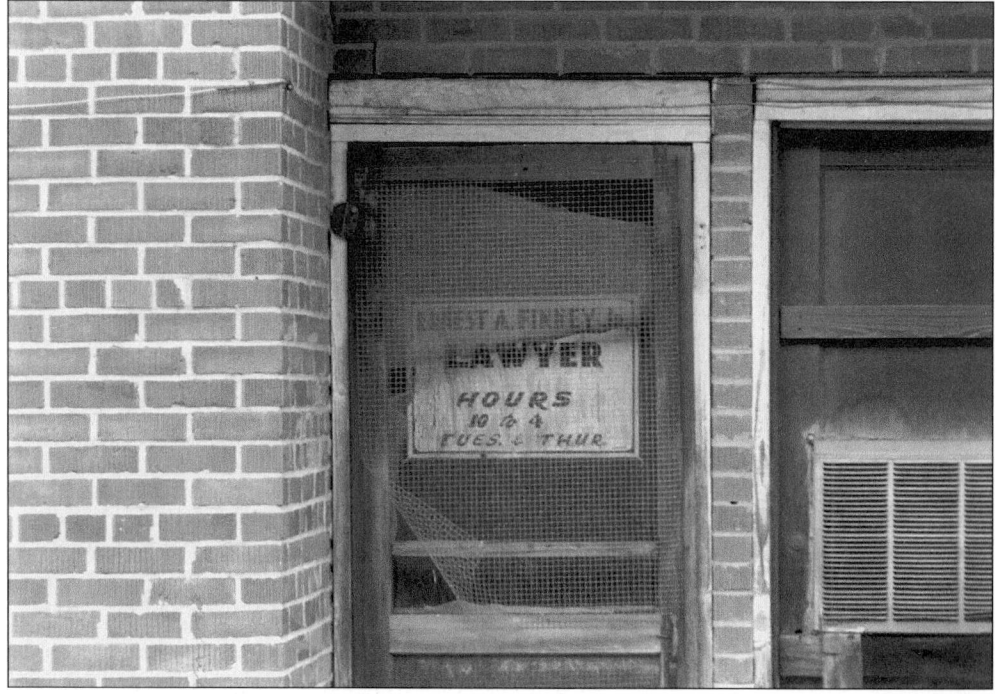

South Carolina Supreme Court Chief Justice Ernest A. Finney had a legal practice in this building on Arch Street. The front of the building housed Gibson's Barber Shop and Inez Fogan's Beauty Shop. (Photo courtesy of Dr. James Blake and Ray Govus.)

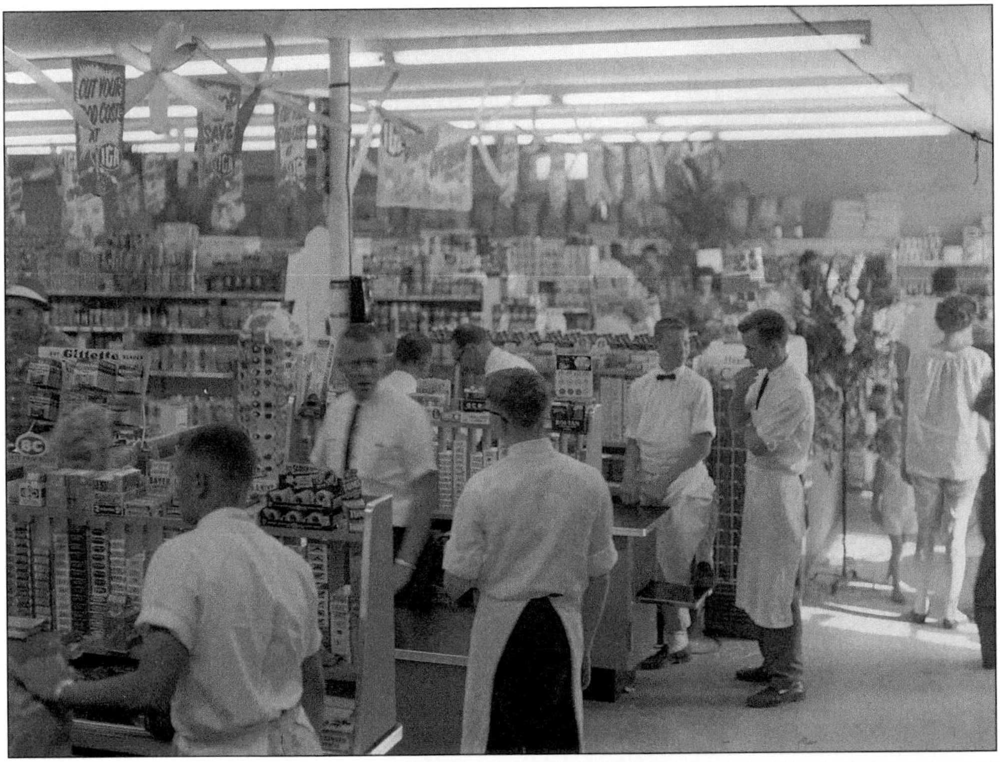

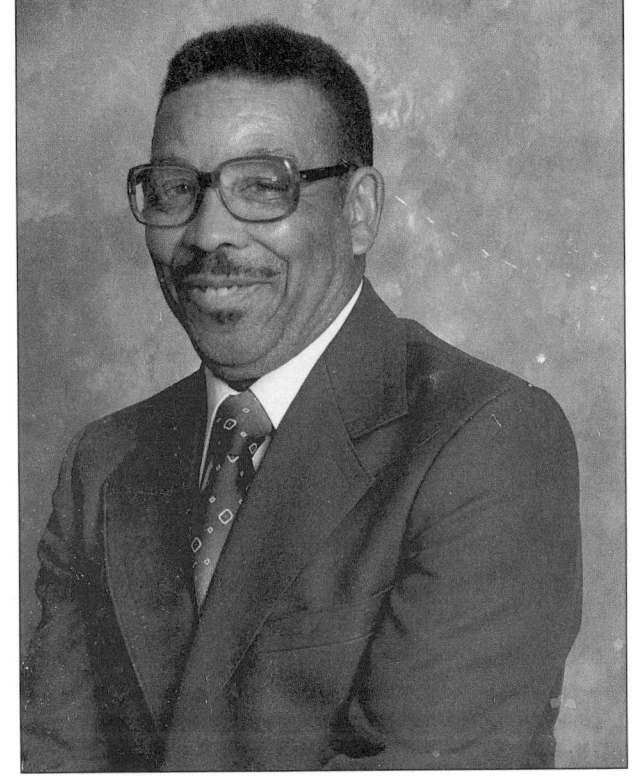

The inside of Ammons IGA Foodliner during the grand reopening in 1962 shows the neatly attired staff with white shirts and ties. (Photo courtesy of Demont Ammons.)

Mr. James "Pop" Dorsey was the operator of Eastside Grocery from 1971 until 1999. Mr. Dorsey got his nickname, "Pop," because the area children thought of him as their very own. He expressed to children that they should always do the best job that they could do. The picnic area located across from Marion High School is named for him, for "Pop" Dorsey touched many lives with his kindness. (Photo courtesy of the Dorsey family.)

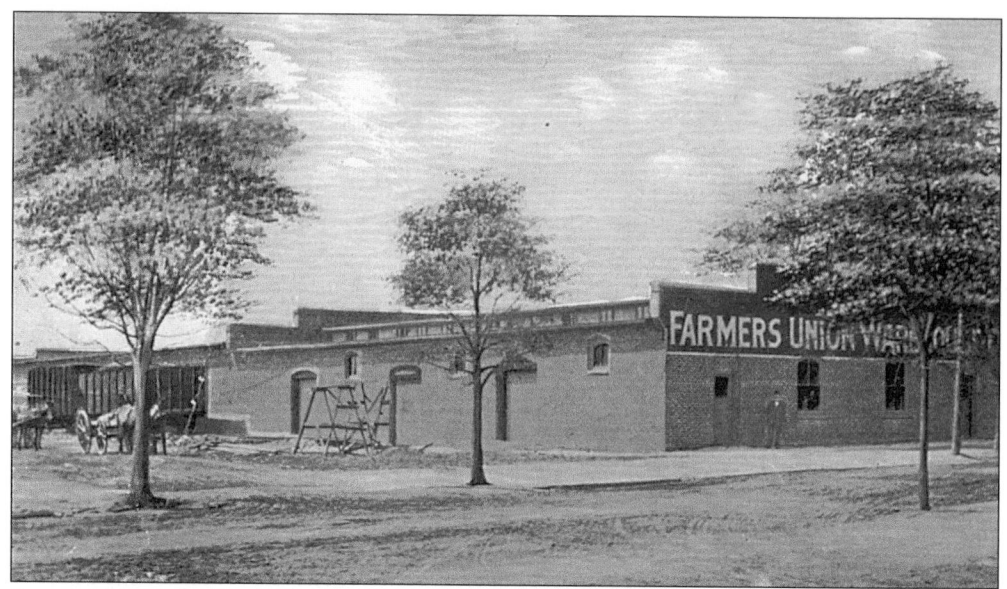

Farmers' Union Tobacco Warehouse was located on Manning Street. (Photo courtesy of James and Nita Neely.)

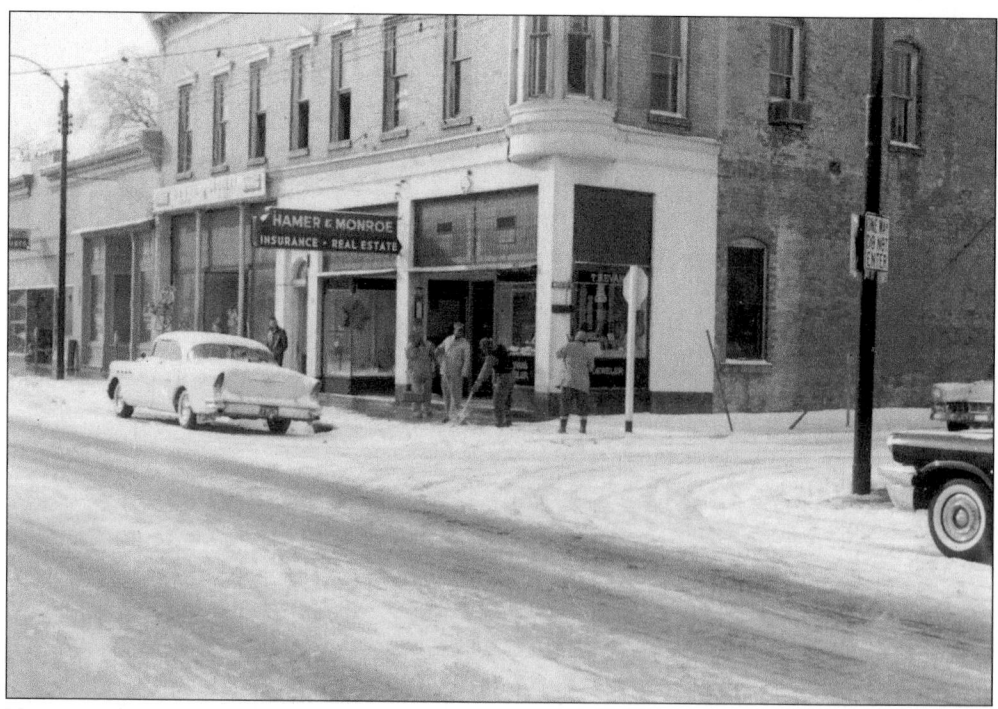

Hamer and Monroe occupied this business site on the corner of Main and Witcover Streets. (Photo courtesy of Mitzi Winesett.)

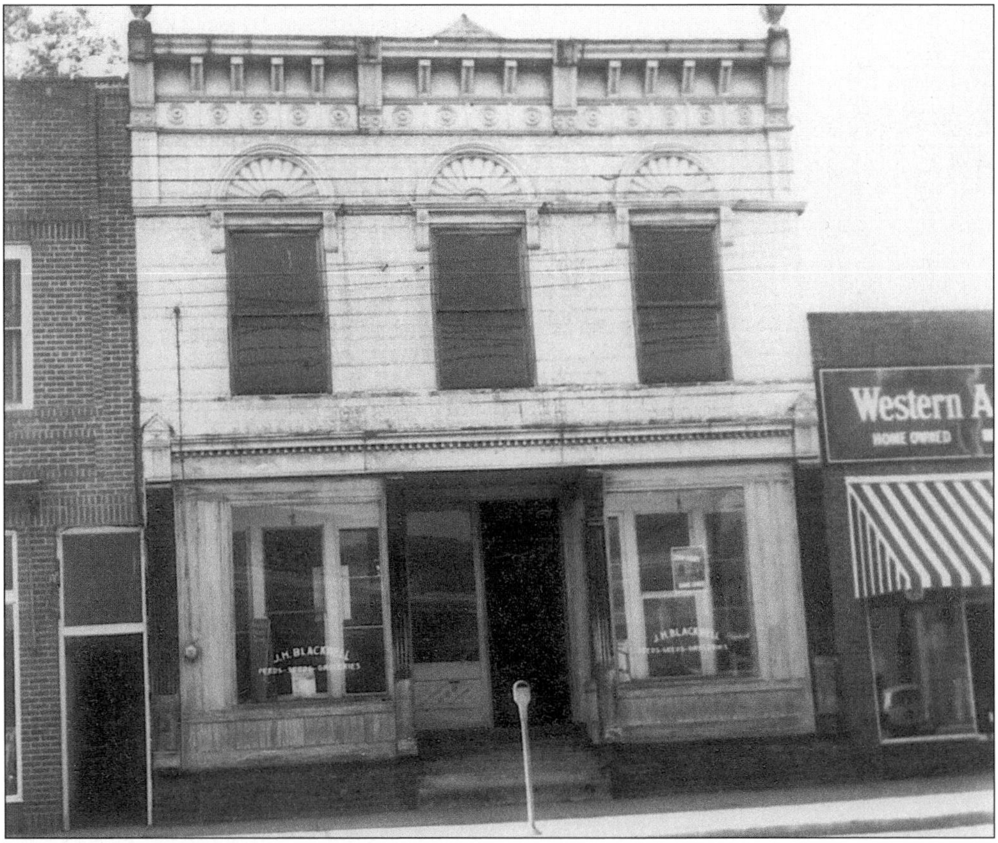

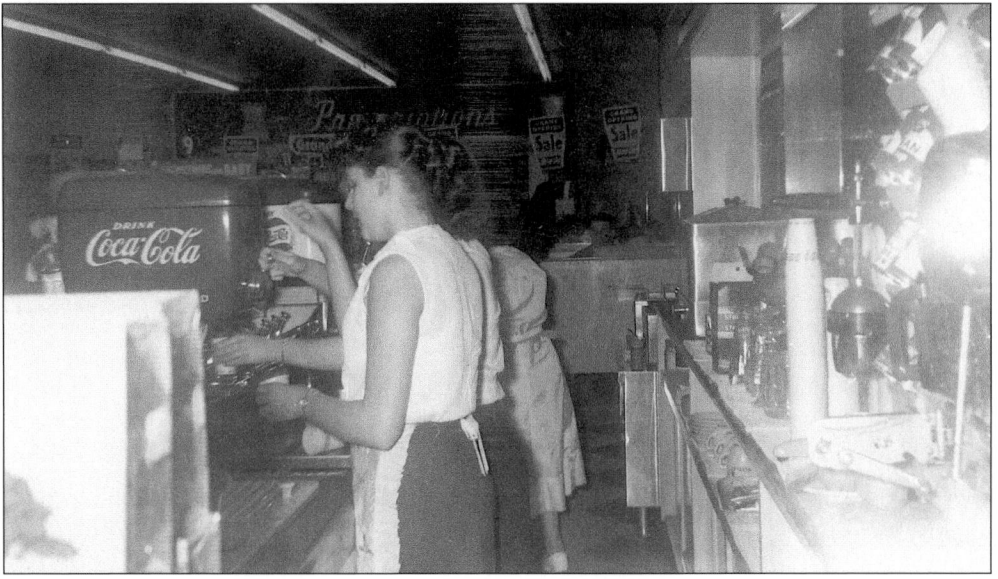

The popular J.H. Blackwell Store, shown in 1957, would later become the Professional Pharmacy. (Photo courtesy of FoxTrot Committee.)

Fountain cokes are still being served today at the Professional Pharmacy on North Main Street. (Photo courtesy of Billie Mishoe.)

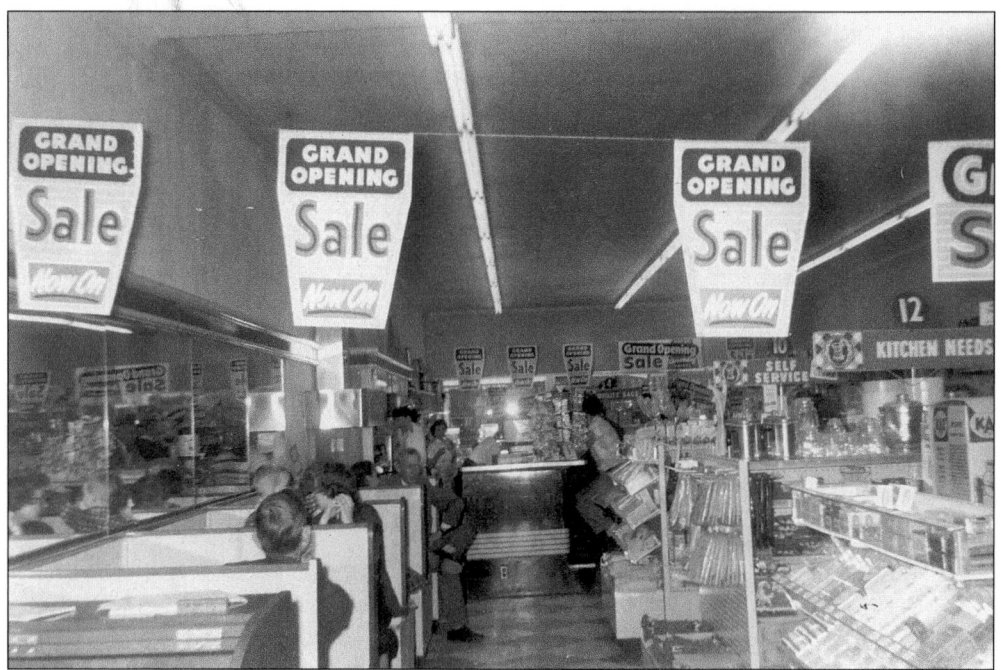

The grand opening of the Professional Pharmacy took place when it was owned by the Paul Mishoe family. (Photo courtesy of Billie Mishoe.)

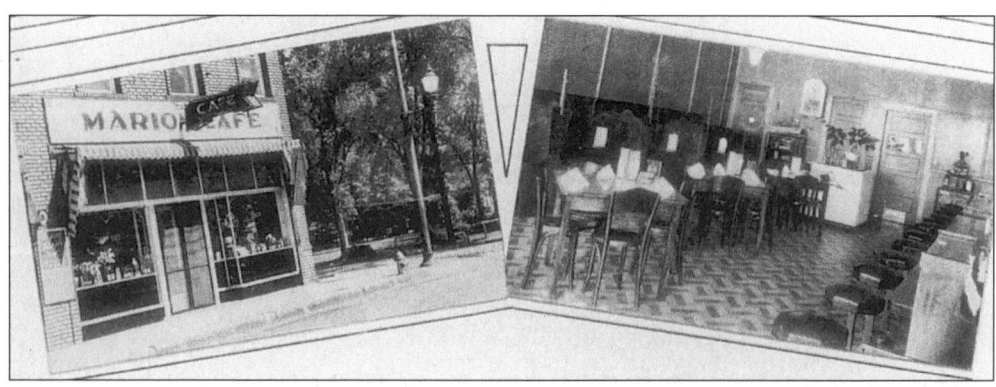

The Marion Cafe on the corner of Dozier and Main Streets was one of the most modern restaurants in eastern South Carolina, according to the proprietor, Angel Bekis. (Photo courtesy of FoxTrot Committee and the Caroliniana Library at USC.)

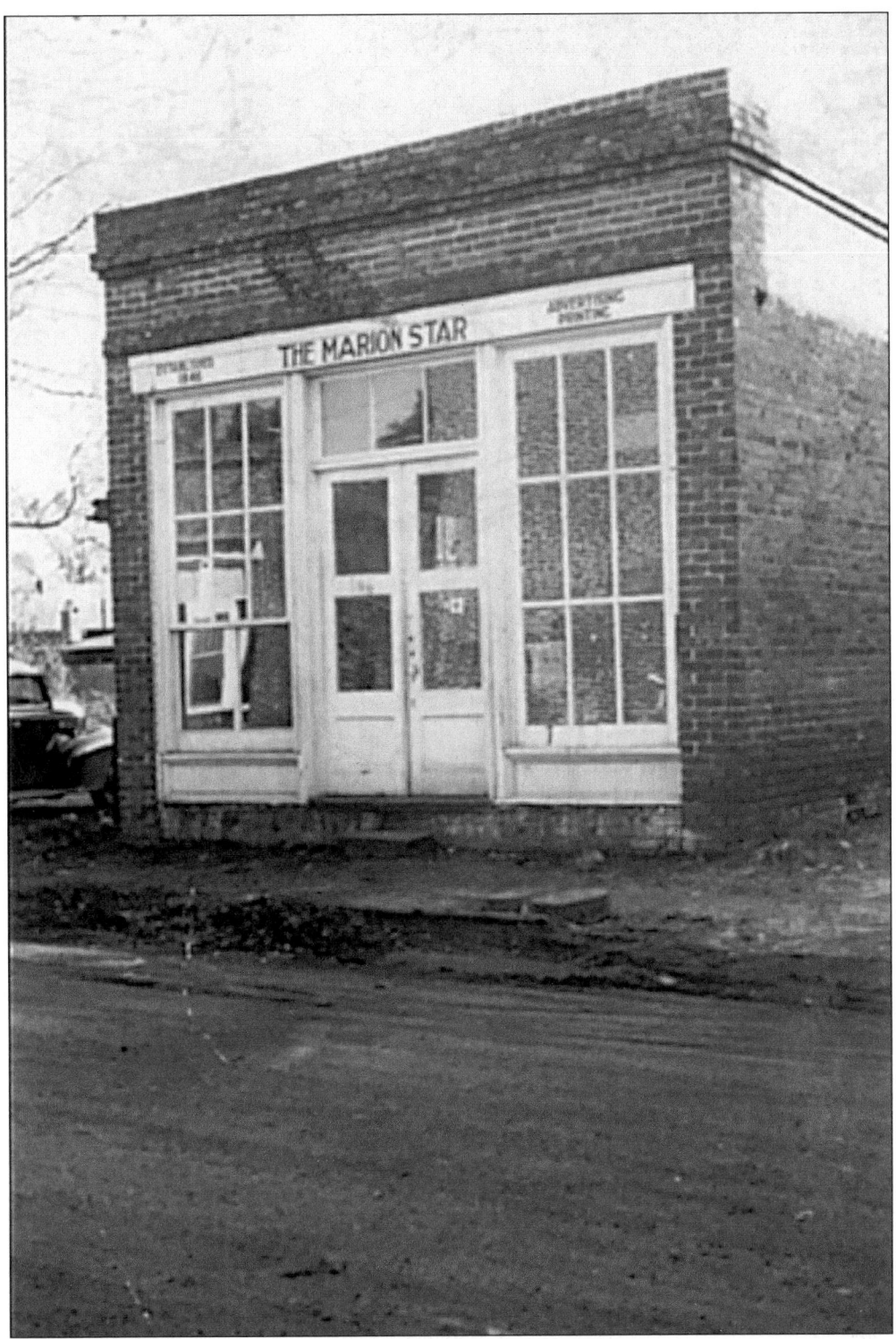

Lem Winesett, the editor and owner of the *Marion Star*, kept generations focused on the heart and soul of the hometown. (Photo courtesy of Mitzi Winesett.)

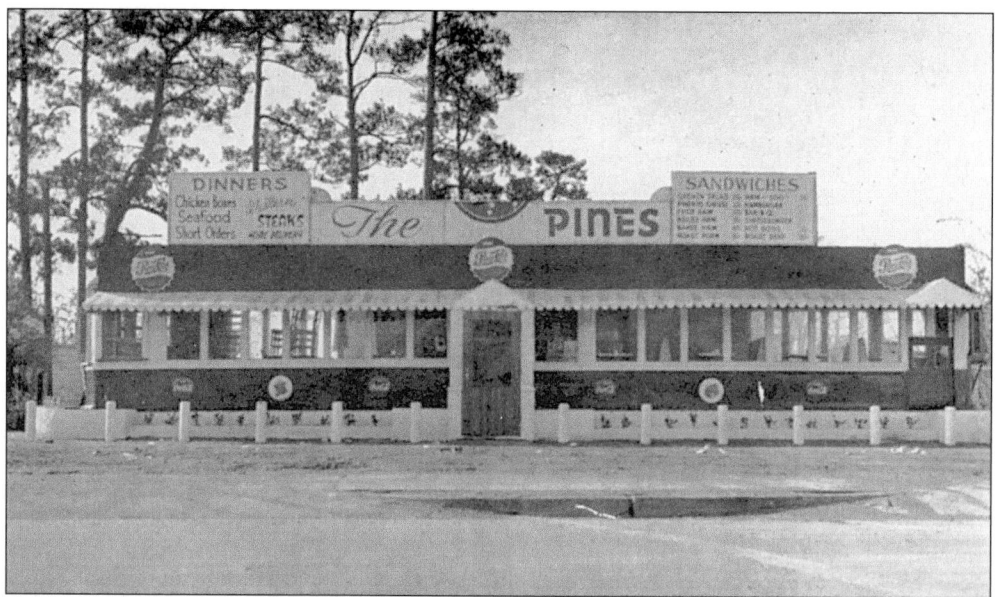

The Pines Diner, located on South Main Street, was a favorite gathering place for the young people. This photo appeared in the advertising section of the 1954 Marion High School annual. (Photo courtesy of Nancy Askins.)

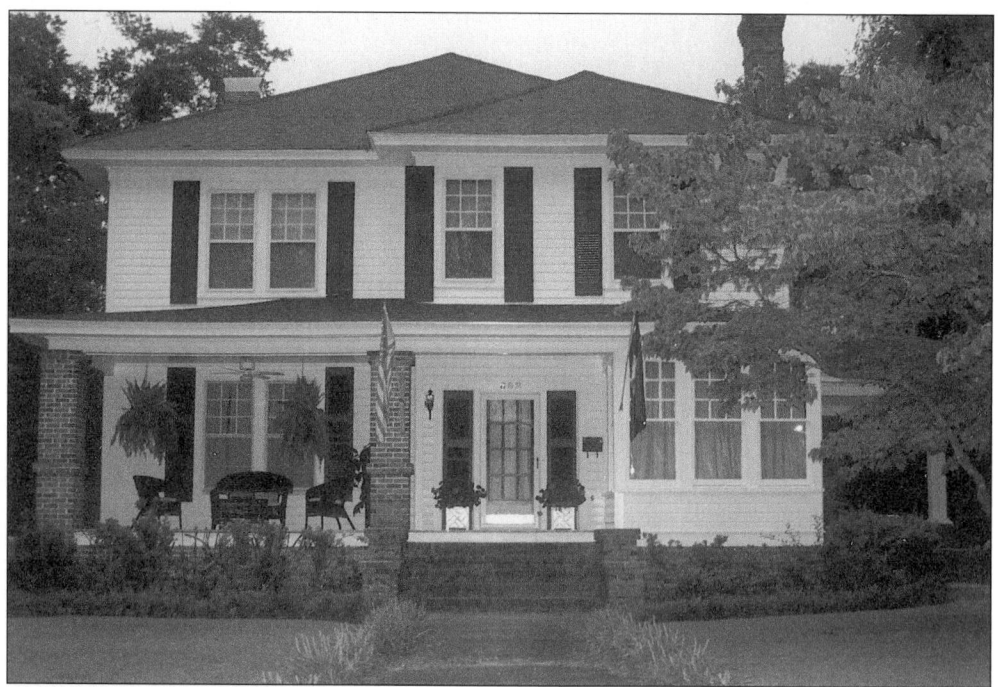

The first hospital located in Marion was in this home on Willcox Avenue. Margaret Cox James remembers entering the hospital from the porte-cochere, where Dr. Carroll Howell set her broken arm. The operating room was located upstairs. (Photo courtesy of David James.)

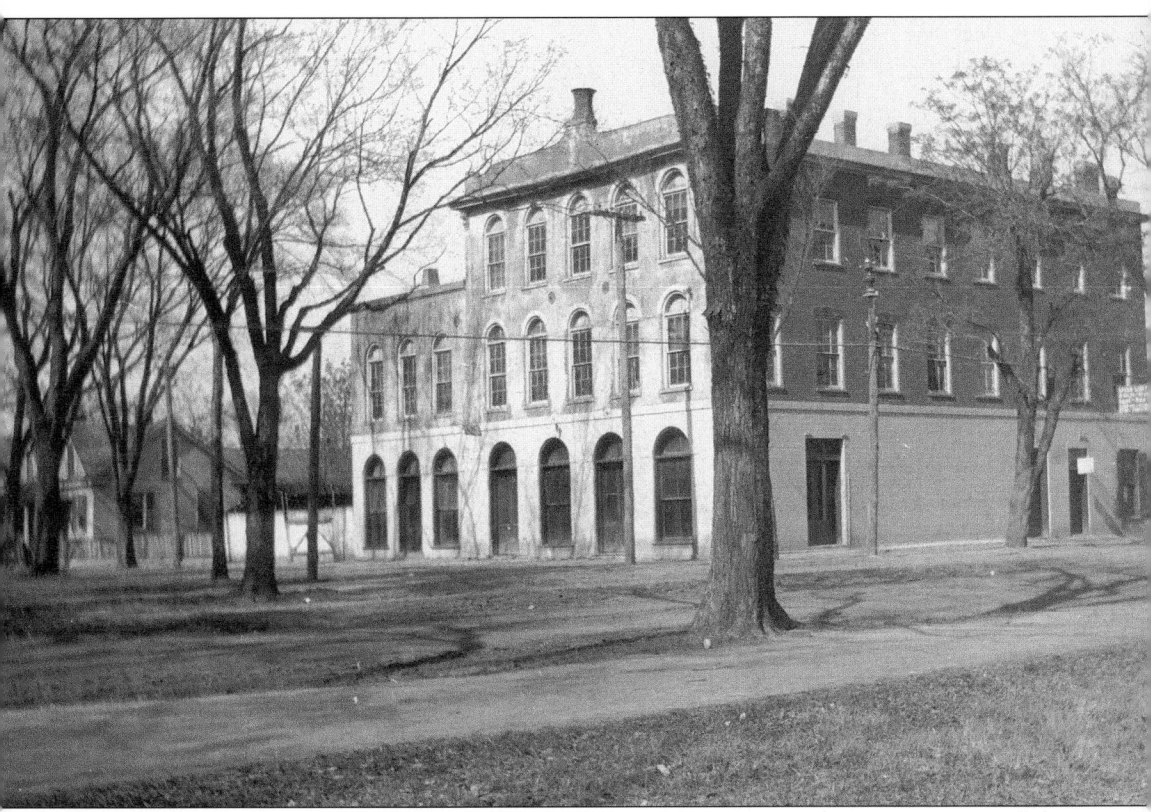

The Jenkins Hotel was situated on the corner of Main and Dozier Streets on the site of the Exxon station. Taylor's Barber Shop was initially located on the street level, and it is possible to see the entrance with the sign over it. Taylor's Barber Shop would later be built across Main Street at its present location. (Photo courtesy of Mike McLendon.)

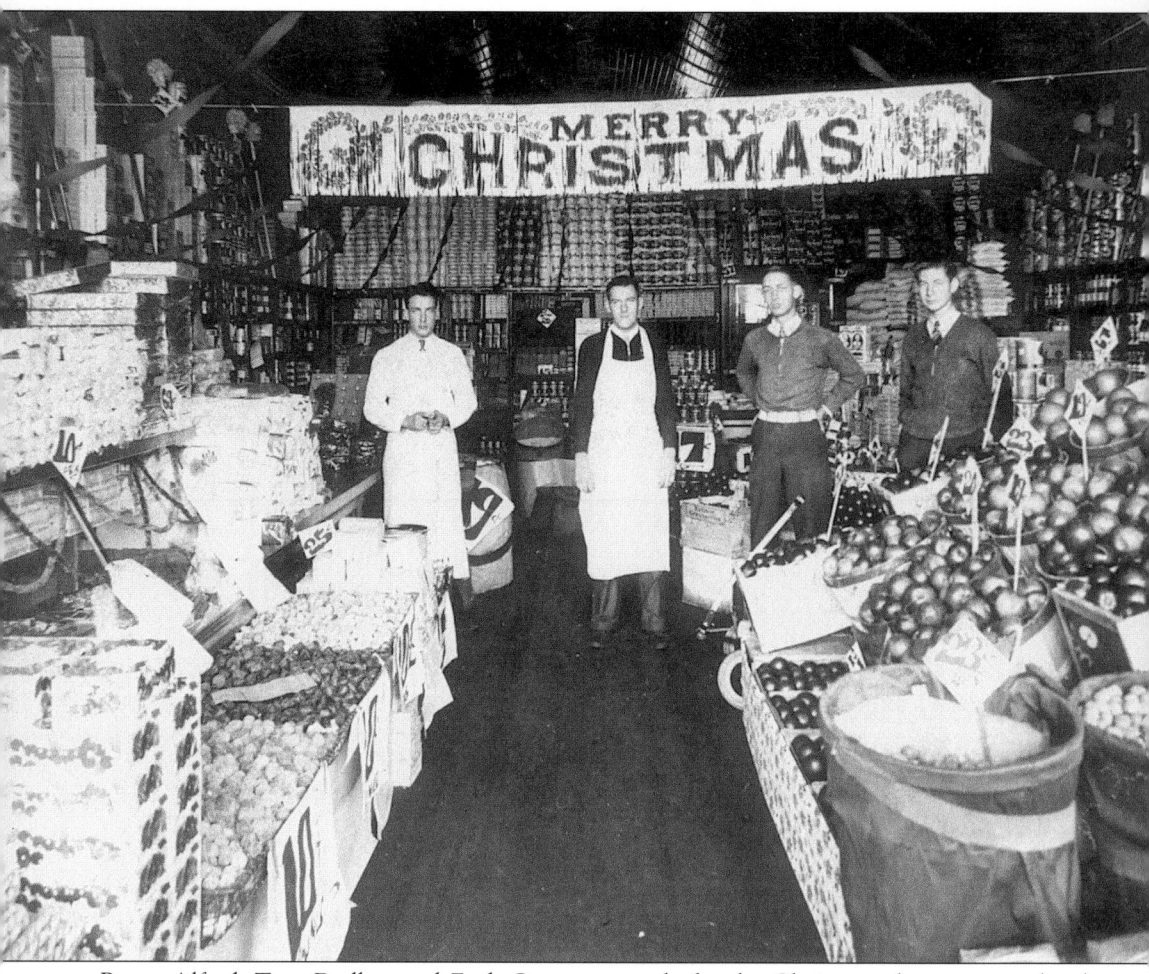

Beans Alford, Tom Dudley, and Zack Gregg are ready for the Christmas shoppers at a local grocery store on Main Street in 1933. (Photo courtesy of Hilda Bullock Lemmon.)

Four

DRAGGIN' MAIN

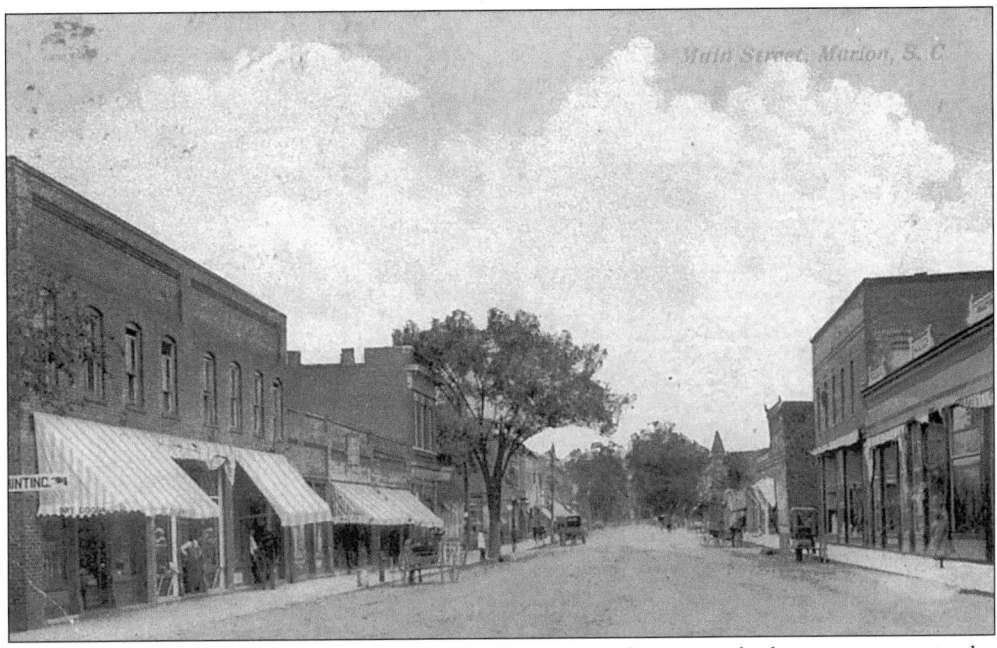

Before 1910, Main Street was still a dirt road. The paving of Main marked major progress in the business district. (Photo courtesy of F.T. Zeman.)

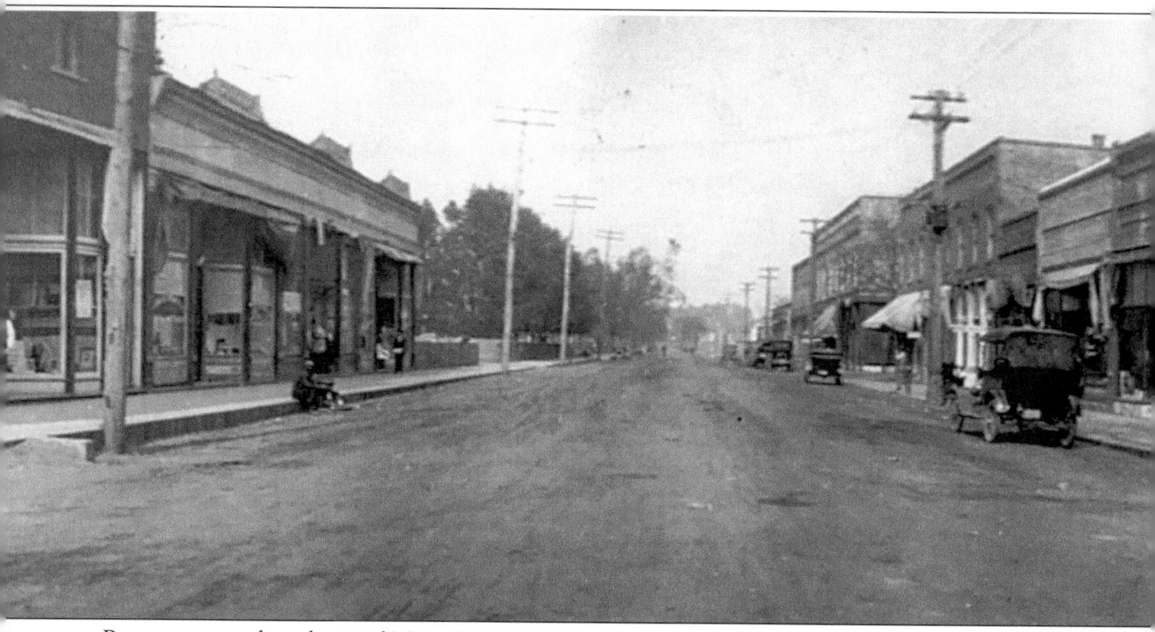

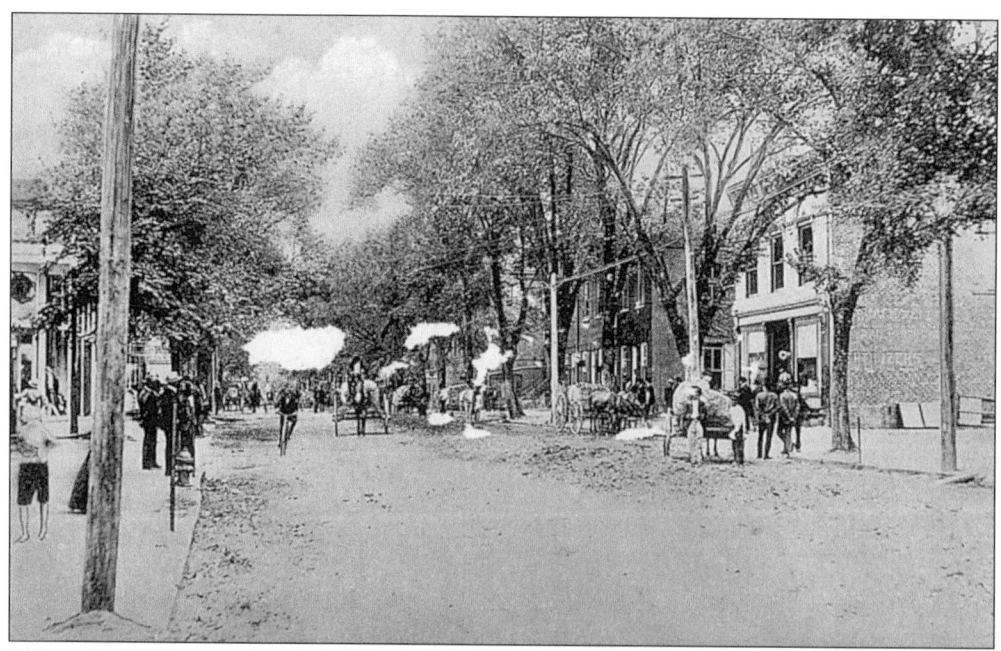

Prominent in this photo of Main Street is the Fleishman Brothers Store next door to Douglas McIntyre Merchandise Store. The Fleishman Store eventually became Ammons Furniture Store. (Photo courtesy of Ginny McIntyre.)

This early-1900s picture postcard features pedestrians, wagons, and bicycles along an unpaved Main Street. It is possible to see the Blackwell Building and the Professional Building on the right-hand side looking south. (Photo courtesy of Mike McLendon.)

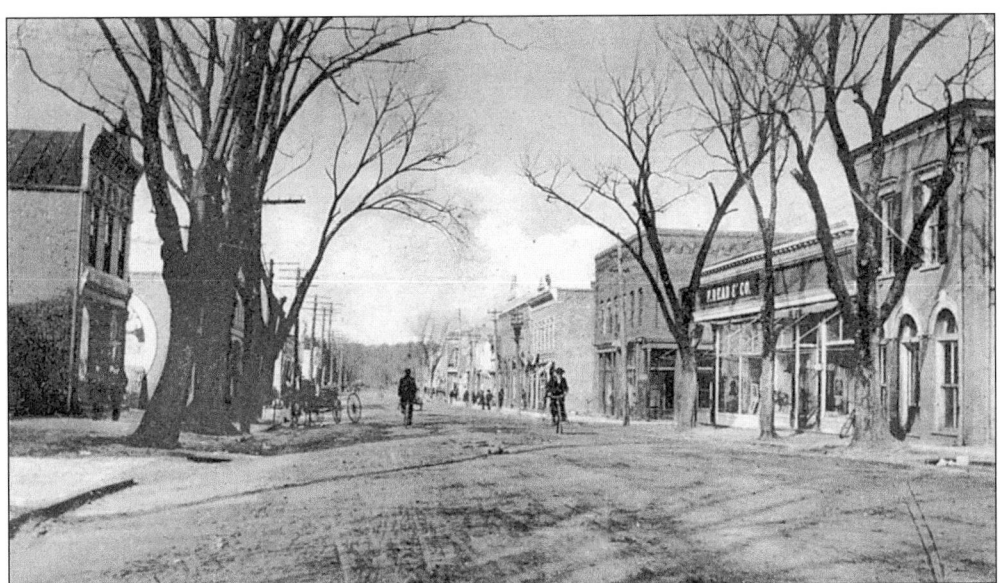

On the left, looking north on Main, is the Professional Pharmacy Building. (Photo courtesy of Valerie Baumrind Bonatis.)

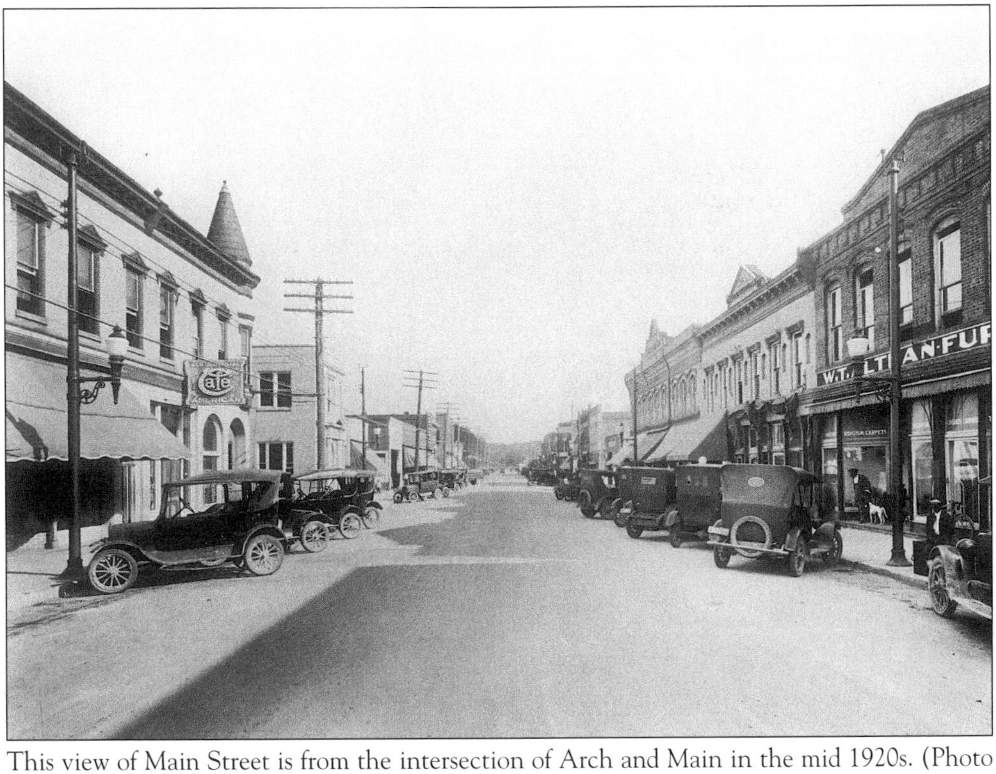

This view of Main Street is from the intersection of Arch and Main in the mid 1920s. (Photo courtesy of the Caroliniana Library, USC.)

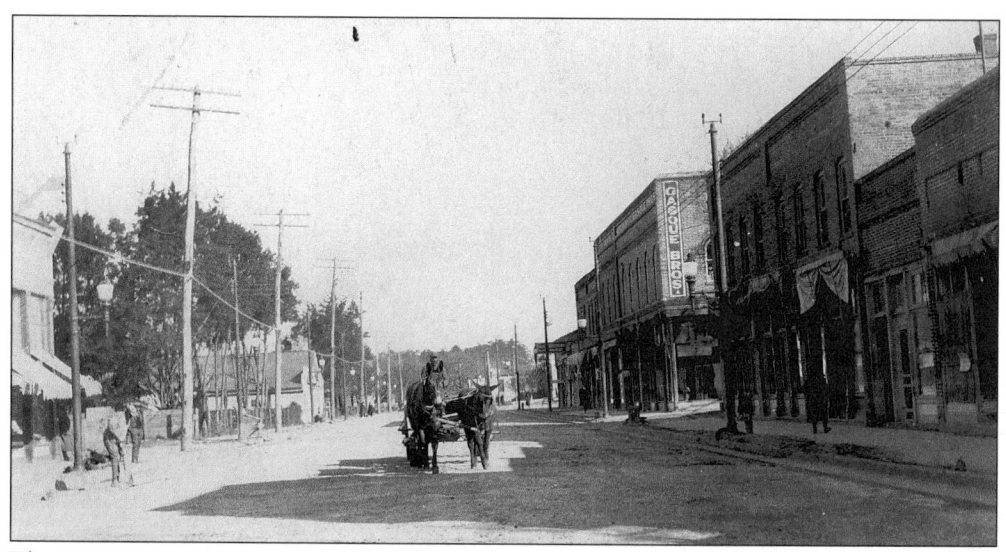

The intersection of Main and Fairlee Streets is seen in this early photograph. (Photo courtesy of Mike McLendon.)

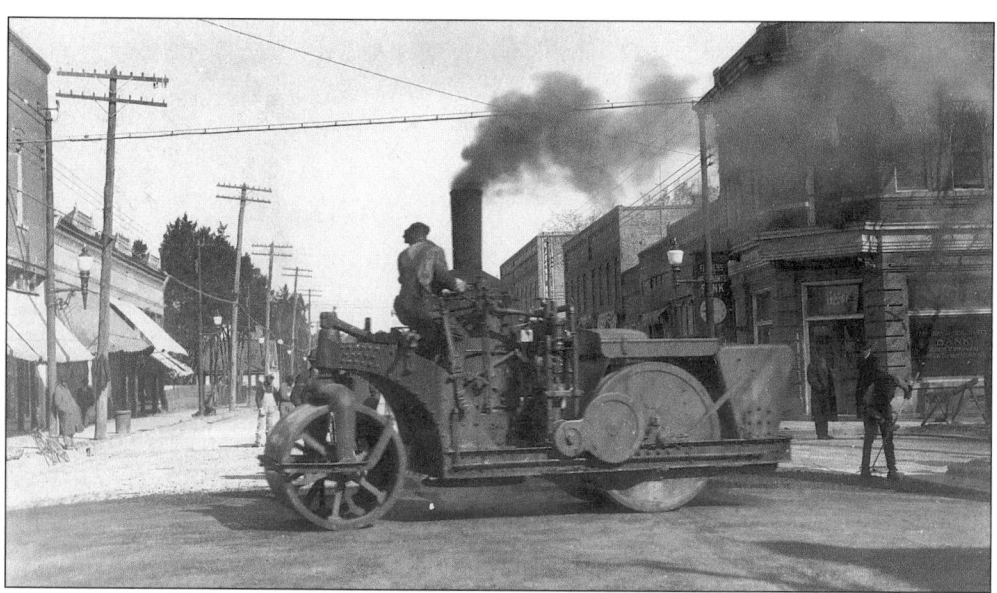

Main Street was first paved in the early 1920s. This early photograph shows the way the corner of Harllee and Main Streets looked during that time. (Photo courtesy of Mike McLendon.)

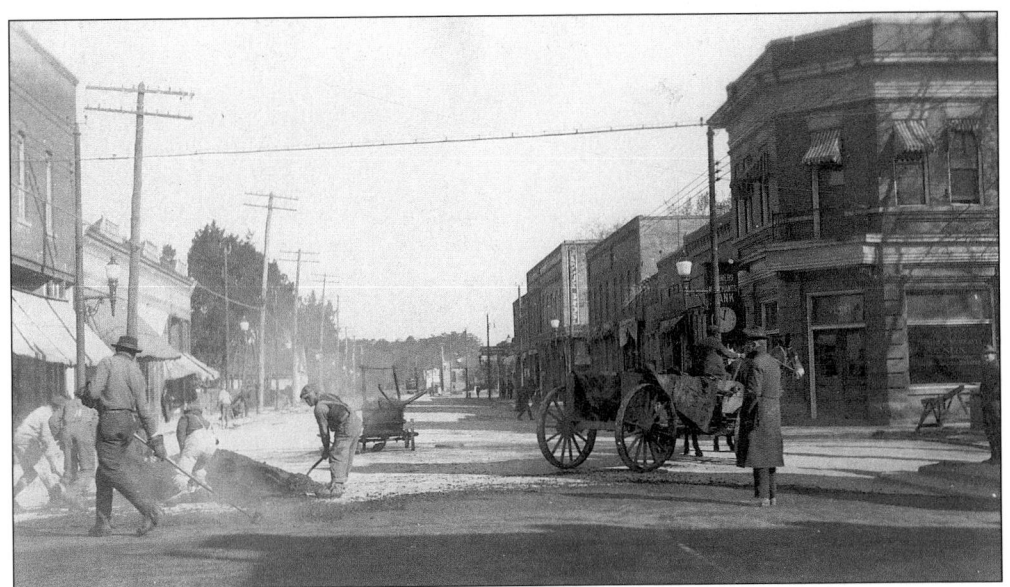

This shot of a North Main Street paving crew shows the mule-drawn construction wagon in 1910. (Photo courtesy of Mike McLendon.)

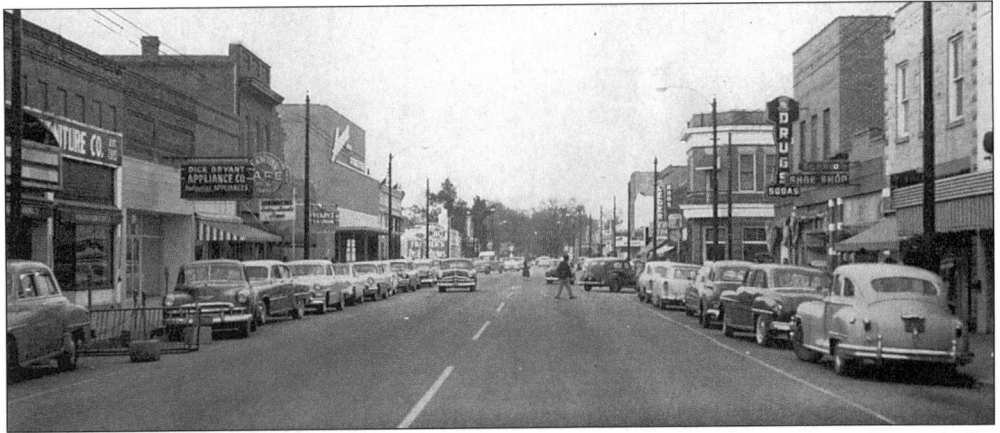

In 1954, a youngster could ride a bike to Downtown Marion, park it in the bike rack, watch the movie at the Rainbow, and then go down the street for an ice cream cone at Perry's Ice Cream Shop. (Photo courtesy of Nancy Askins.)

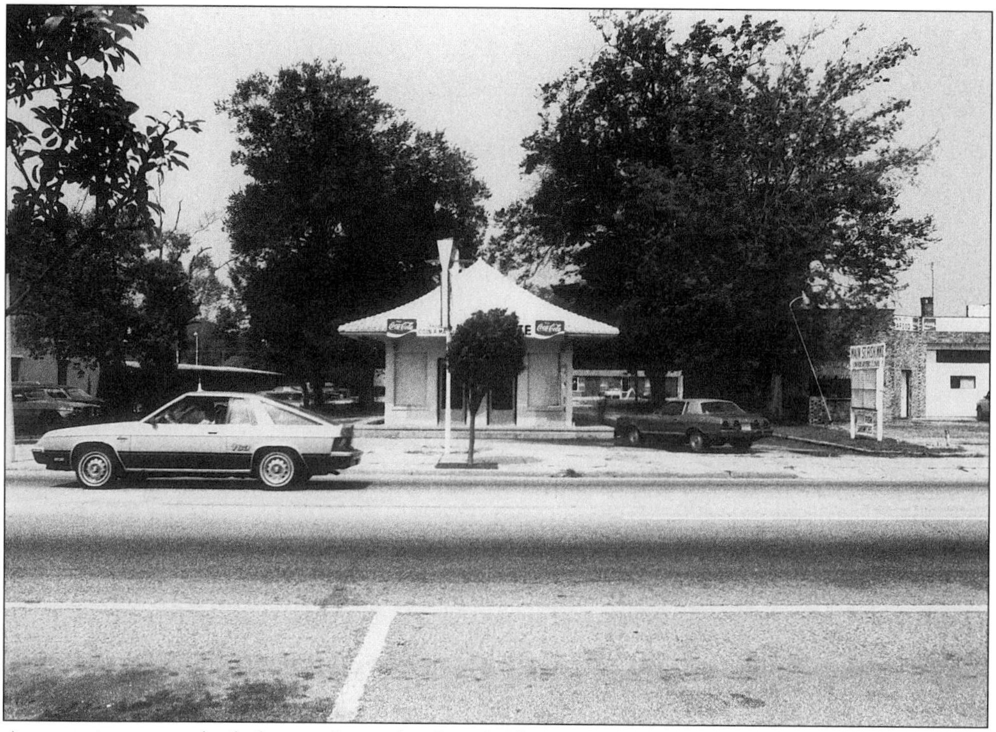

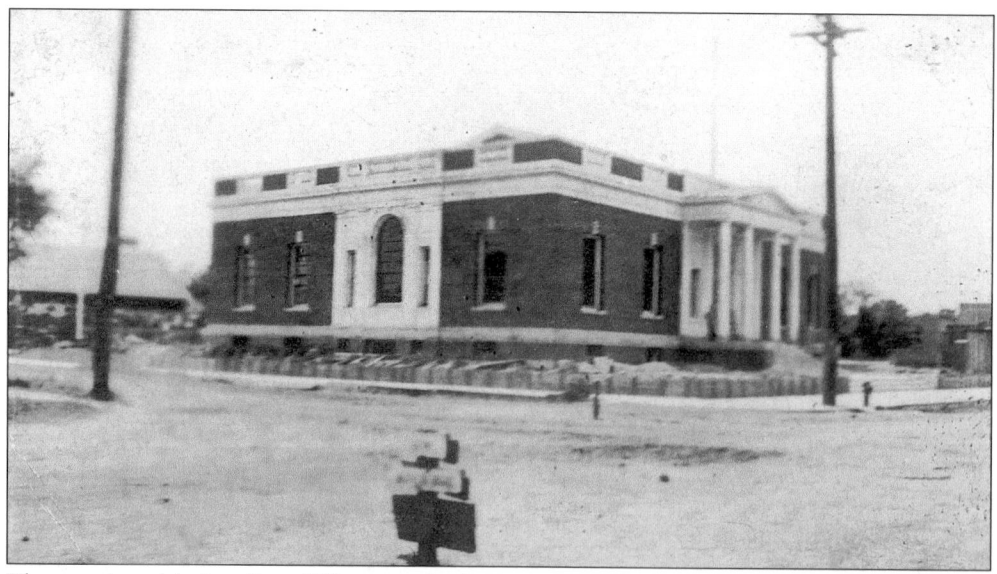

At one time, everybody knew about the Snack Shop. Next door was a Texaco service station that eventually became the Swamp Fox Shell Station. Located behind the station was Atkinson Motor Company, a Pontiac dealership. (Photo courtesy of Maggie Riales.)

The previous Marion Post Office was built in 1916 and operated until February 1976. It was located at the corner of Main Street and Railroad Avenue. (Photo courtesy of Ben and Beth Mullins.)

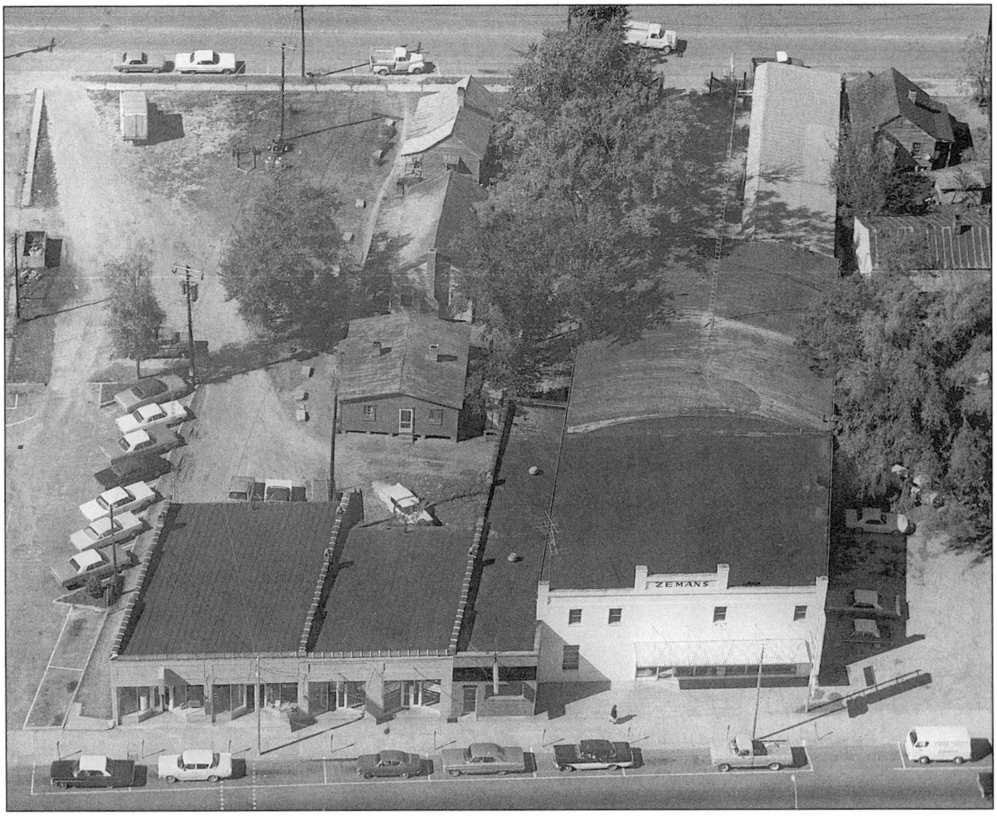

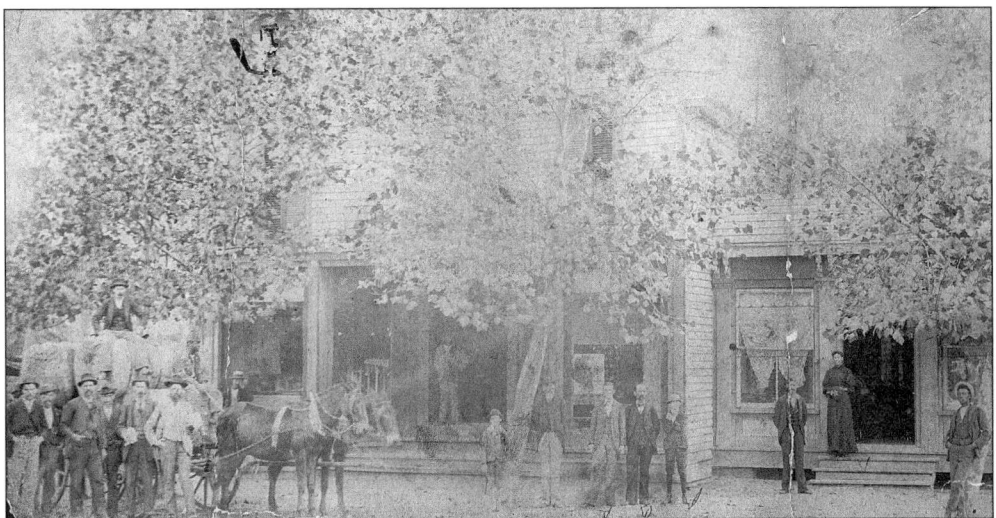

This is a 1967 aerial view of businesses, such as Zeman's, and simple "shotgun" houses in the rear, before T. Carroll Atkinson Jr. Boulevard connected Main Street to Tom Gasque Avenue (Academy Street). The businesses that were once housed to the left were Pargas, Baker's Radio and TV, Daniel's Barber Shop, Brown Insurance Agency, and Piedmont Insurance Agency. (Photo by Slim Mims; courtesy of F.T. Zeman.)

This photograph illustrates the Gasque Mercantile Company as it appeared in 1892. (Photo courtesy of Suzanne Gasque McIntyre.)

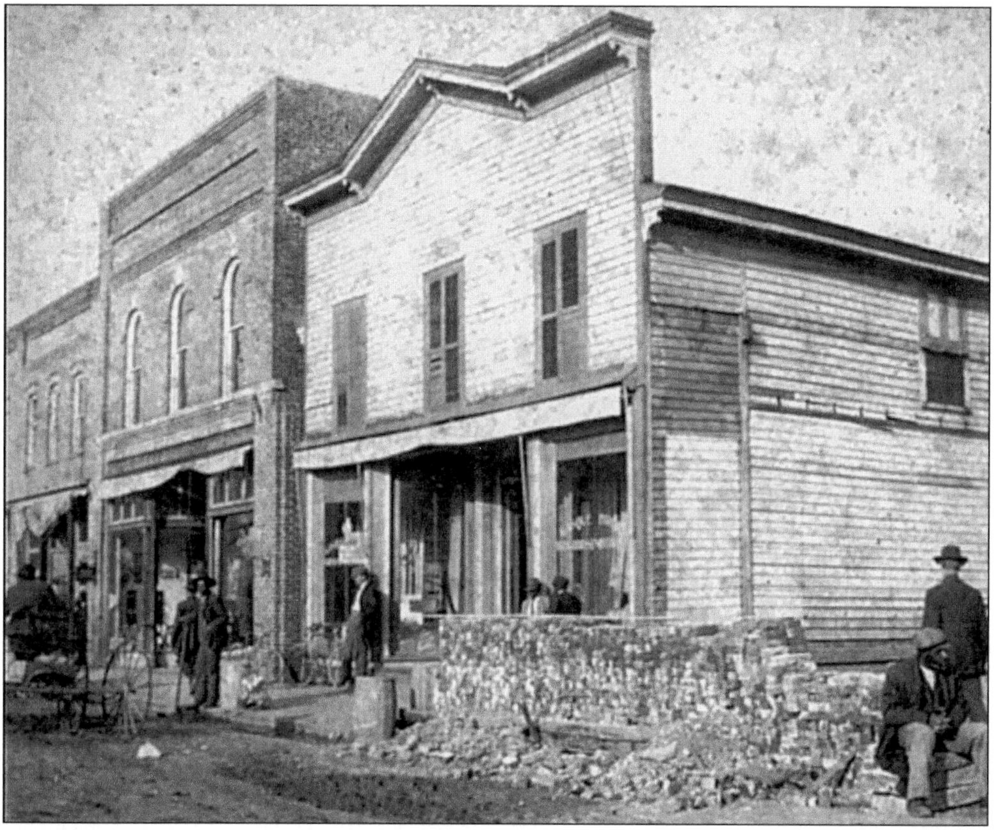

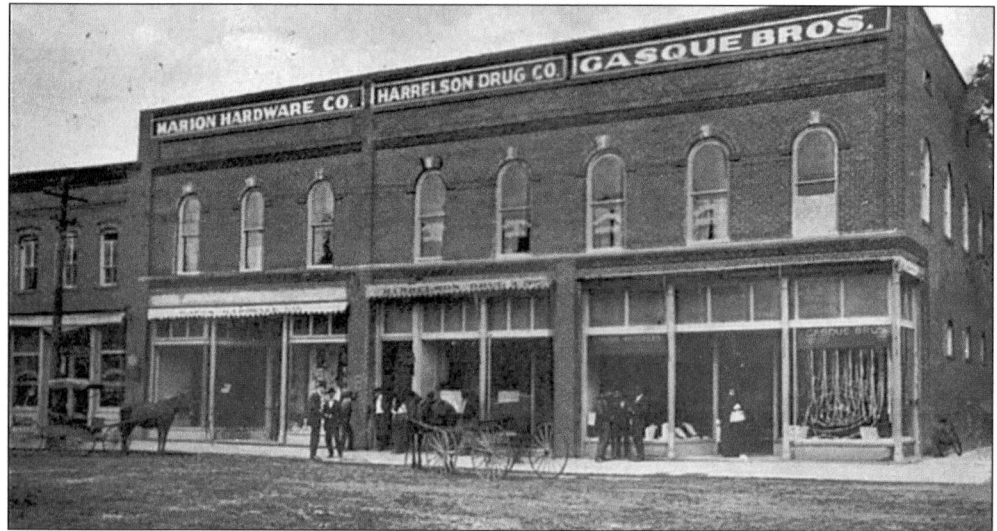

The 1906 version of the Gasque Mercantile Company shows that the millinery store had been torn down. Preparations by the Gasque family were being made to turn the wooden building into a brick structure. (Photo courtesy of Suzanne Gasque McIntyre.)

After changing the facade to brick, the Gasque Building housed Gasque Brothers, Harrelson Drug Company, and Marion Hardware Company. (Photo courtesy of Suzanne Gasque McIntyre.)

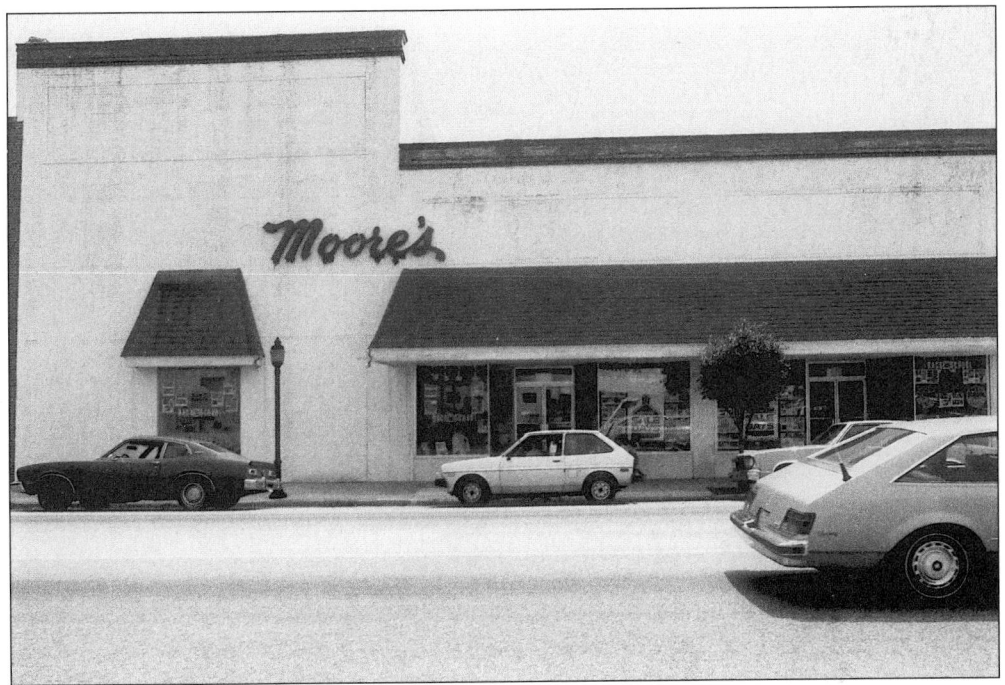

The Gasque Building eventually became B.C. Moore's Department Store, c. 1970. (Photo courtesy of Maggie Railes.)

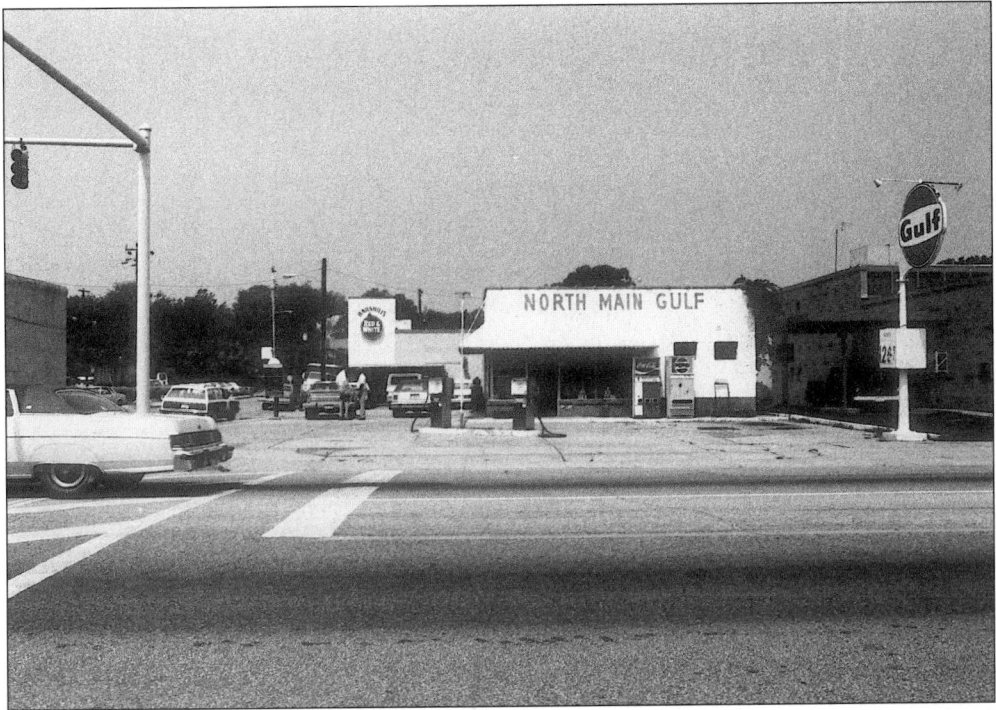

This picture is of the North Main Gulf service station, formerly Martin's Texaco. The Red and White Grocery Store and, at one time, the Colonial Store were just a step off of Main Street. (Photo courtesy of Maggie Riales.)

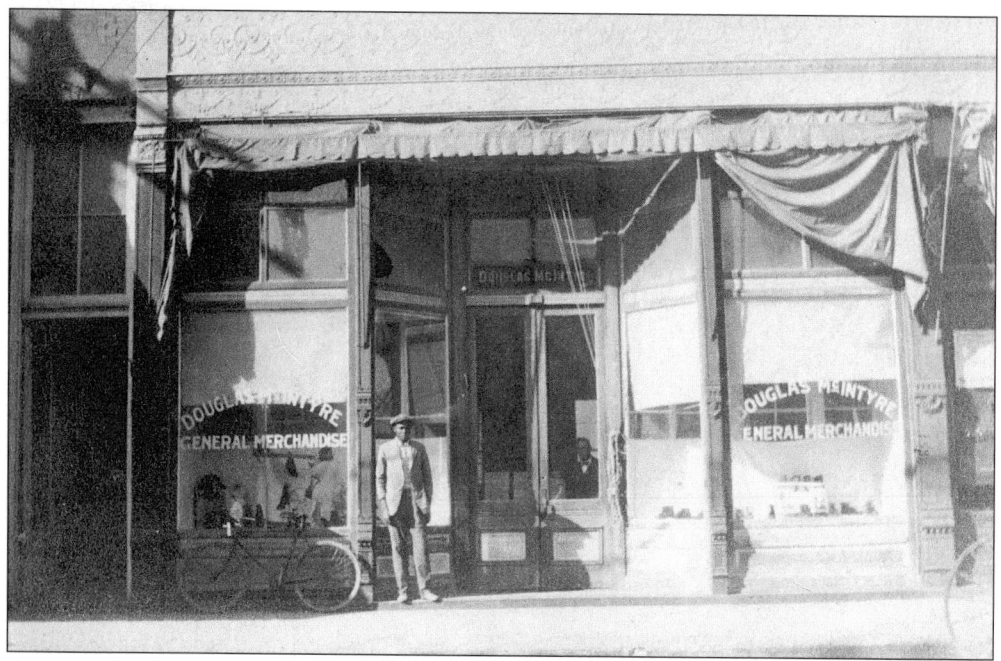

An example of a Victorian-pressed metal facade can be seen on the Douglas McIntyre General Merchandise Store. This store was built by Cornelius Graham. (Photo courtesy of Ginny McIntyre.)

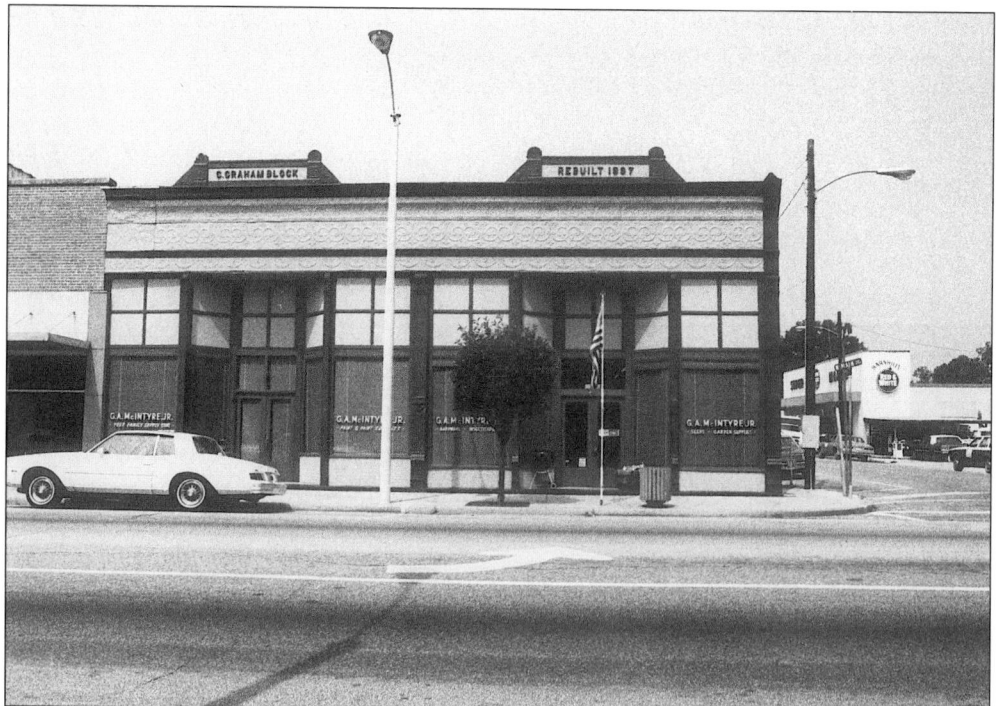

This 1970s photograph shows the change from the Douglas McIntyre General Merchandise Store, as it was known previously, to G.A. McIntyre Jr. Hardware. (Photo courtesy of Ginny McIntyre.)

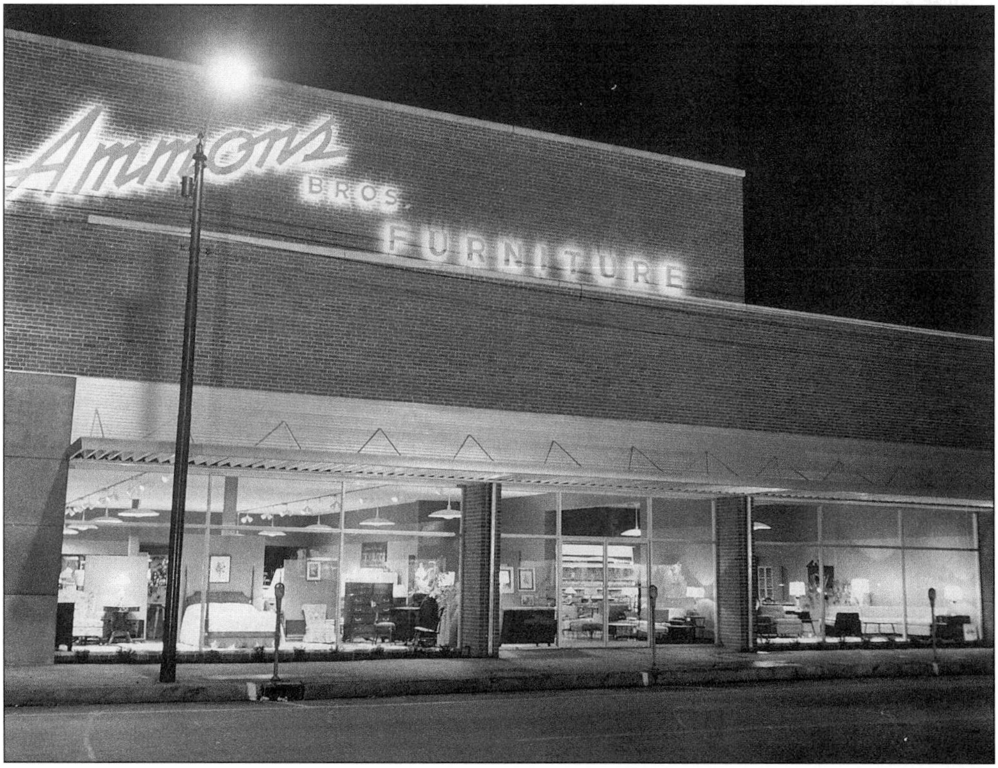

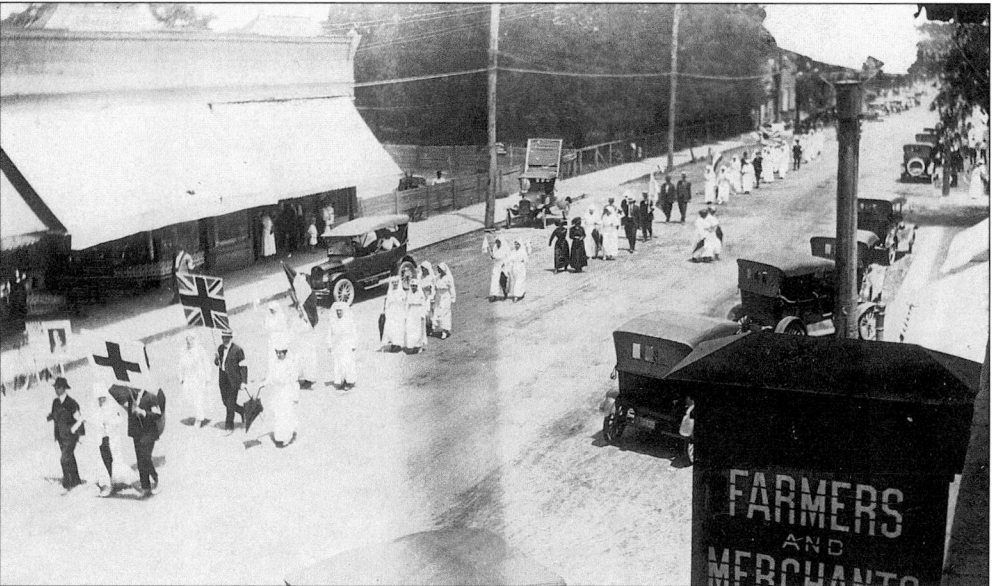

Parking meters were still being used on Main Street when this evening photograph was taken of Ammons Furniture Company. This building once housed the Fleishman Brothers Store. (Photo courtesy of Demont Ammons.)

From the balcony of the Farmers and Merchants Bank, employees could view the Red Cross parades during World War I. These parades were an effort to raise consciousness regarding the war effort and to increase membership. (Photo courtesy of Mike McLendon.)

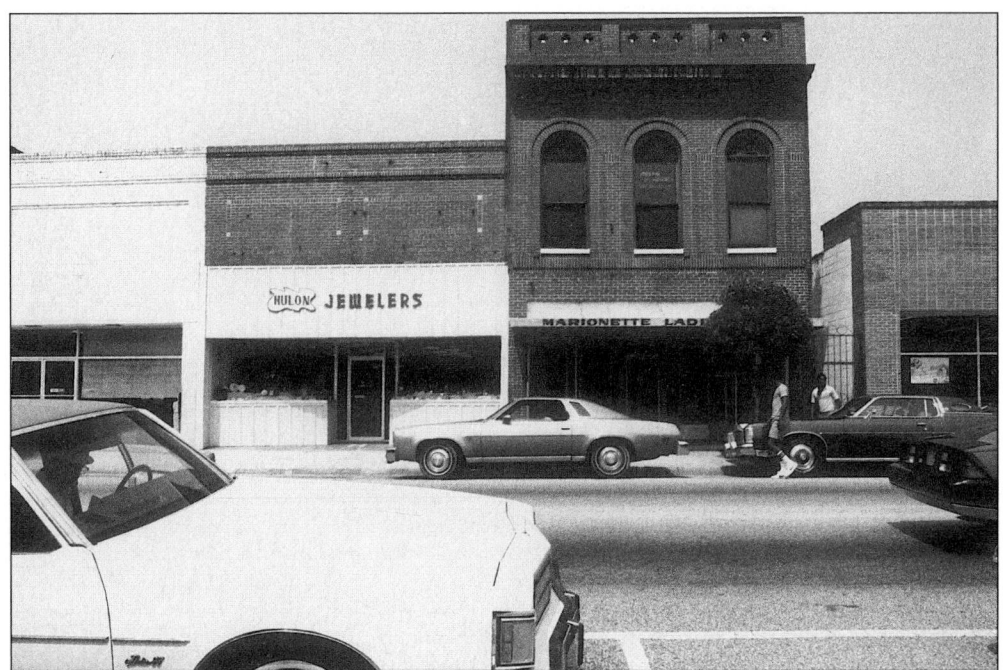

Presently housing Hulon Jewelers, the building shown in this photograph was once the Candy Kitchen, operated by Mr. and Mrs. Harry Andrews. The Marionette Shop was once Horinbein's Ladies Shop. Presently doing business here is Judy's Flowers. This building was the post office until 1916. (Photo courtesy of Maggie Riales.)

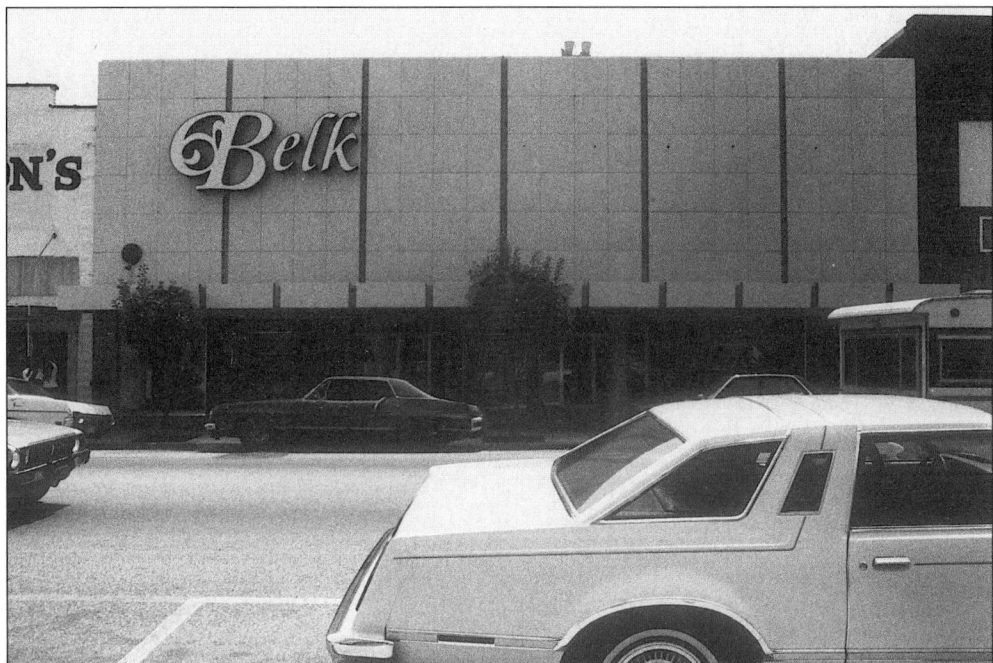

One of several department stores that used to be on Main Street was Belk Department Store, which is seen in this 1970s photograph. Many years prior, this was the location of Evans Service Station. (Photo courtesy of Maggie Riales.)

90

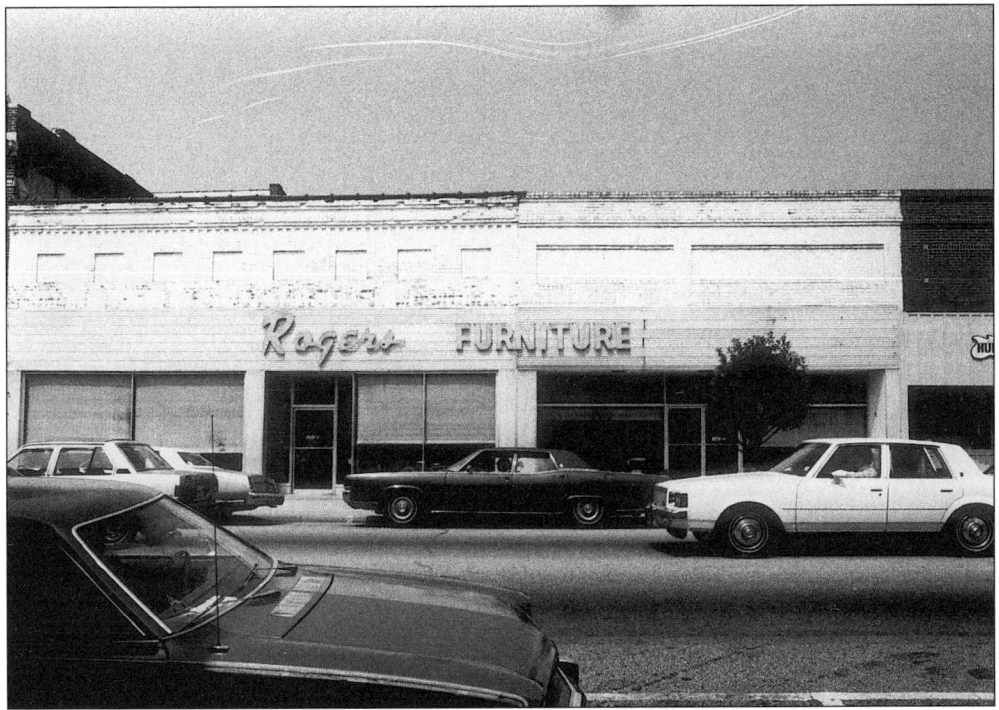

The part of the building that housed Rogers Furniture Company was built in 1898. (Photo courtesy of Maggie Riales.)

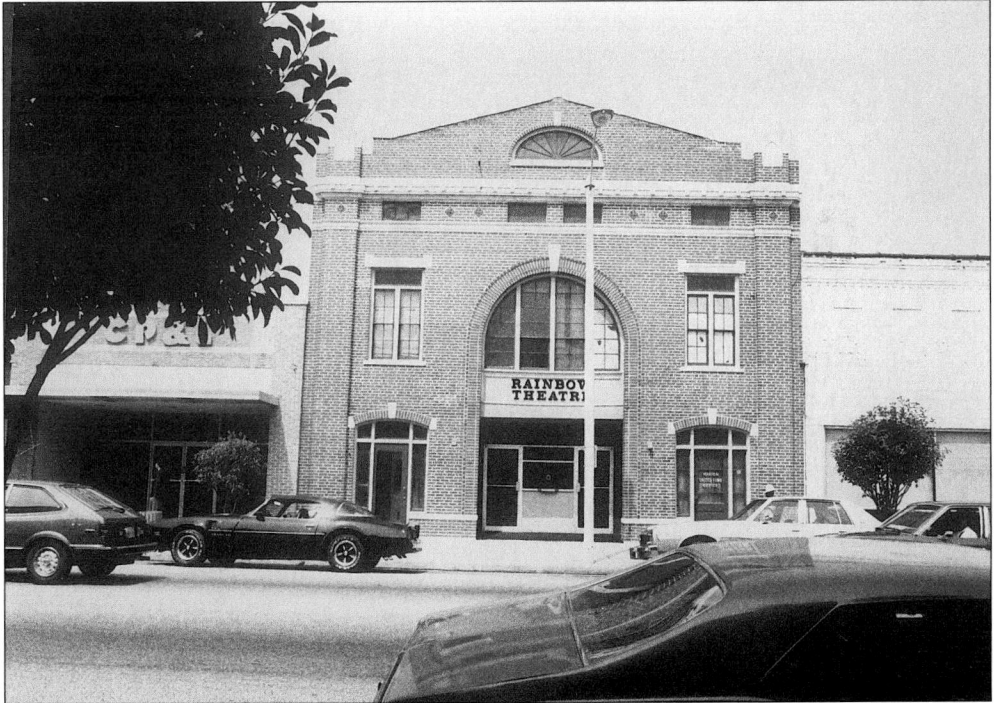

The Rainbow, or Marion Theater, was adjacent to the offices of the Carolina Power and Light Company. (Photo courtesy of Maggie Riales.)

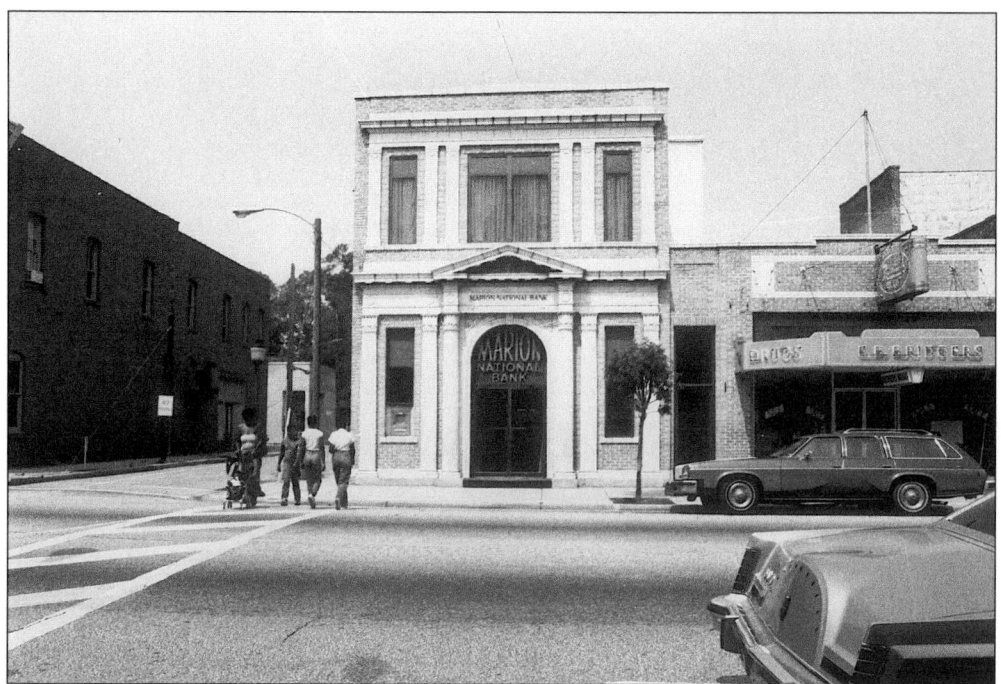

The Marion National Bank, built in 1922, was located at the intersection of Main and Witcover Streets. (Photo courtesy of Maggie Riales.)

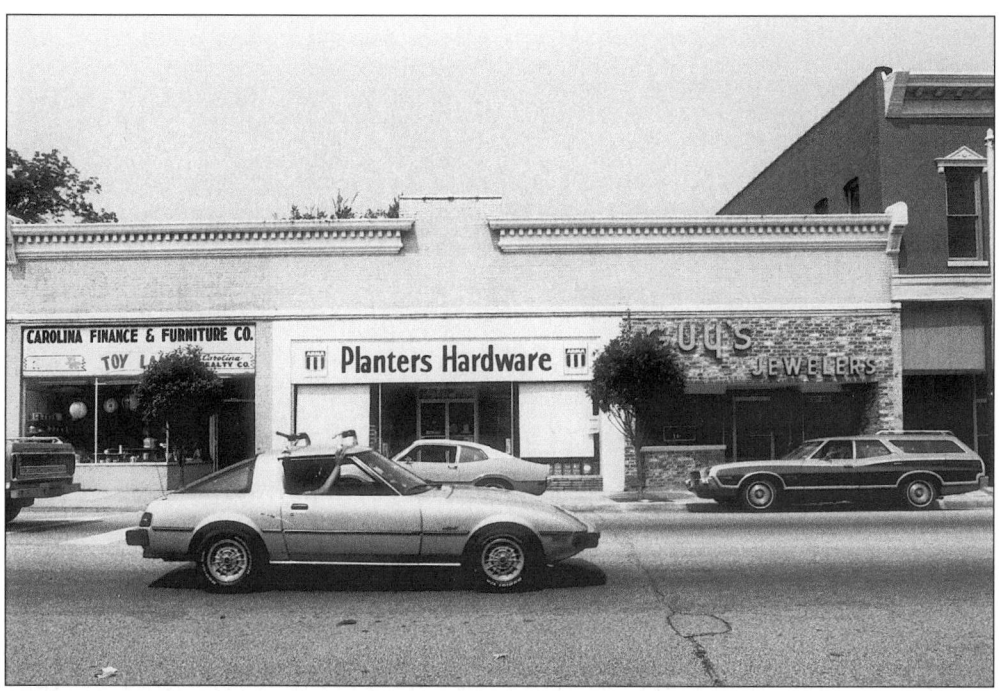

This large building was the site of Carolina Finance and Furniture Company, Planters Hardware, and Guy's Jewelers in the late 1970s. In earlier times, this building was a grocery store owned by Mr. Clark Willcox. (Photo courtesy of Maggie Riales.)

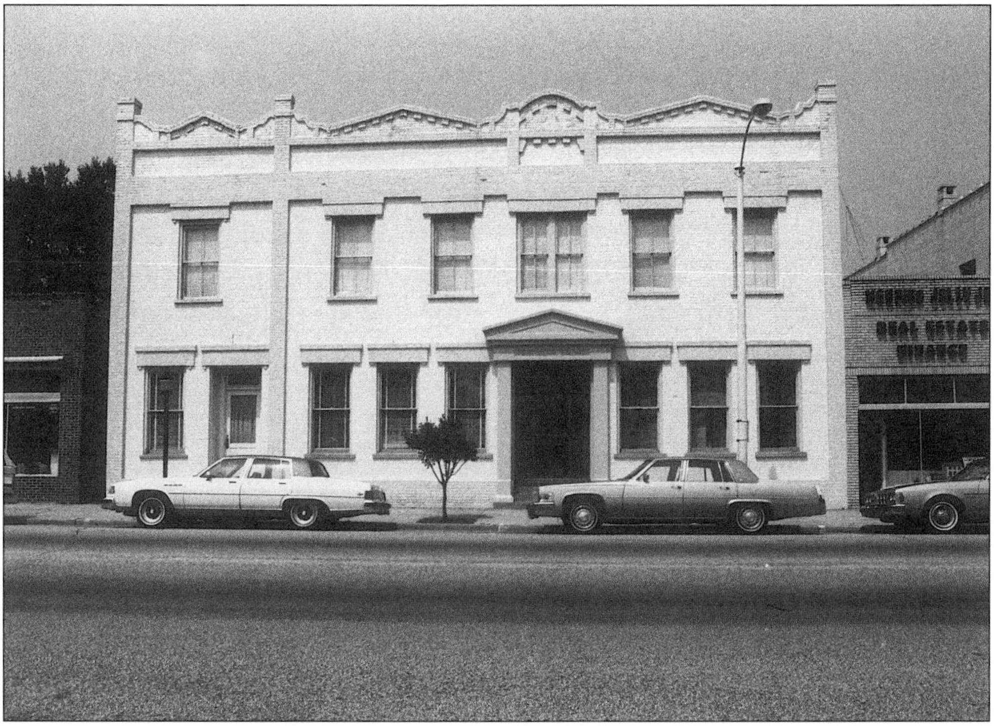

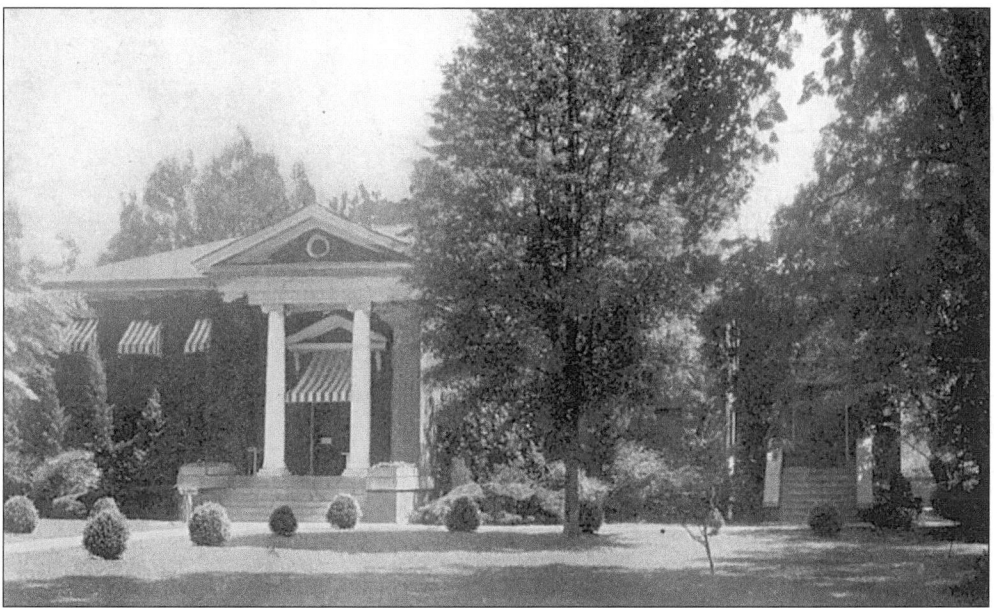

The Professional Building was built in 1885 and has housed attorneys' offices and business offices. The first bank in the area, the Bank of Marion (later Marion National Bank), was located in this building. Housed in four rooms above the bank were the beginnings of what was to become the Marion County Public Library. (Photo courtesy of Maggie Riales.)

The Marion County Library was opened in 1906. The new wing (on the right) was constructed onto the original building, which was ivy covered. (Photo courtesy of Valerie Baumrind Bonatis.)

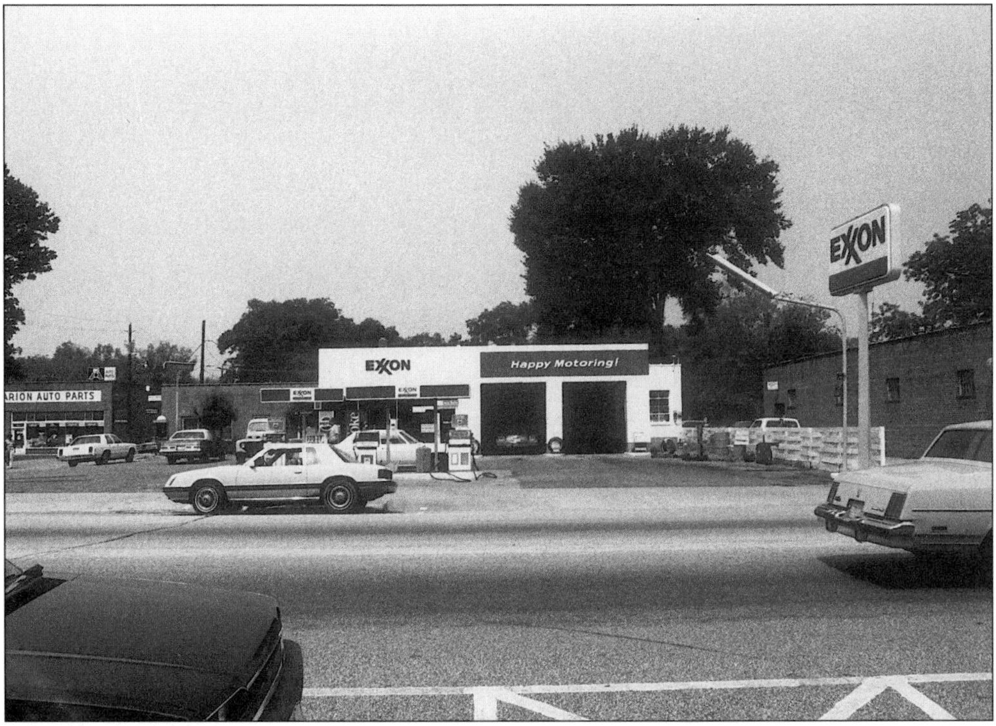

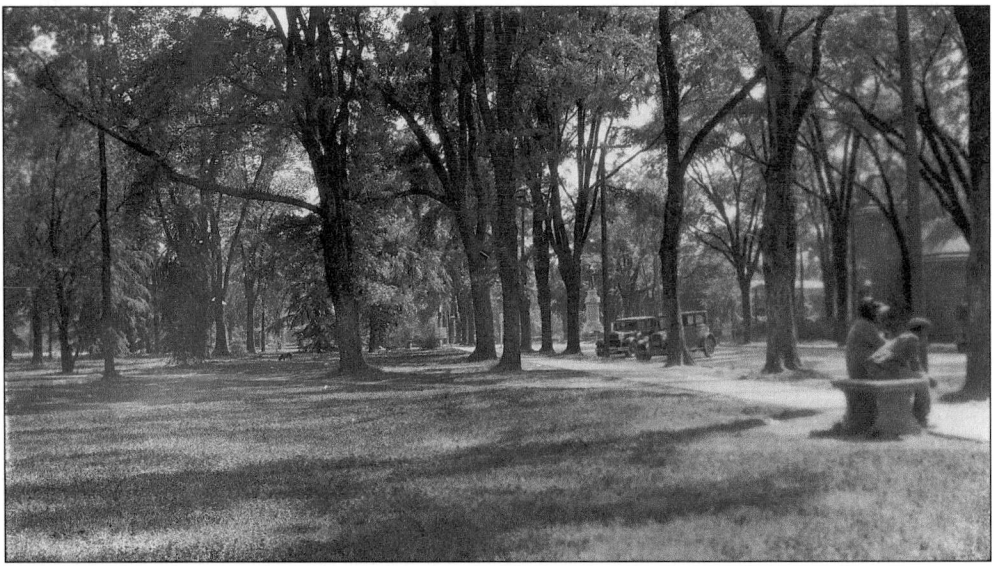

This is a photograph of the corner of Main and Dozier Streets. On West Court Street, which runs into Dozier, is Marion Auto Parts. Other businesses have been located on this site, such as a Chevrolet automobile dealership, a drugstore operated by W.C. McMillan, and the Jenkins Hotel. (Photo courtesy of Maggie Riales.)

This view, looking southward, shows how the Public Square on Main Street appeared in the 1920s. (Photo courtesy of Ginny McIntyre.)

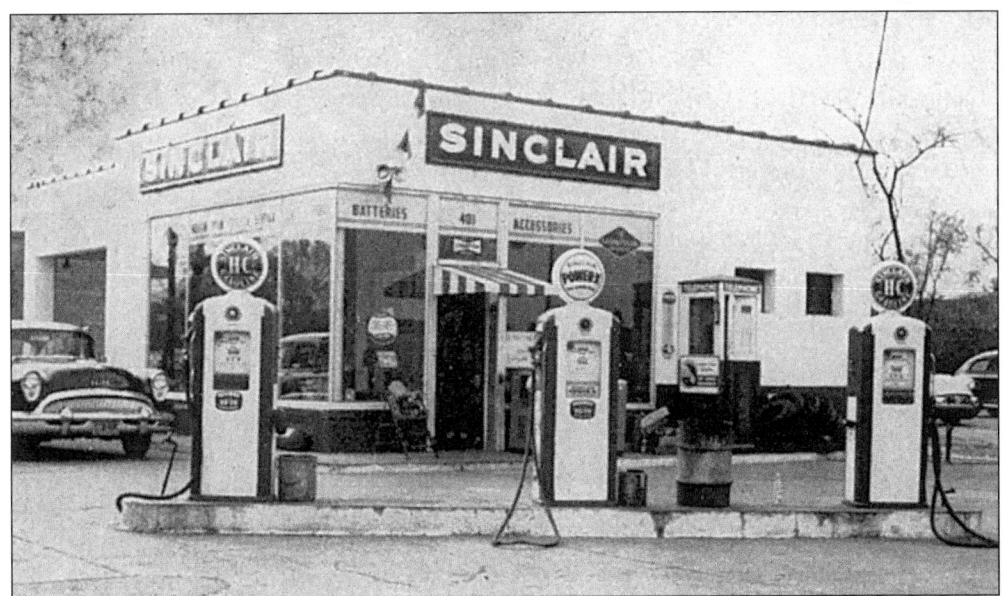

America's love affair with the automobile would not have been possible without full-service gasoline stations. The North Main Service Station stood at the corner of Main and Fairlee Streets. The symbol of Sinclair Oil Company was a dinosaur. (Photo courtesy of Nancy Askins.)

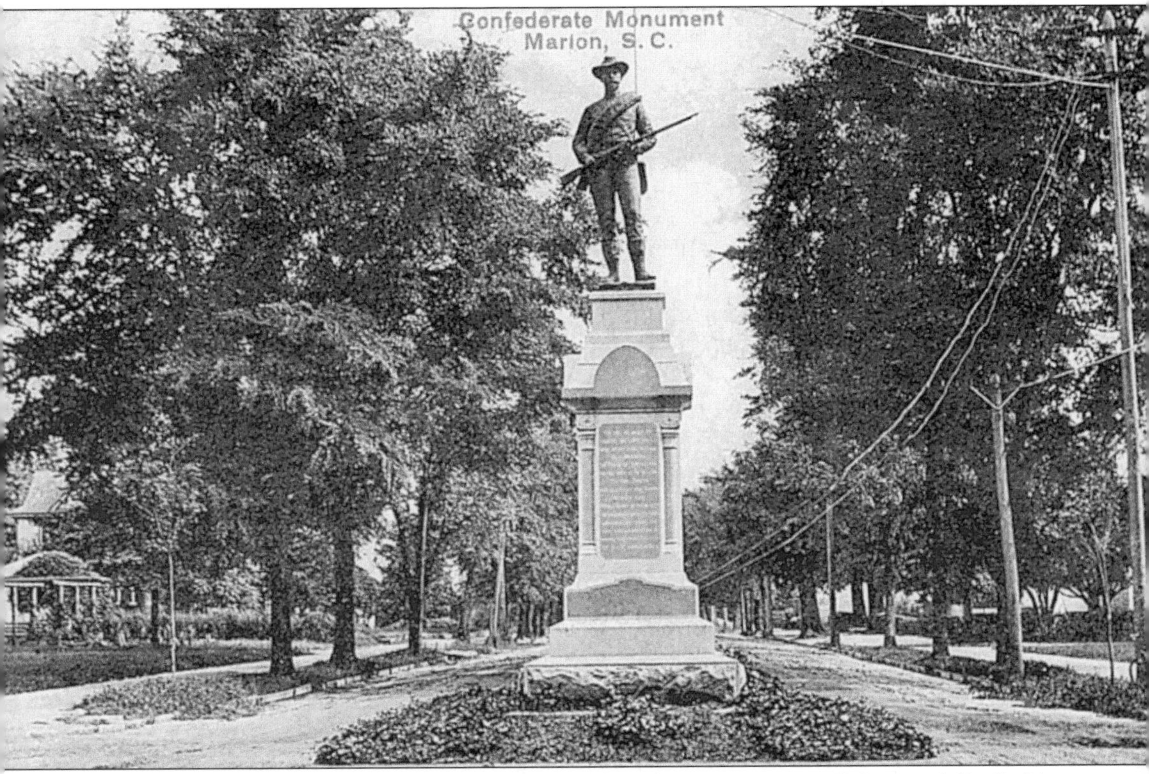

The Confederate Monument, erected in 1903, stood in the intersection of Main and Godbold Streets. (Photo courtesy of Ginny McIntyre.)

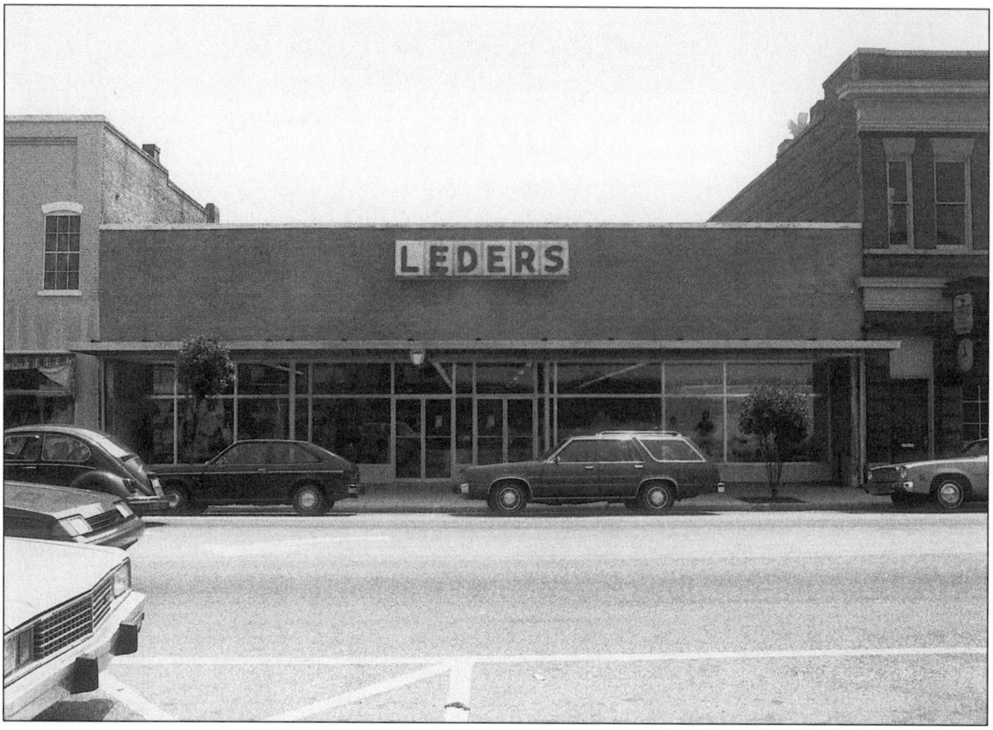

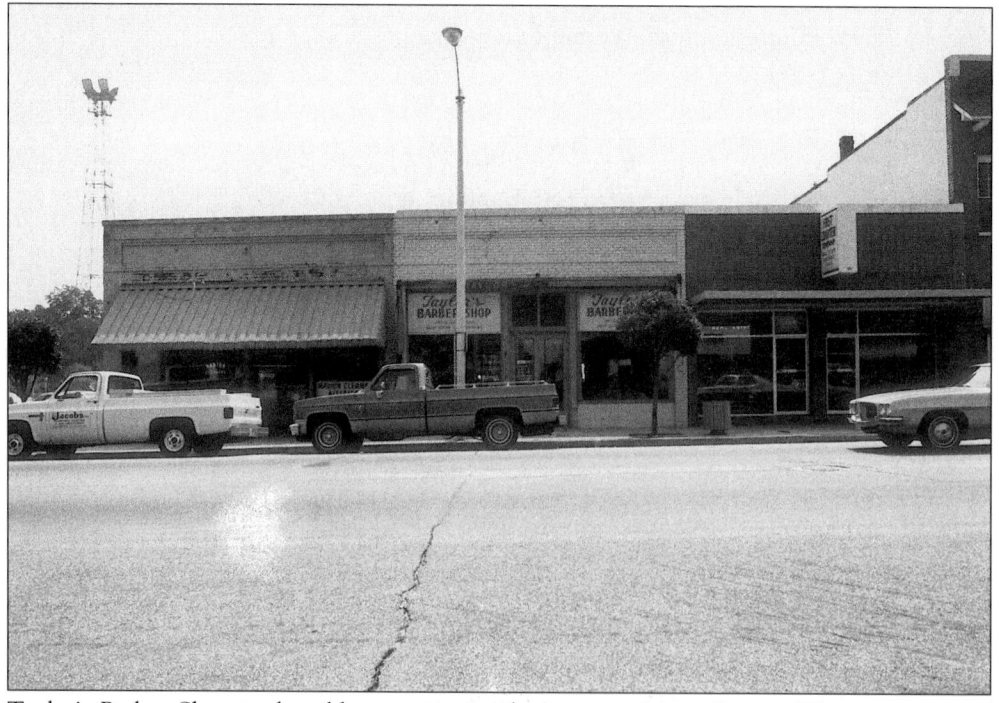

Leders Department Store was a mainstay in Downtown Marion for many years. (Photo courtesy of Maggie Riales.)

Taylor's Barber Shop is the oldest continuing business on Main Street. (Photo courtesy of Maggie Riales.)

Five

TRAVELIN'

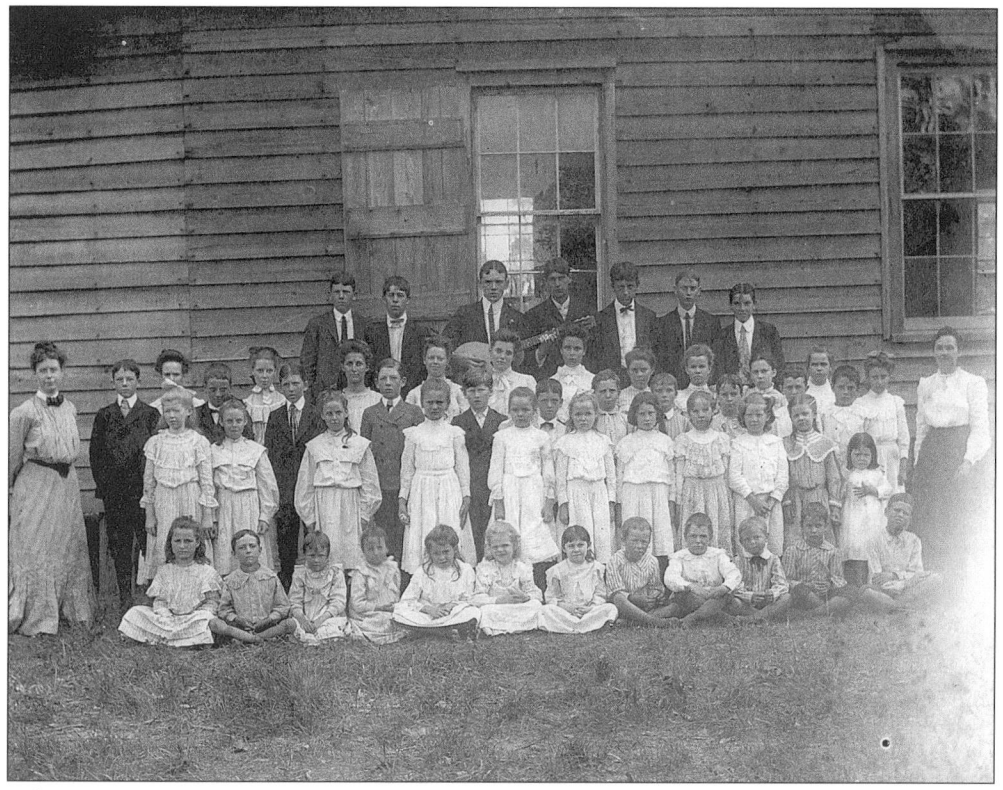

Palmer School teachers and students posed outside their building for this school picture. Palmer School was located in Centenary. (Photo courtesy of Viola Gibson.)

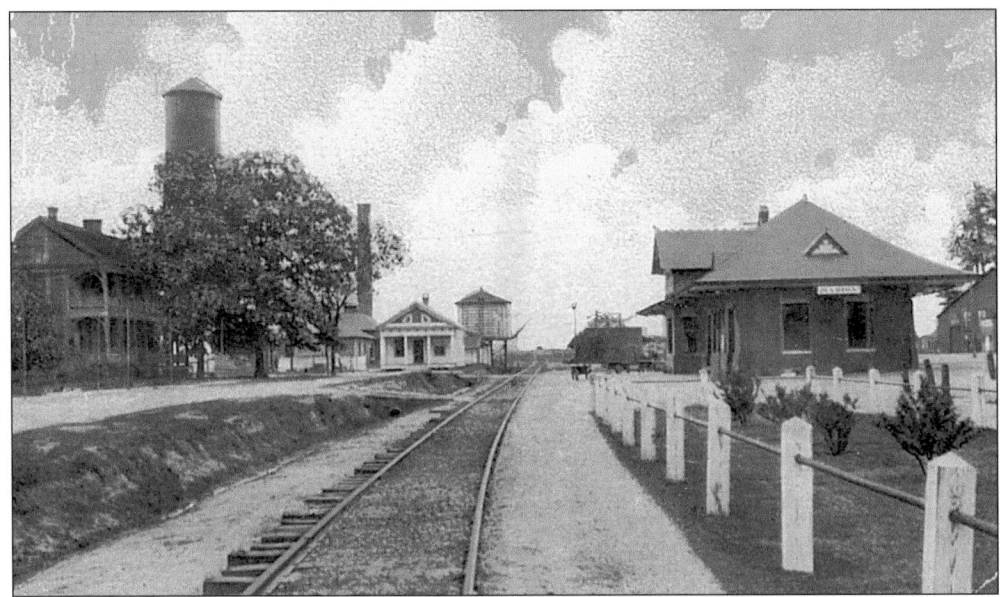

Marion once heard the sounds of the trains either with freight or passengers. The ACL Depot is located on the right and still stands in Marion, South Carolina. (Photo courtesy of James and Nita Neely.)

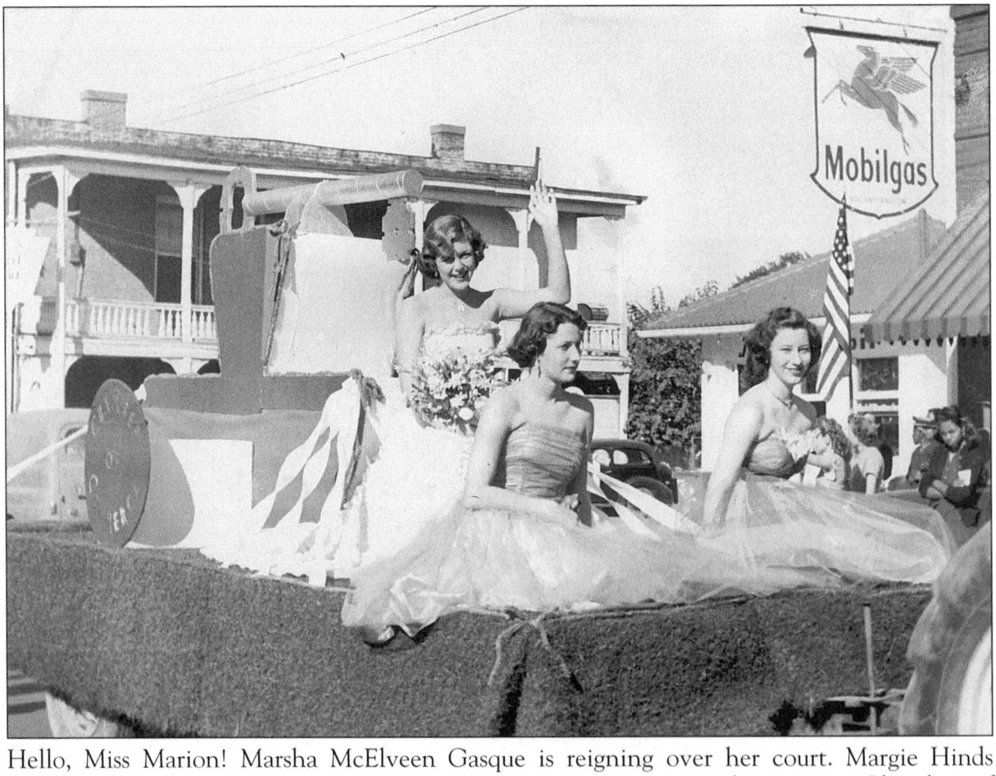

Hello, Miss Marion! Marsha McElveen Gasque is reigning over her court. Margie Hinds Skipper and Martha Britt Dozier travel down Main Street on the Marion Chamber of Commerce float. Bill's Mobile and Dr. Dibble's office can be seen in the background. (Photo by Marion Photo Service; courtesy of Martha B. Dozier.)

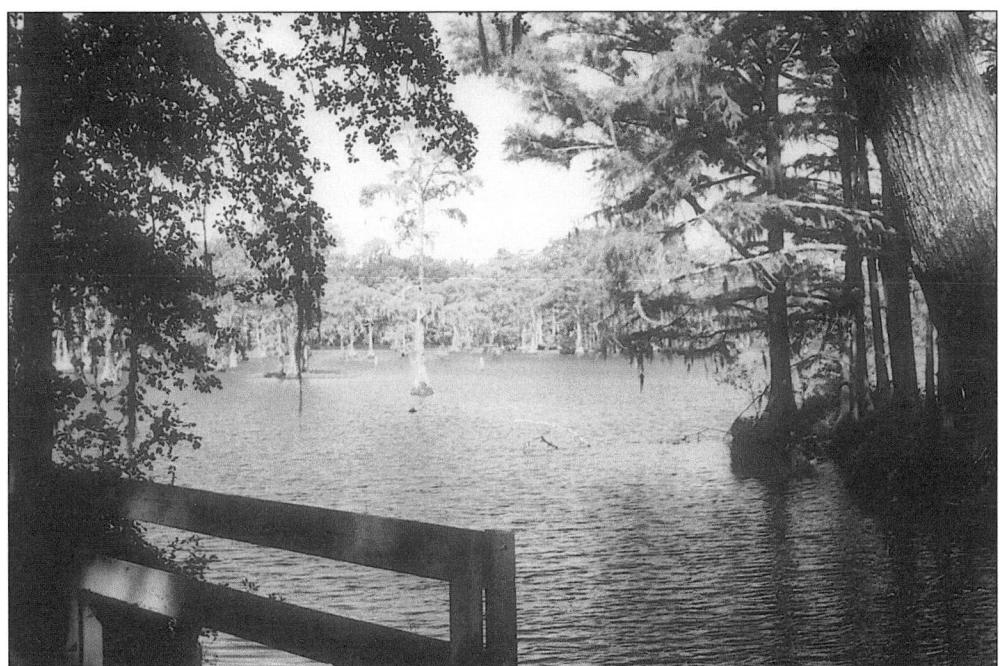

Lushly draped cypress trees still can be seen when traveling to Legette's Mill Pond, near Centenary. (Photo courtesy of Viola Gibson.)

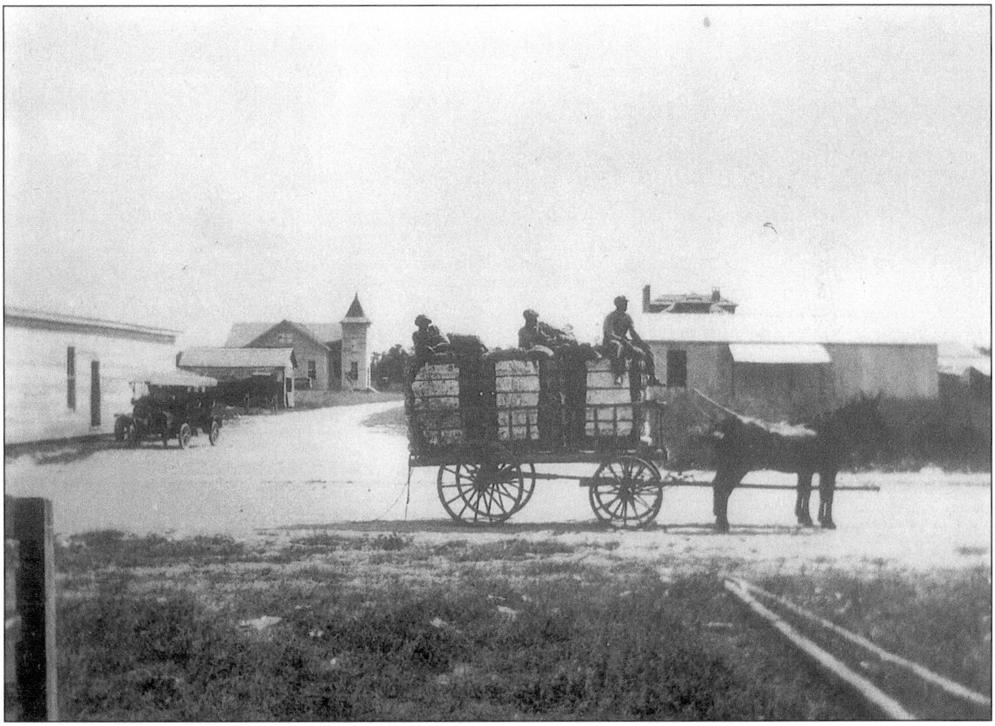

Around 1900, traveling to market in Centenary, South Carolina, are a horse-drawn wagon and three bales of cotton with a handsome car parked in front. The Baker Store is on the right. (Photo courtesy of Viola Gibson.)

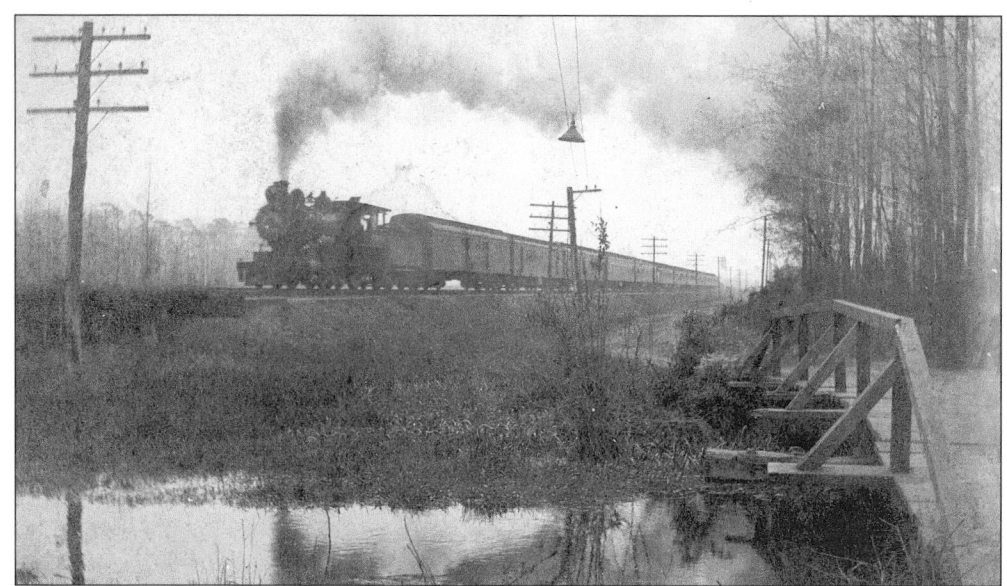

With its whistle blowing and a full head of steam, this locomotive is traveling near Pee Dee in the early 1900s. (Photo courtesy of Dot D. McIntyre.)

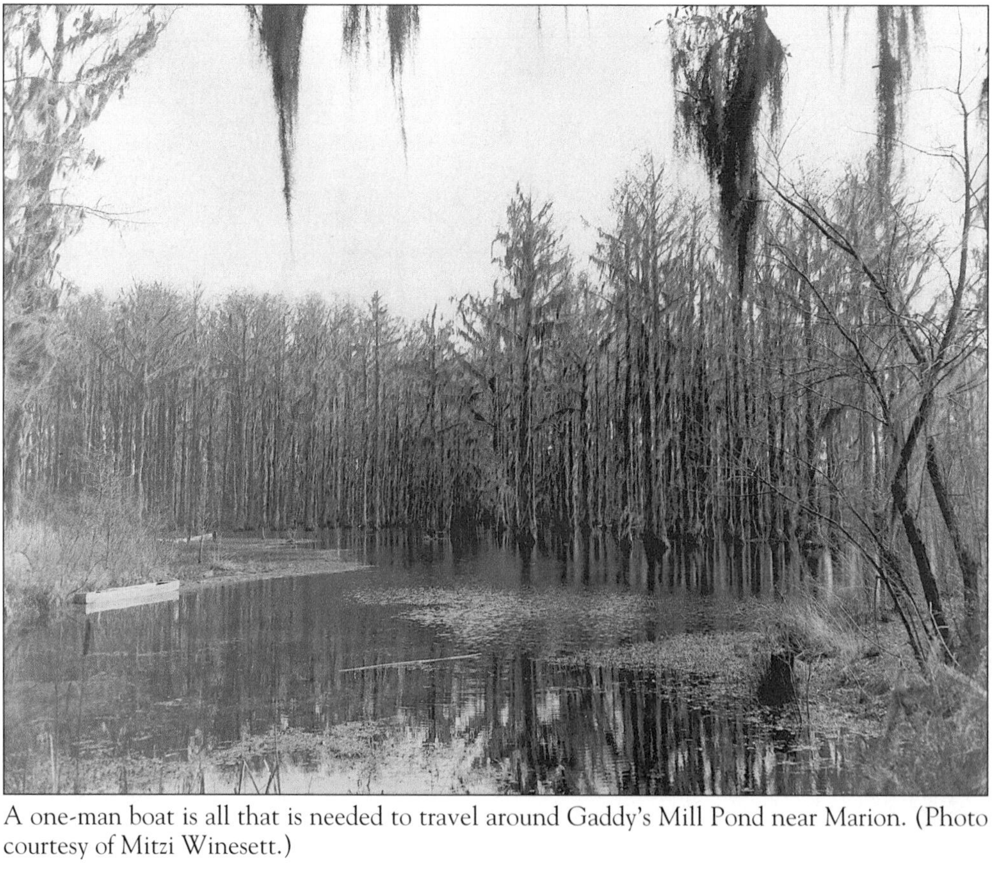

A one-man boat is all that is needed to travel around Gaddy's Mill Pond near Marion. (Photo courtesy of Mitzi Winesett.)

Traveling in style and turning heads are Wilma Wall and Lillian Miles. In 1890, Marion had a bicycle club. Lillian's father was the sheriff of Marion County. (Photo courtesy of Libby Stanley.)

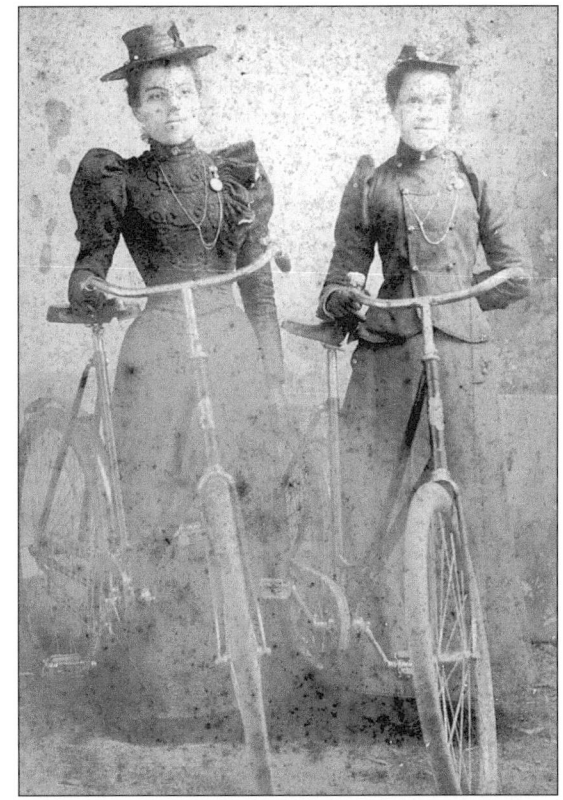

Legette's Mill Pond was home to a gristmill in years past and also grew rice commercially until the 1920s. (Photo courtesy of Viola Gibson.)

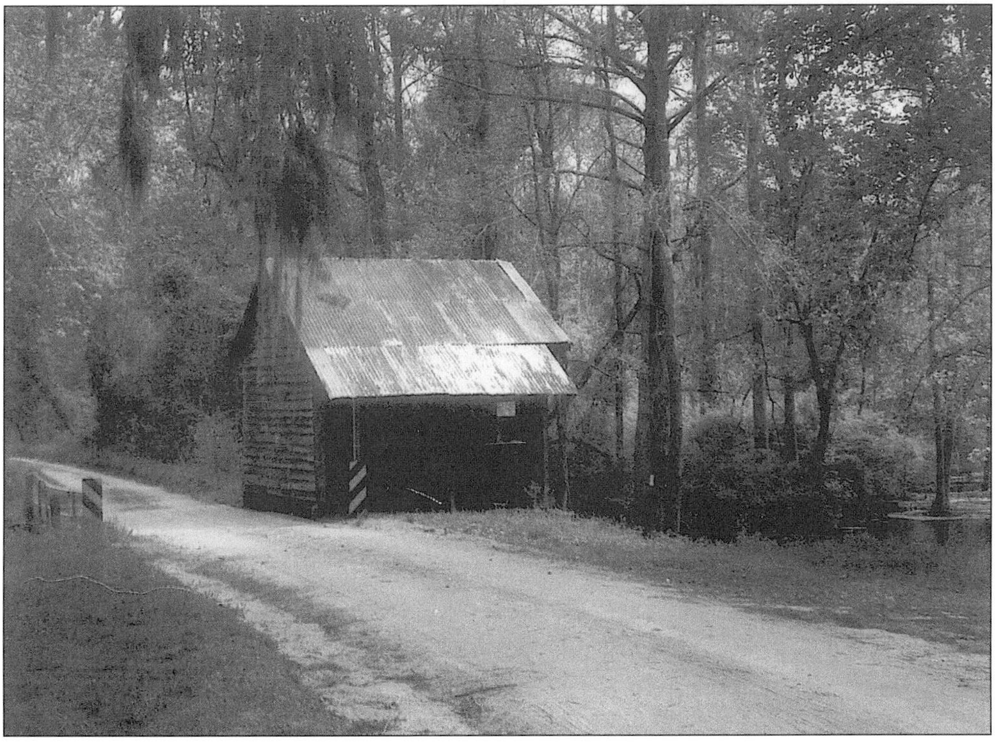

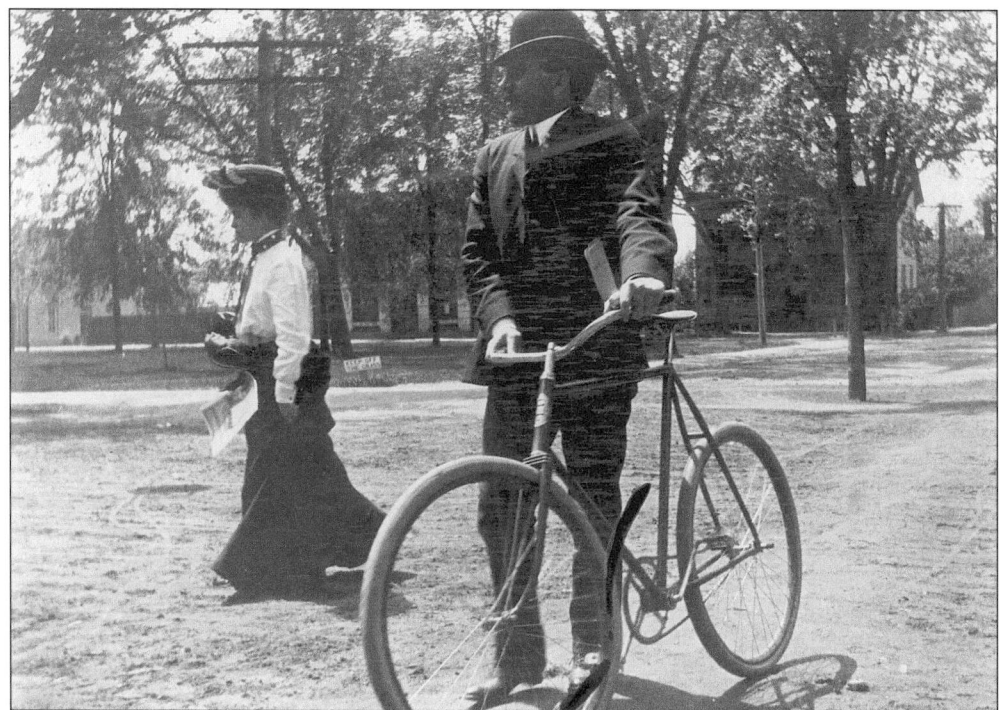

Kathryn Pratt Gasque and her cousin are pictured, *c.* 1909, on the Square with the courthouse in the background. His bicycle was not built for two! (Photo courtesy of Suzanne Gasque McIntyre.)

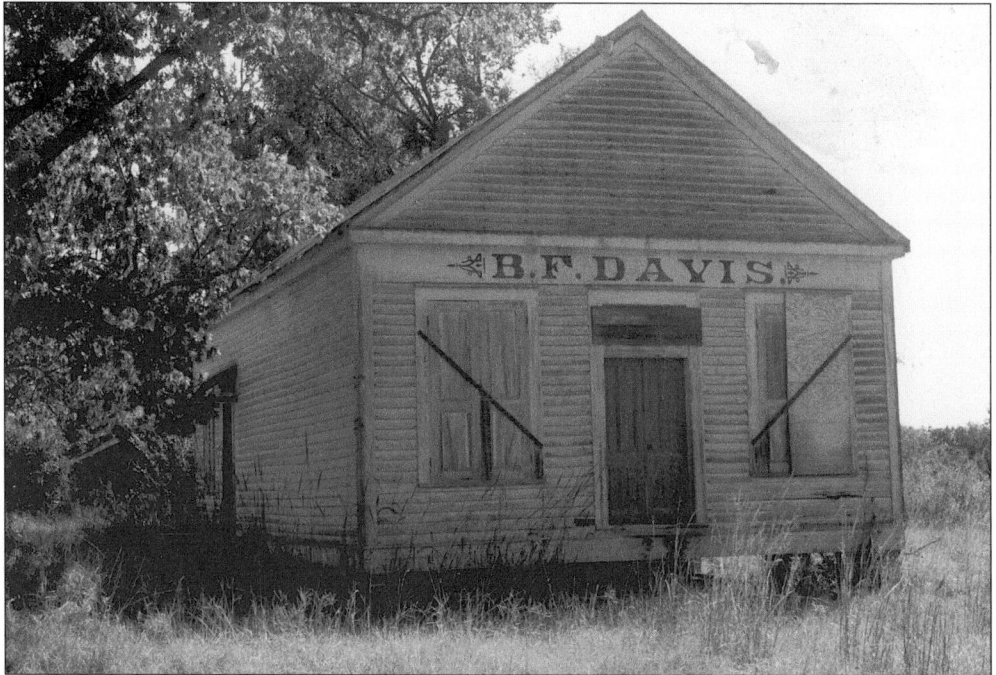

The B.F. Davis store, one of the oldest stores in Centenary, closed in the 1940s. (Photo courtesy of Viola Gibson.)

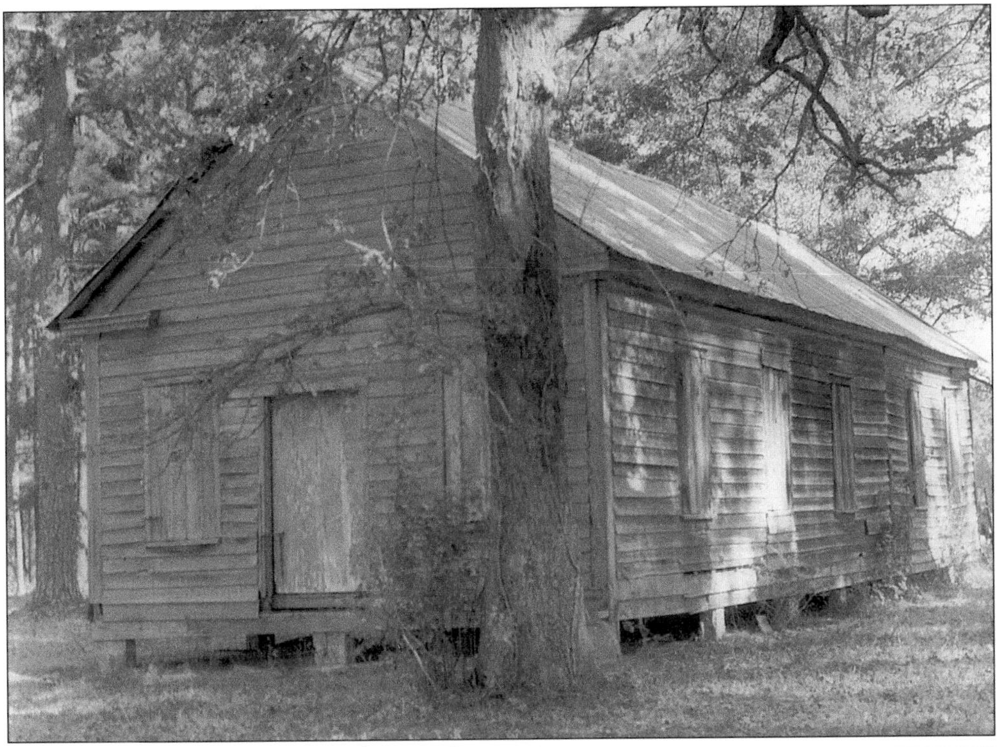

When traveling to Centenary, a glimpse of what is left of the Palmer School can be seen. The Palmer School was built in 1887. (Photo courtesy of Viola Gibson.)

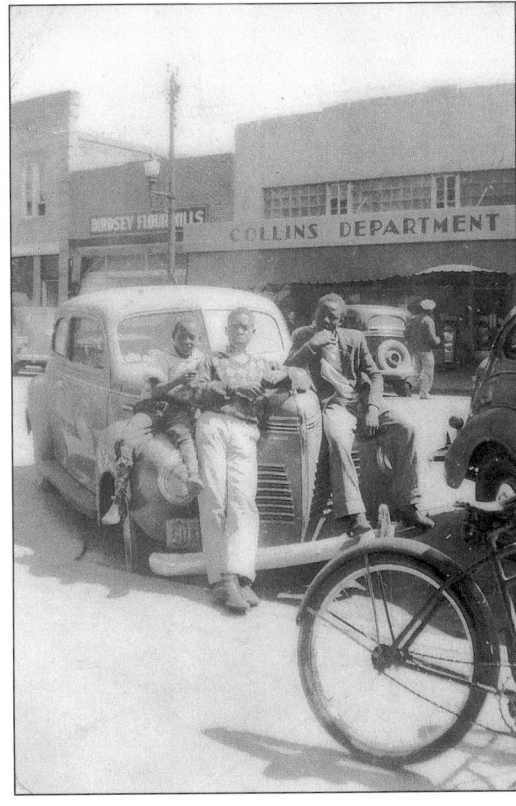

These fellows are apparently relaxing on their automobile while the ladies are shopping in Downtown Marion. Collins Department Store is located across Main Street in the background. (Photo courtesy of Ginny McIntyre.)

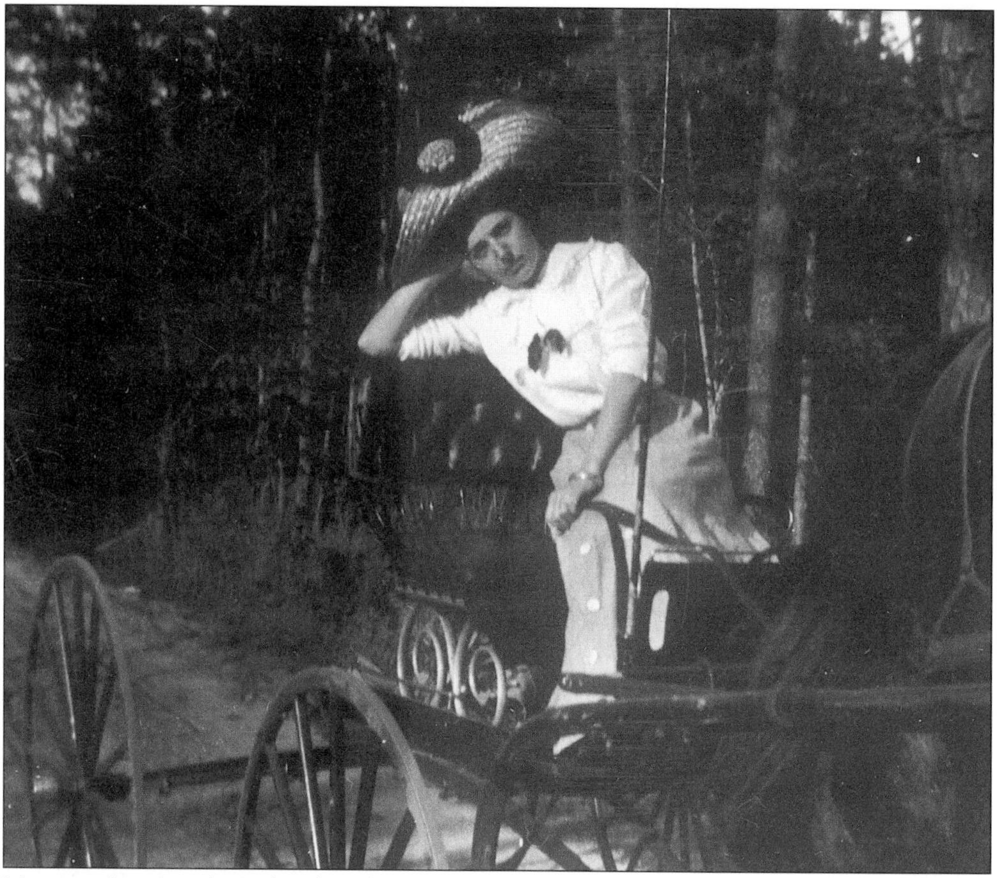

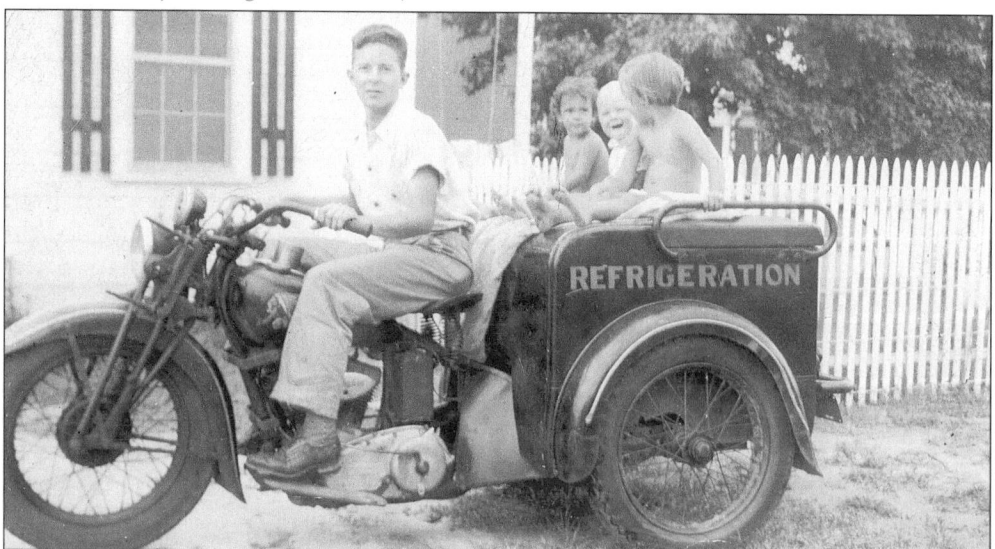

Margaret Layton takes a break in her horse and buggy while traveling the roads of Marion. (Photo courtesy of Margaret E. Wood.)

Everyone loved traveling with Freddie Zeman on his business motorcycle. Here, Eleanor Zeman, Beth Dixon, and Valerie Baumrind enjoy a ride. (Photo courtesy of F.T. Zeman.)

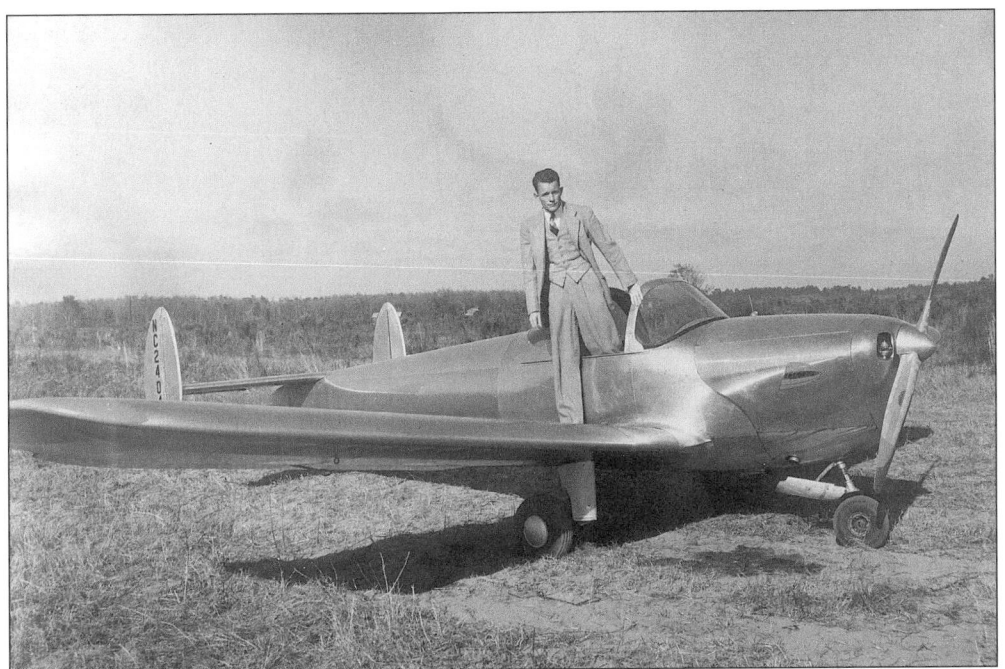

Doyel Cotton enjoys another mode of travel. Cotton is shown at the landing strip at Ellerbe Heights after flying high in 1946. (Photo by Pete Johnson; courtesy of LeeAnne E. Owens.)

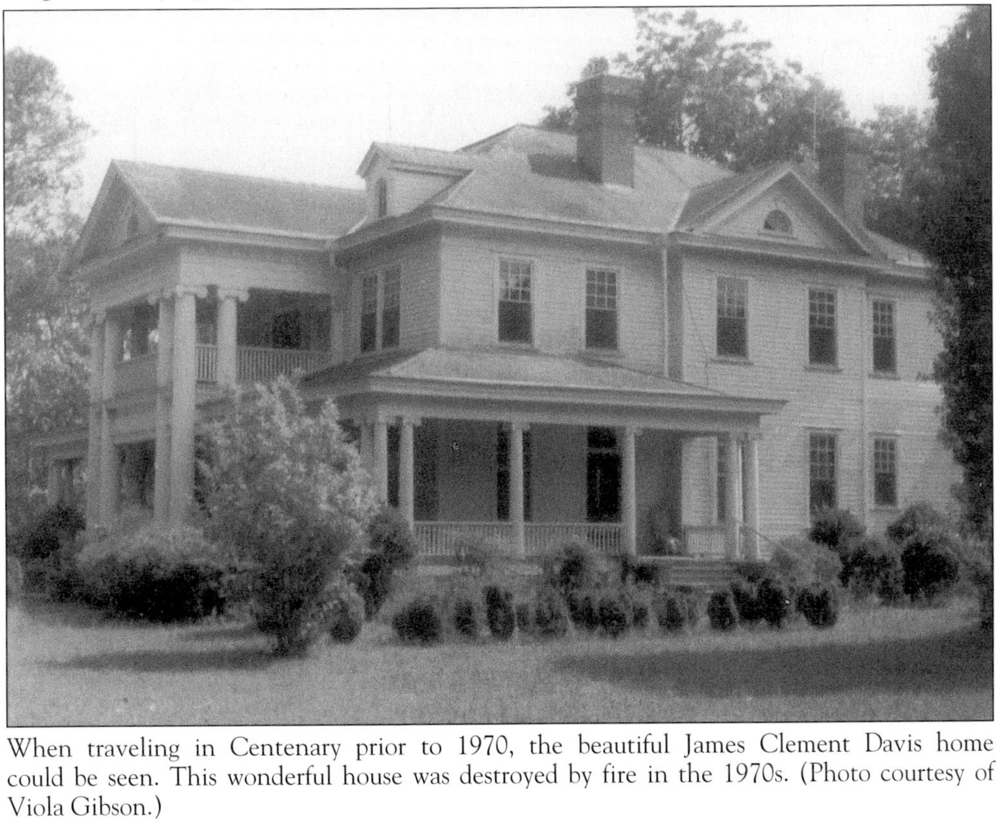

When traveling in Centenary prior to 1970, the beautiful James Clement Davis home could be seen. This wonderful house was destroyed by fire in the 1970s. (Photo courtesy of Viola Gibson.)

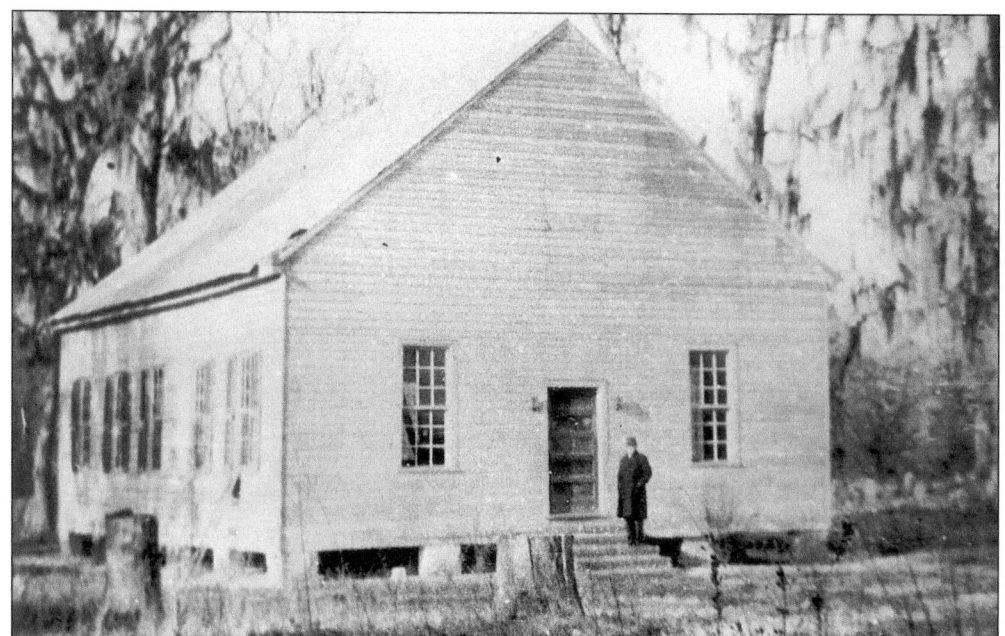

Shiloh Methodist Church was established in 1815. The original building was located in the Springville community. The church building was dismantled, and the materials were transported in wagons to a location in the present church cemetery. This building was used until 1939. The Reverend F. Carlisle Smith of Mullins is pictured here in 1939. (Photo courtesy of Mike Jackson.)

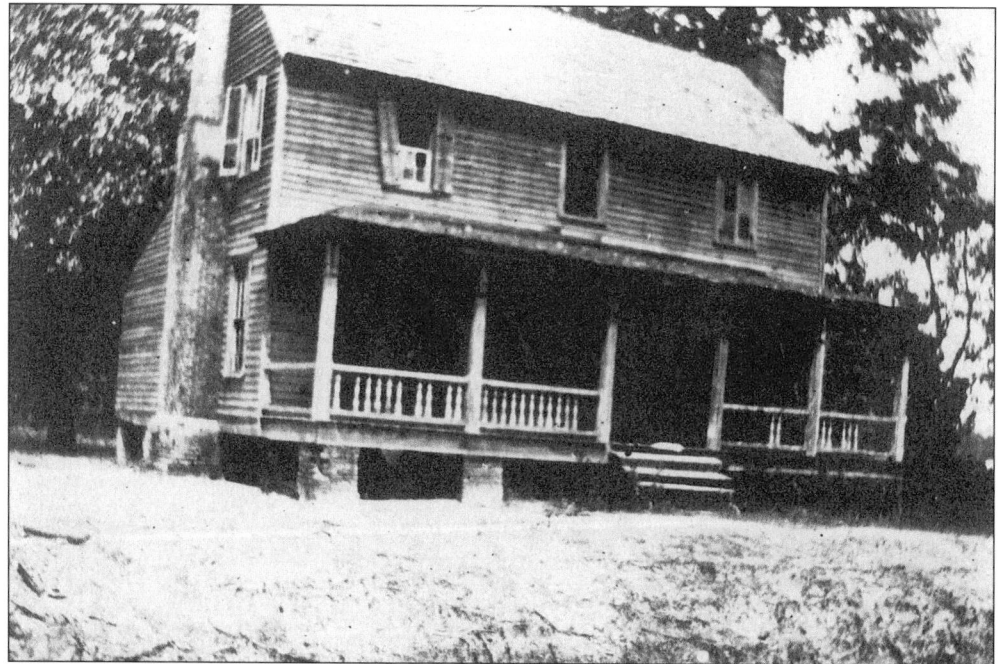

Traveling to the Three Mile Fork, south of Marion, would take you to the Annis Phillips Baker home. Annis Phillips was first married to Hugh Giles Jr., c. 1800s. (Photo courtesy of Libby Stanley.)

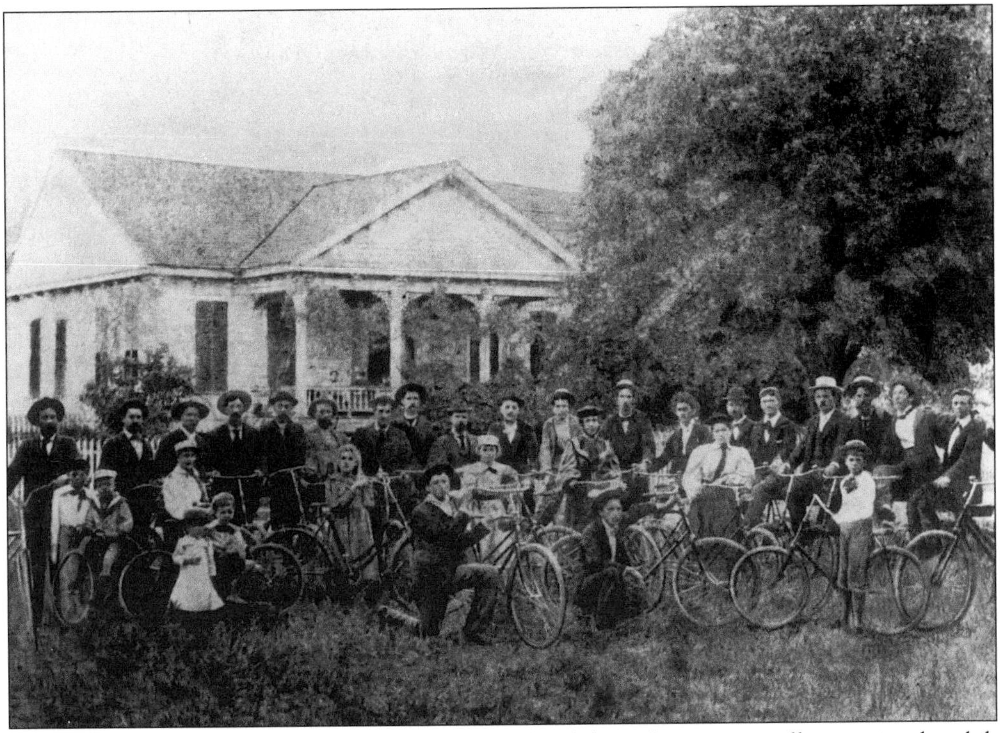

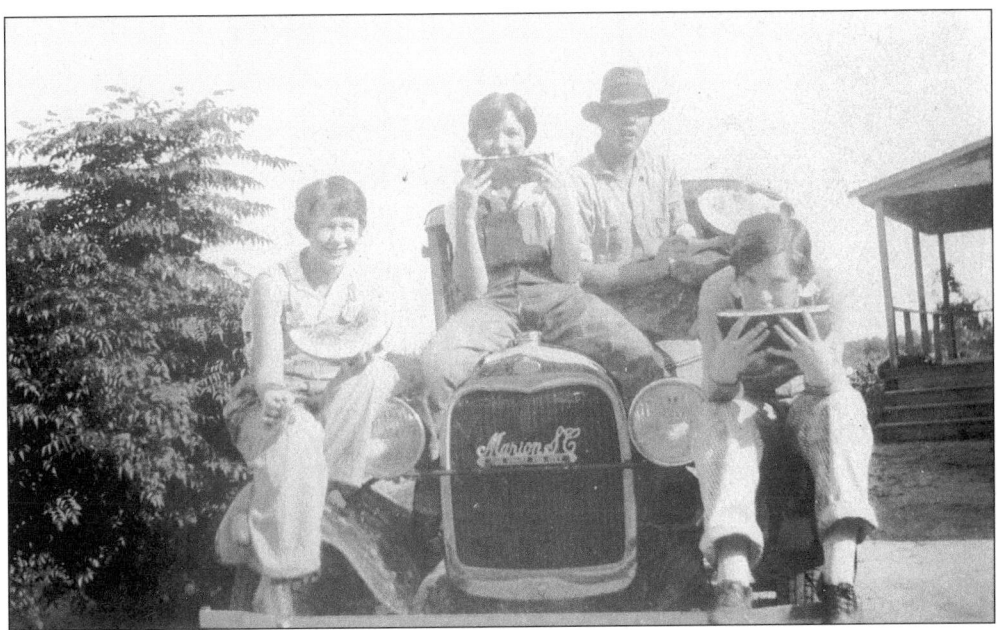

Getting ready to travel is the 1898 Marion Bicycle Club. Before setting off on a trip, the club posed in front of the Archibald McIntyre house. (Photo courtesy of Suzanne Gasque McIntyre.)

Pride in Marion is exhibited on the grille of the Bryant family car. William Lide Bryant, wearing a hat, is enjoying a delicious watermelon grown on the farm. (Photo courtesy of Judy Alderman and Gene Wiggins.)

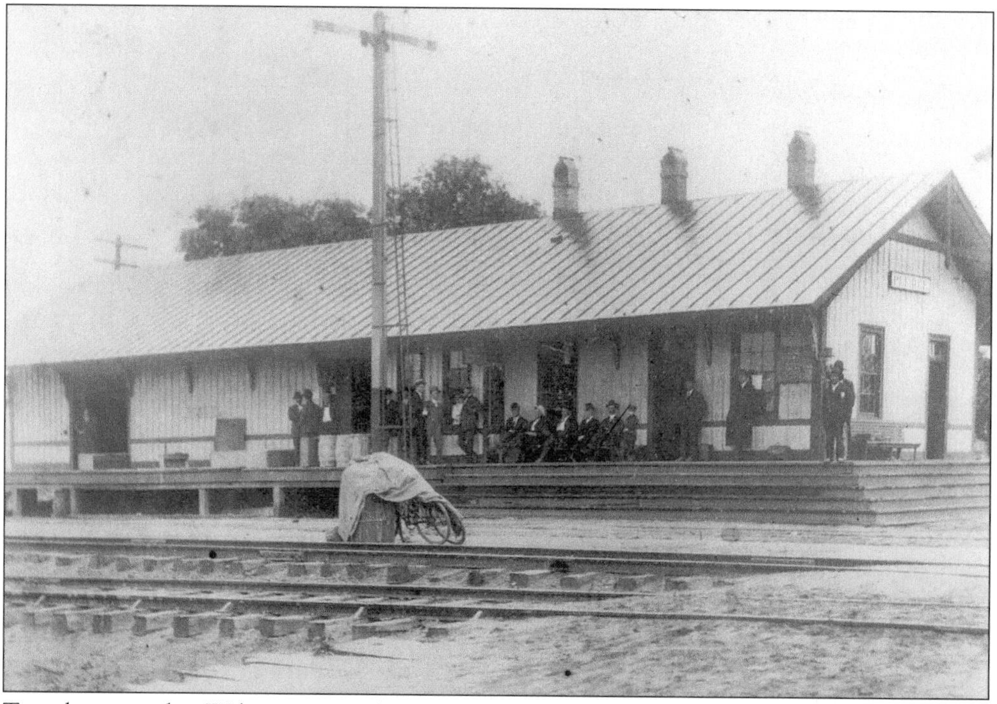

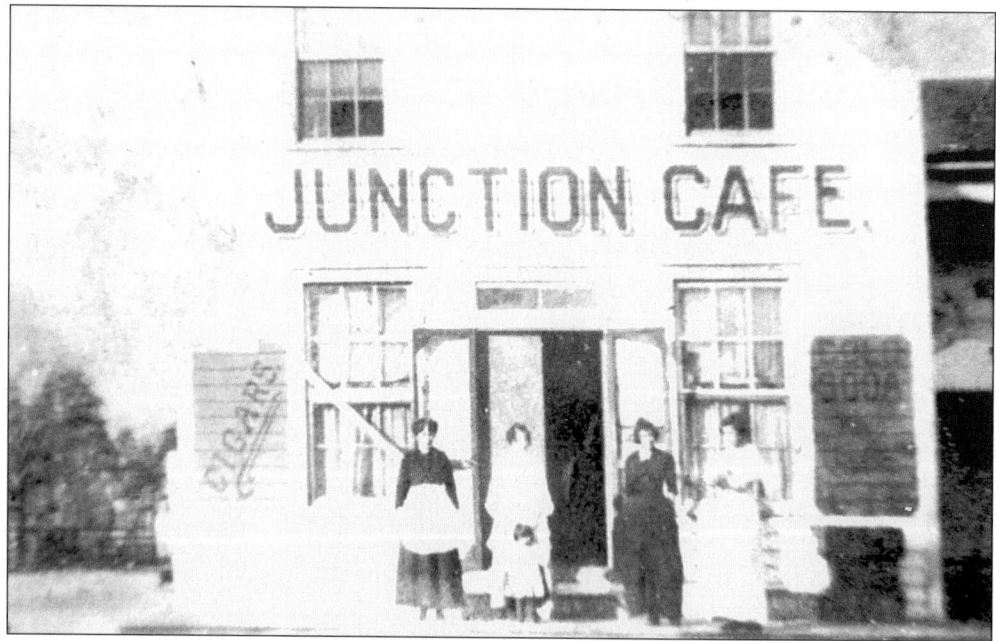

Traveling on the Wilmington-Columbia-Augusta Line and the Main Line (Fayetteville-Richmond) would bring travelers to the Pee Dee Depot. Marion residents sometimes found it necessary to board the train at Pee Dee. (Photo courtesy of Mike Jackson.)

When traveling through Pee Dee, a visitor could see the Junction Cafe and Hotel, located across the railroad track from the depot. This picture was made in 1914. The structure was destroyed by fire in 1927. Mrs. W.T. Collins, stands behind her little girl, Alice. (Photo courtesy of Mike Jackson.)

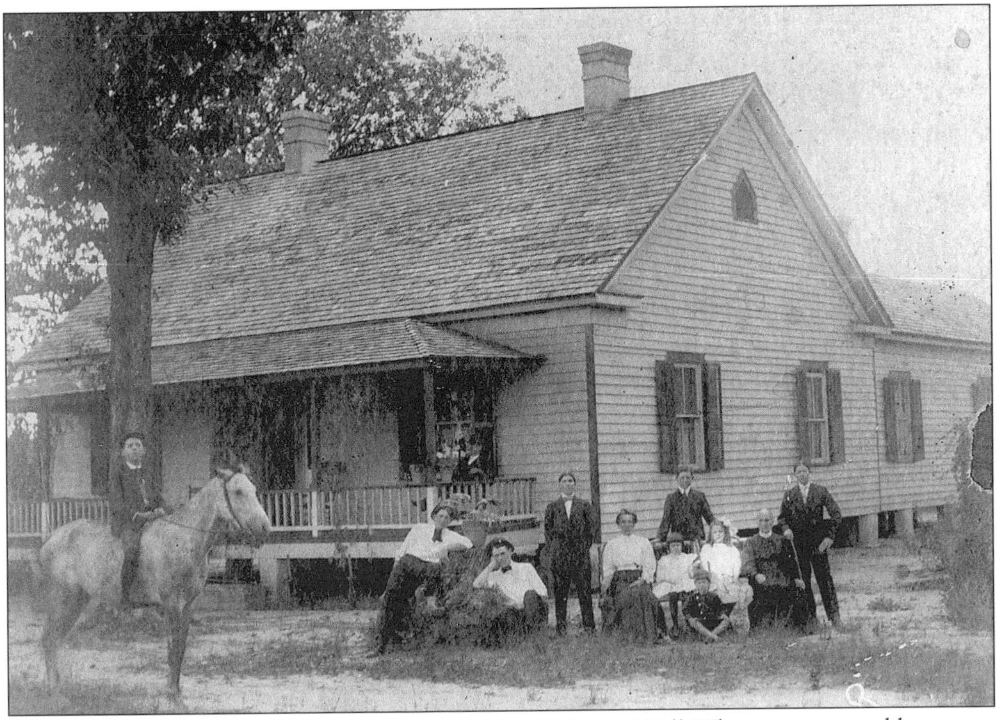

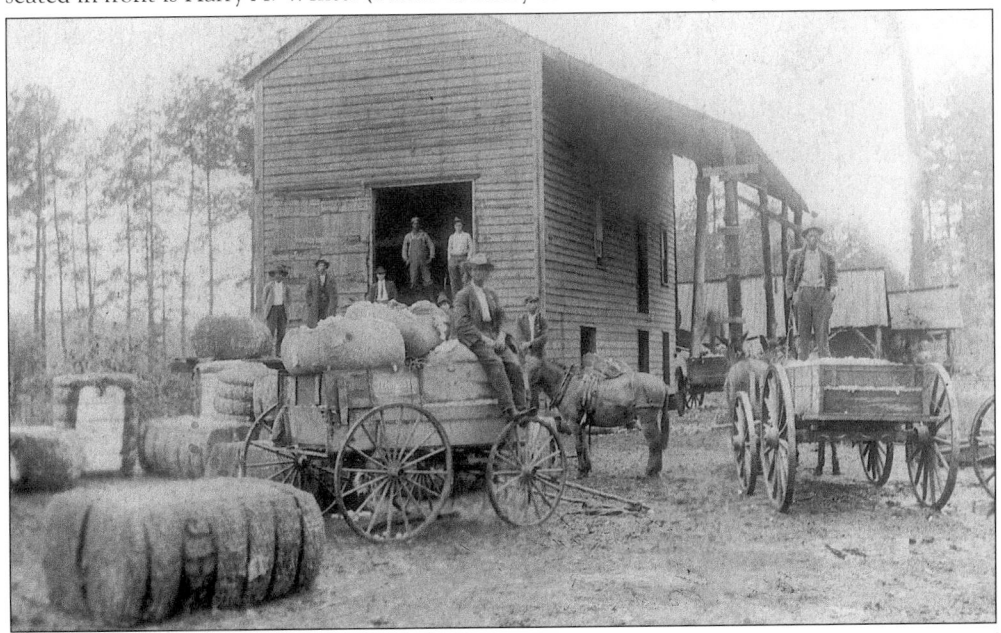

The family of Preston C. White (on the porch) and Hattie Wall White are pictured here near Centenary, *c.* 1910. On the horse is Warren T. White. In the middle, from left to right, are twins Wayland D. White and Herbert S. White, Pearley C. White, Hattie Wall White, Forrest G. White, little Olive M. White, little Ruth L White, Leonora A. Wall, and Leon P. White; seated in front is Harry A. White. (Photo courtesy of Viola Gibson.)

This cotton gin in the Centenary area was situated on LeGette property. (Photo courtesy of Viola Gibson.)

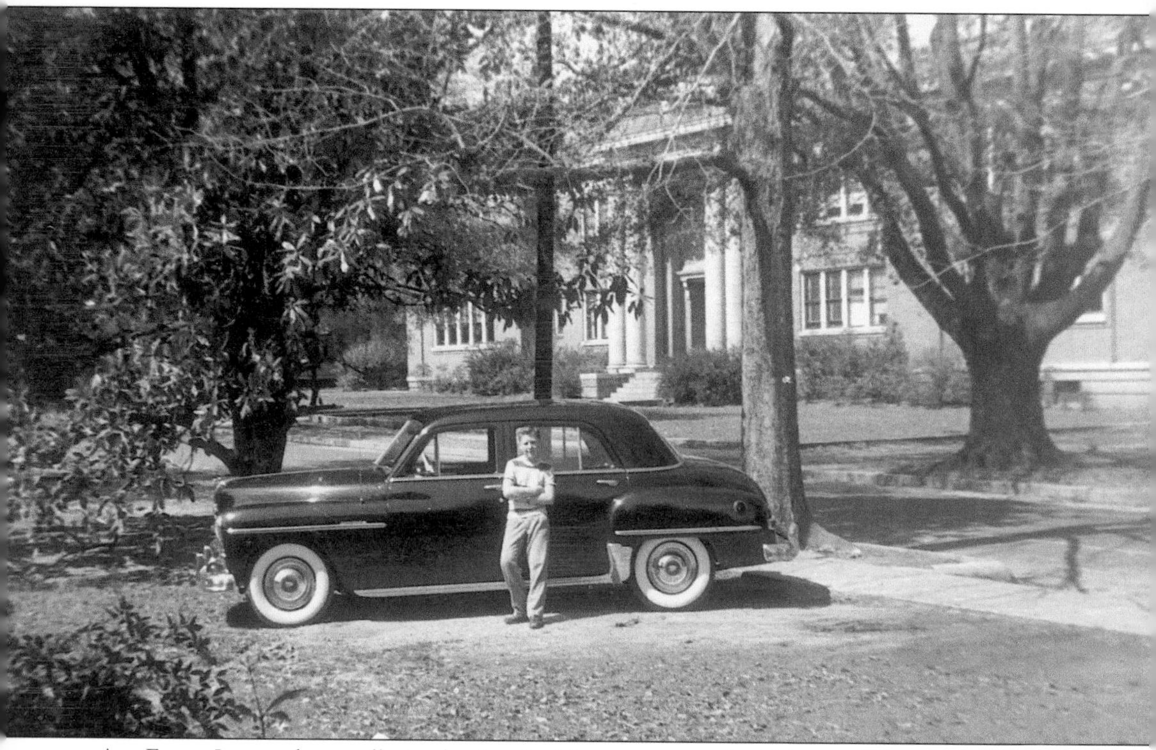

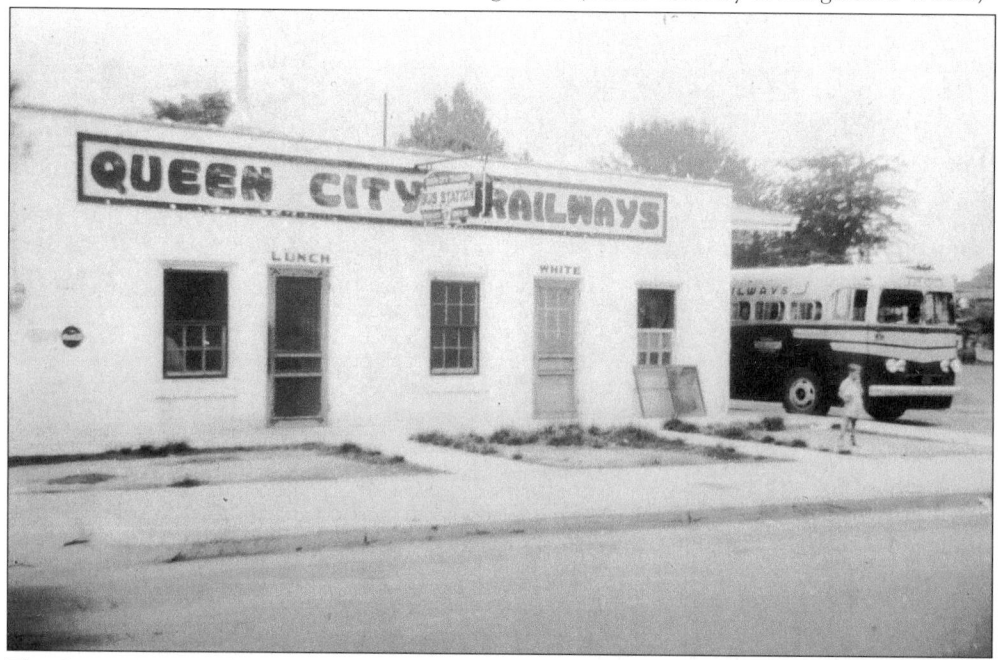

Asa Evans Jr. stands proudly in the family driveway on Godbold Street before going cruising. Marion Grammar School is visible in the background. (Photo courtesy of Margaret E. Wood.)

The Queen City Trailways Bus Station, operated in the 1940s by Ann Bryant Bayless and Bill Bayless, was situated next to the Coca-Cola Bottling Company on Railroad Avenue across from the train depot. (Photo courtesy of Judy Alderman and Gene Wiggins.)

Six

WORKIN' AND PLAYIN'

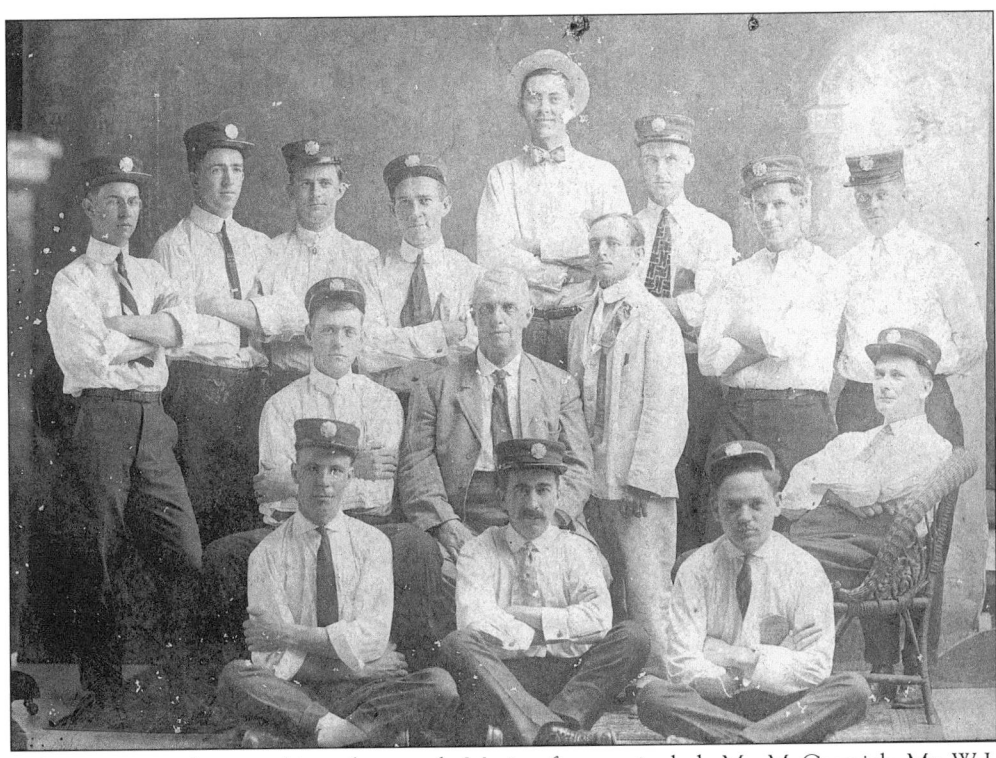

Taking time out from working, these early Marion firemen include Mr. McCormick; Mr. W.J. Orr; Mr. Madge McLendon; Mr. John Atkinson; and Mr. L. Thomas, who was the driver of the fire horses. (Photo courtesy of Suzanne Gasque McIntyre.)

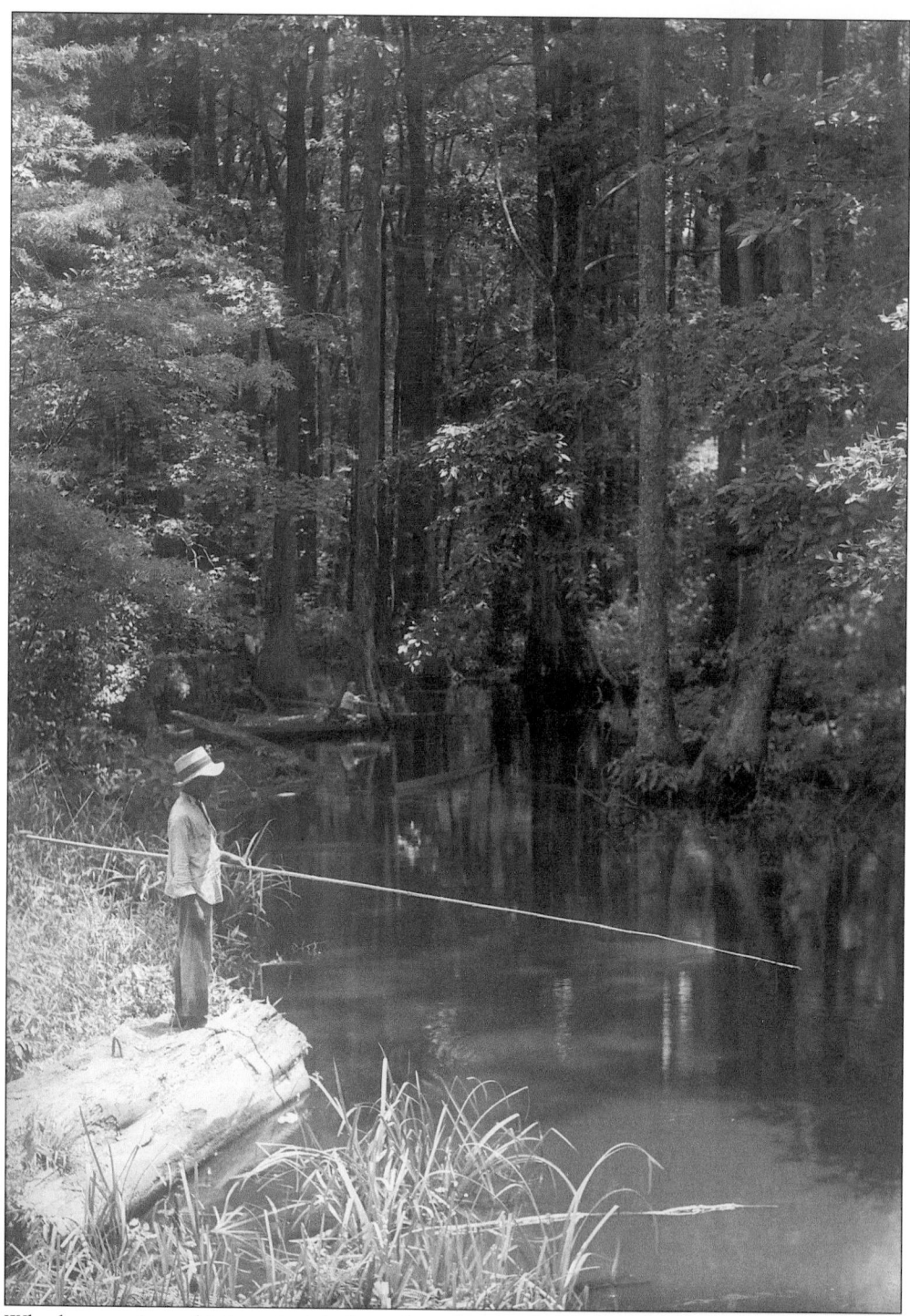

Whether one is workin' or playin', depends on how you look at it, but these folks look pretty serious as they fish along Catfish Creek. (Photo courtesy of FoxTrot Committee and the Caroliniana Library.)

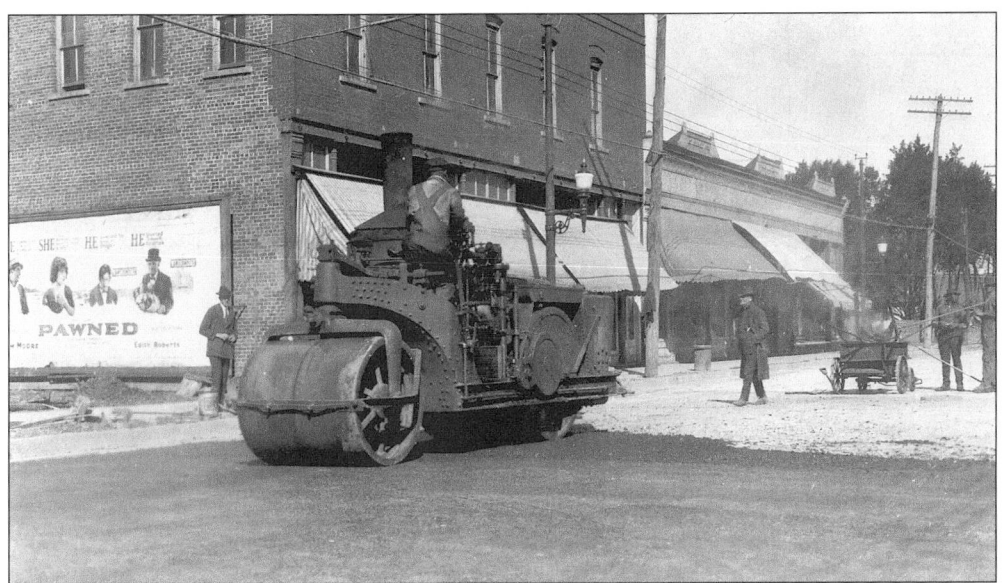

In this view looking north, with Harllee Street on the right, these men are hard at work paving Marion's Main Street in 1929. (Photo courtesy of Ginny McIntyre.)

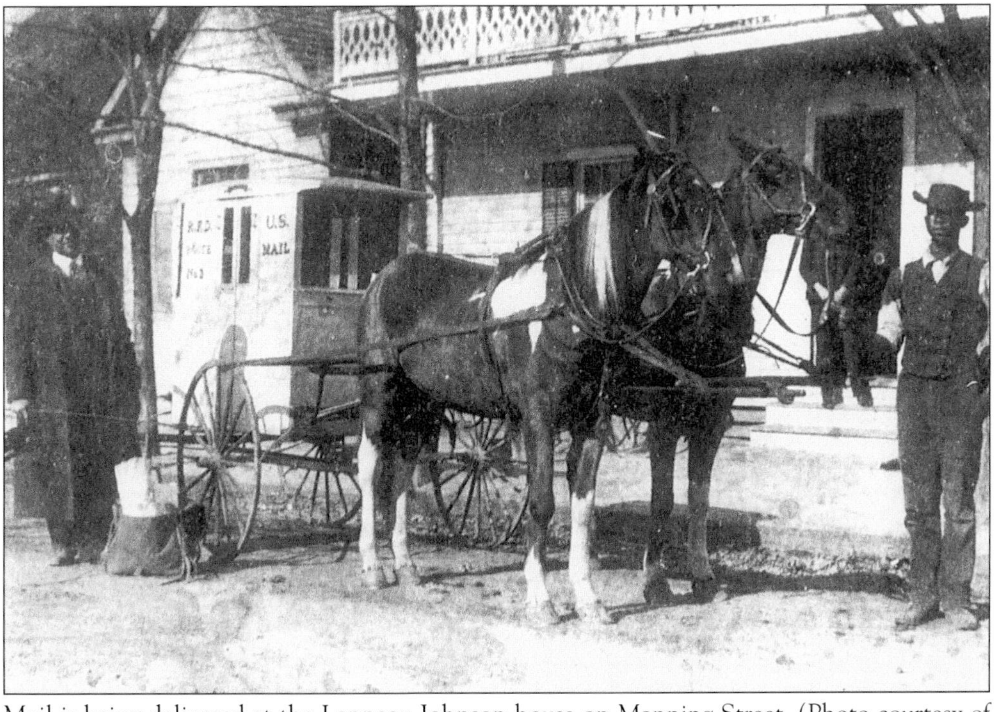

Mail is being delivered at the Lanneau Johnson house on Manning Street. (Photo courtesy of FoxTrot Committee.)

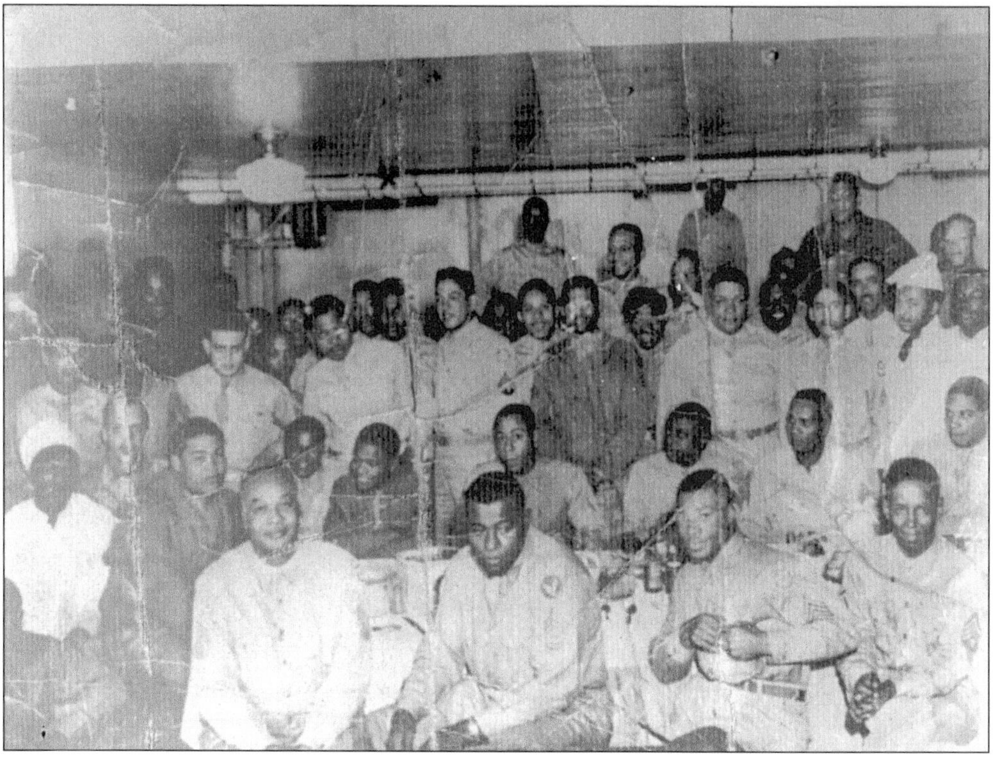

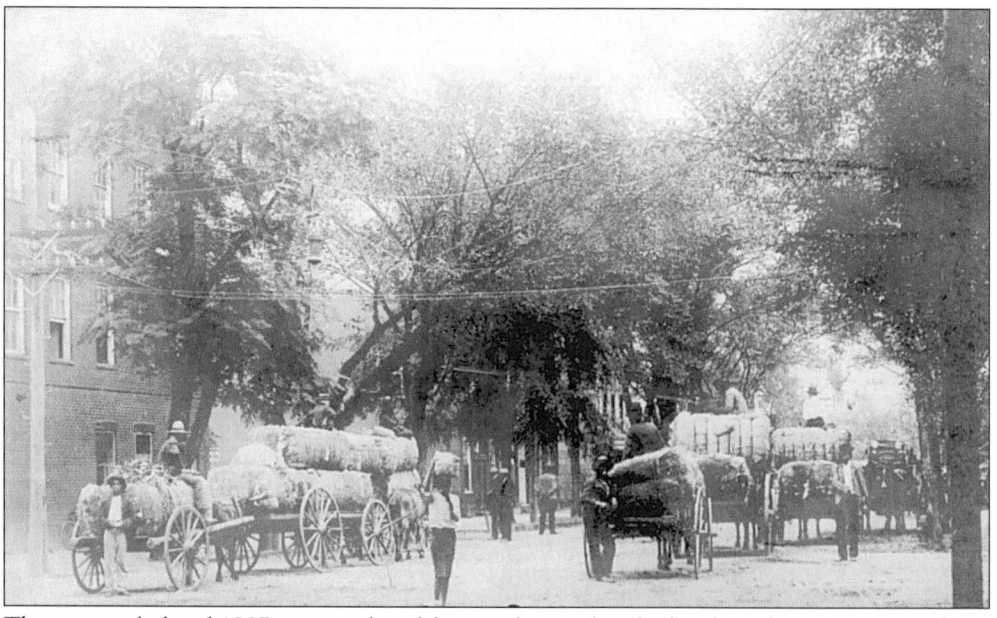

The late Ransom Rowell was sergeant of the 1695 C Company of Engineers. Fellow members of his company included boxing greats Joe Lewis and Sugar Ray Robinson. (Photo courtesy of Jerry Rowell.)

This postcard, dated 1907, was produced from a photo taken by local resident Bruce Hamilton. This shows cotton being hauled to market on Court Street behind the courthouse. (Photo courtesy of Valerie Baumrind Bonatis.)

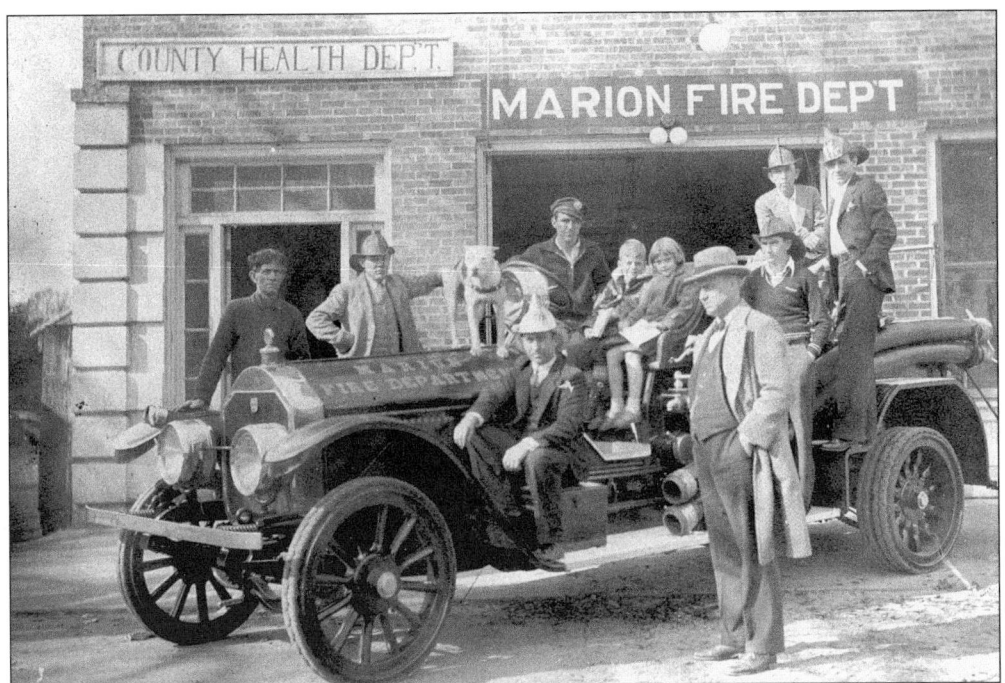

The 1933 Marion Fire Department photograph includes the following, from left to right: Charlie Whittington, Lee Boatwright, Butch (or Spot), David Frank Owens Sr., Emerson Scott Jr., Mary Bee Scott, Clyde Bellamy, Emerson Scott Sr., Joe Boatwright, Berry Richardson, and Clarence Richardson. At that time, the Marion Fire Department and County Health Department were located on West Court Street. (Photo courtesy of Doris Gasque.)

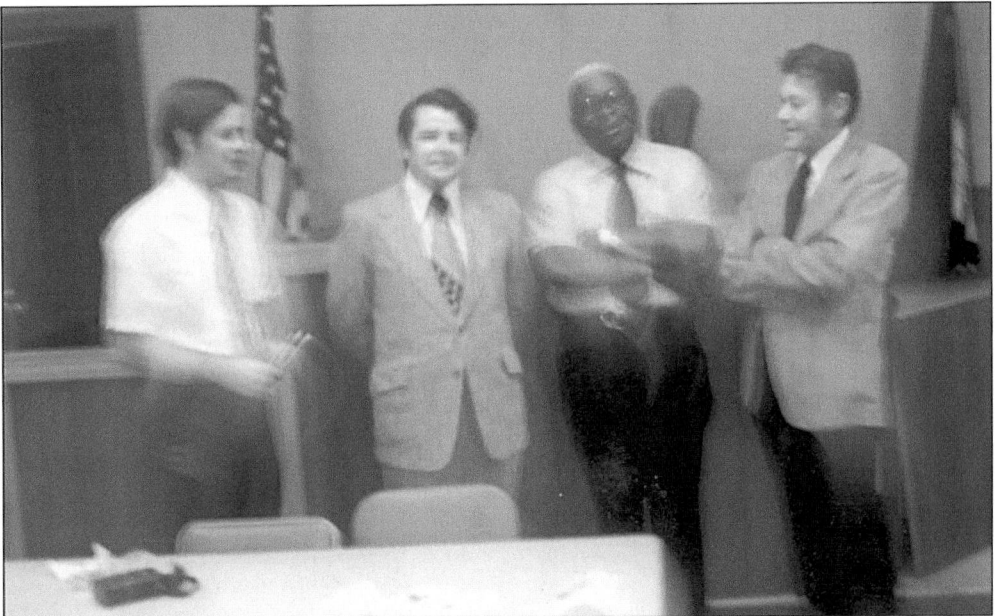

Working hard for the people are Republicans Wayne Taylor and Archie McIntyre, as they welcomed the first black Republican, as well as city councilman, Willie Boykin. (Photo courtesy of Ginny McIntyre.)

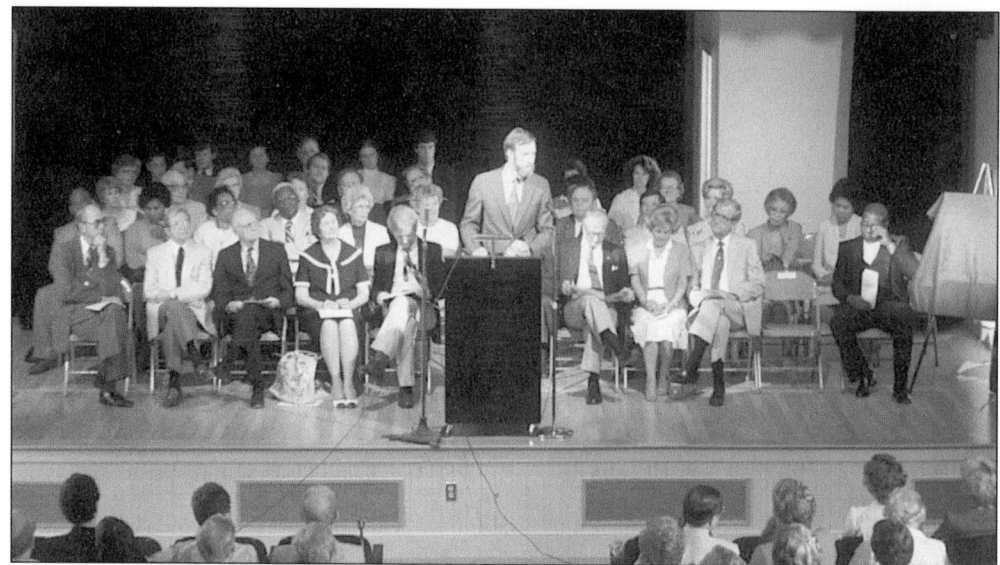

This photograph shows a group of citizens who worked very hard to renovate and preserve the Old Town Hall and Opera House. It was dedicated on May 15, 1983. (Photo courtesy of Mike McLendon.)

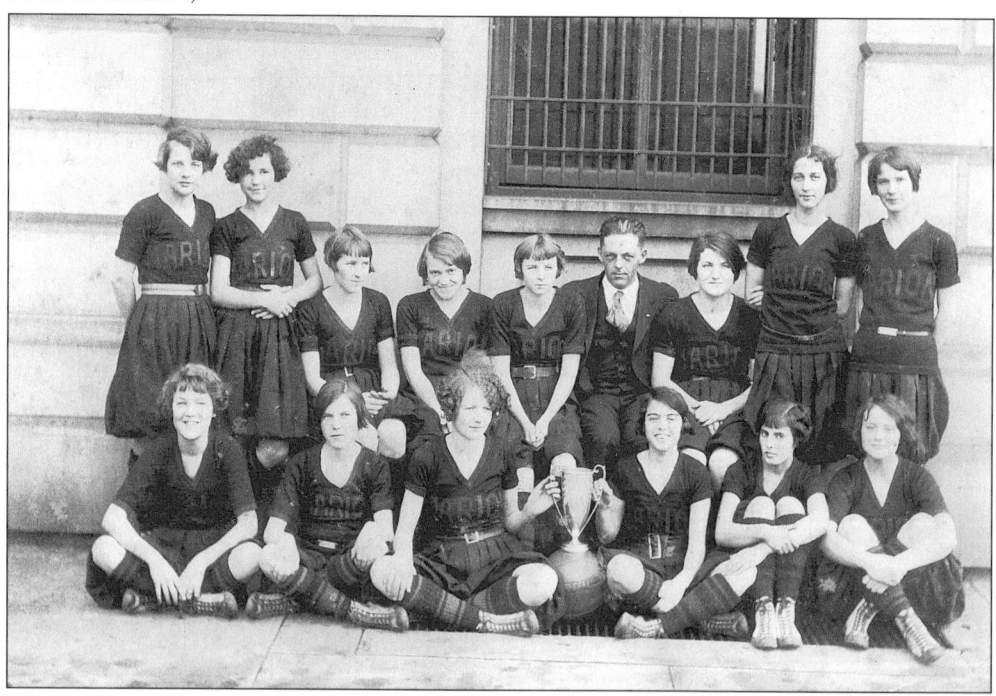

The 1926 Lassifoxes basketball team was the South Carolina basketball champion. They played a U.S. championship tournament and were runner-up U.S. basketball champions. Team members included Dorothy Lewis, Virginia McIntyre (Allison), Mary Hough, Ellen Moore (Guirkin), Lorretta Atkinson, Nora Tew, McKeiver Alford (Dudley), Margaret Willcox (Skinner), Christine Evans (Jones), Mary Worsham (Hite), Mary Dickson, Coach J.C. BeVier, Edna Lamb (Bellamy), Elizabeth Gresham, and Grace Gresham. (Photo courtesy of Suzanne Gasque McIntyre and Mary Elizabeth H. Wilson.)

The interior of a tobacco warehouse, formerly located at the corner of Railroad Avenue and Wheeler Street, is decorated for a party. (Photo courtesy of Mike McLendon.)

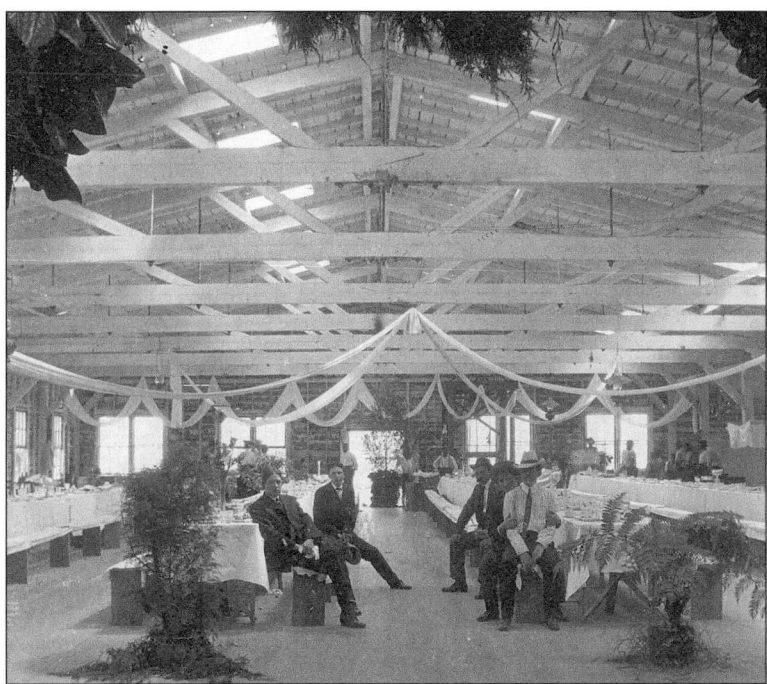

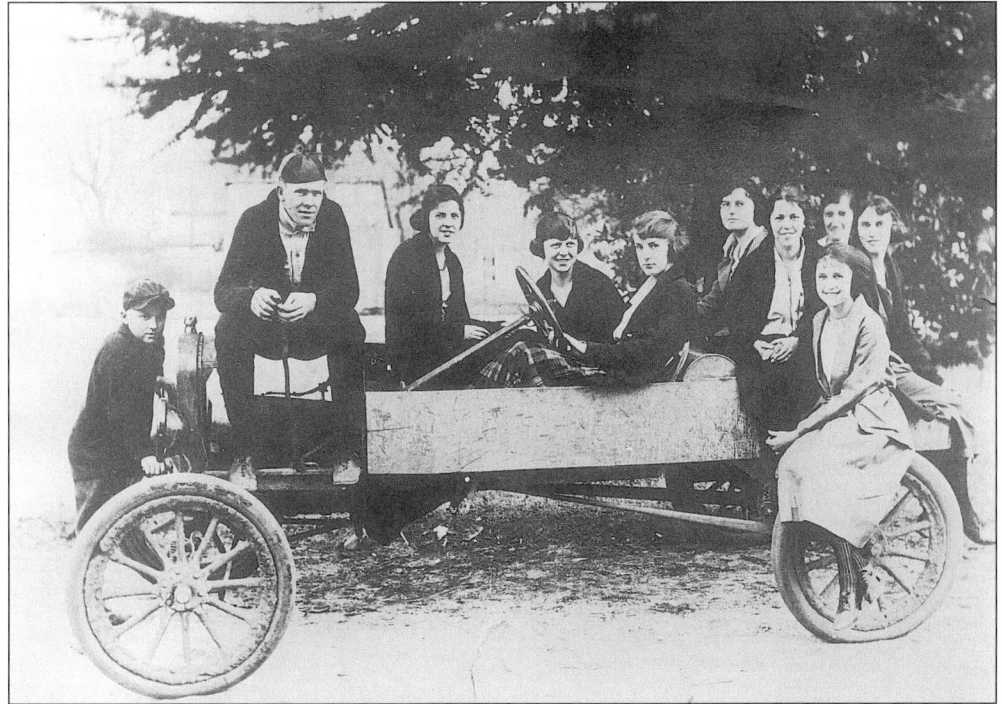

Headed for a picnic in their 1920 "Stripdown," these folks include Bob Jones, Mr. Colin Seaborn, Margaret Davis Stilley, Louise Lawrence, Gladys McLucas, Catherine Smith, Mary Moore, Louise Norwood Haskell, Wilma Jenkins, and Tot Smith. This photograph was taken under the cedar tree in front of the present Marion County Museum. (Photo courtesy of Billy Cornelius.)

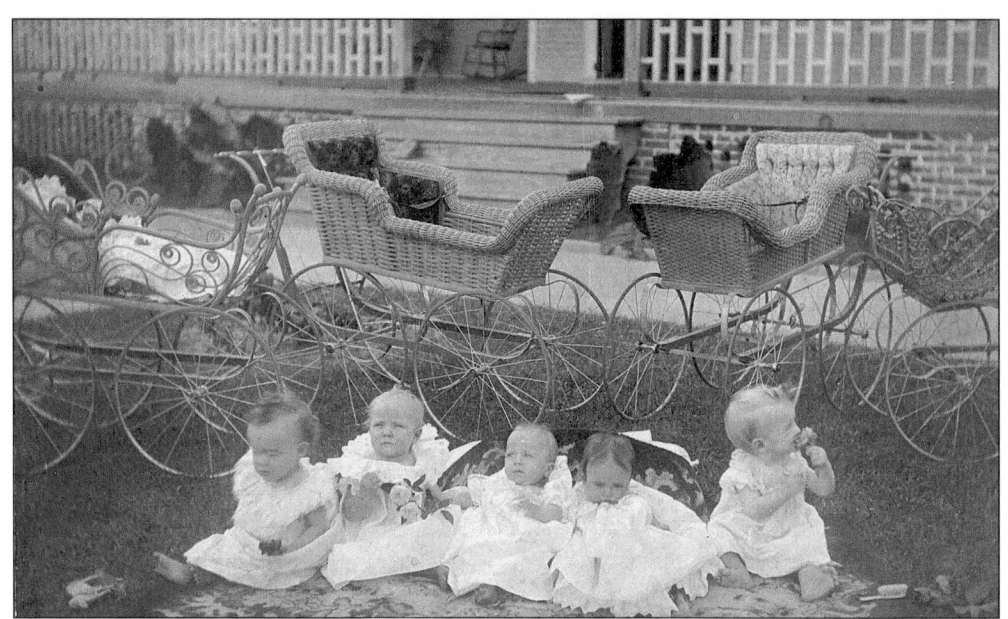

Playing and posing are Mary Clark Willcox Lawrence and neighborhood children in front of the Willcox home on Willcox Avenue in the early 1900s. (Photo courtesy of Joyce Willcox.)

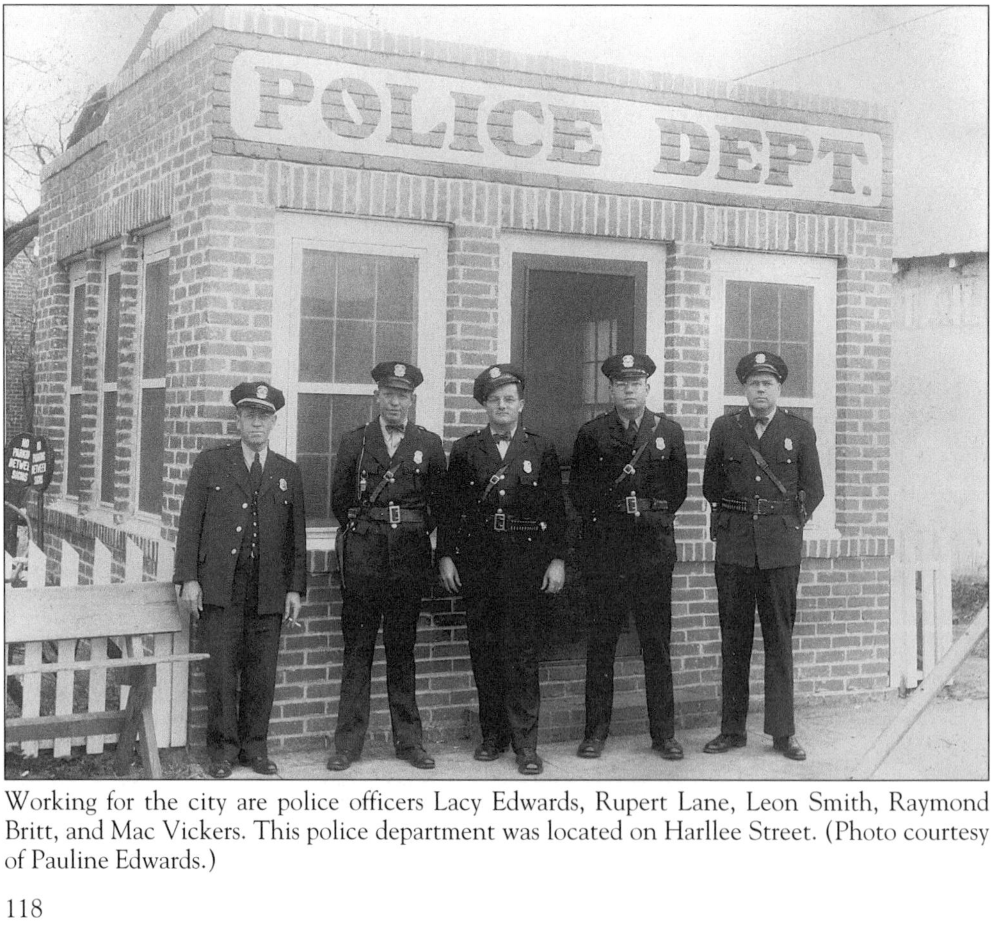

Working for the city are police officers Lacy Edwards, Rupert Lane, Leon Smith, Raymond Britt, and Mac Vickers. This police department was located on Harllee Street. (Photo courtesy of Pauline Edwards.)

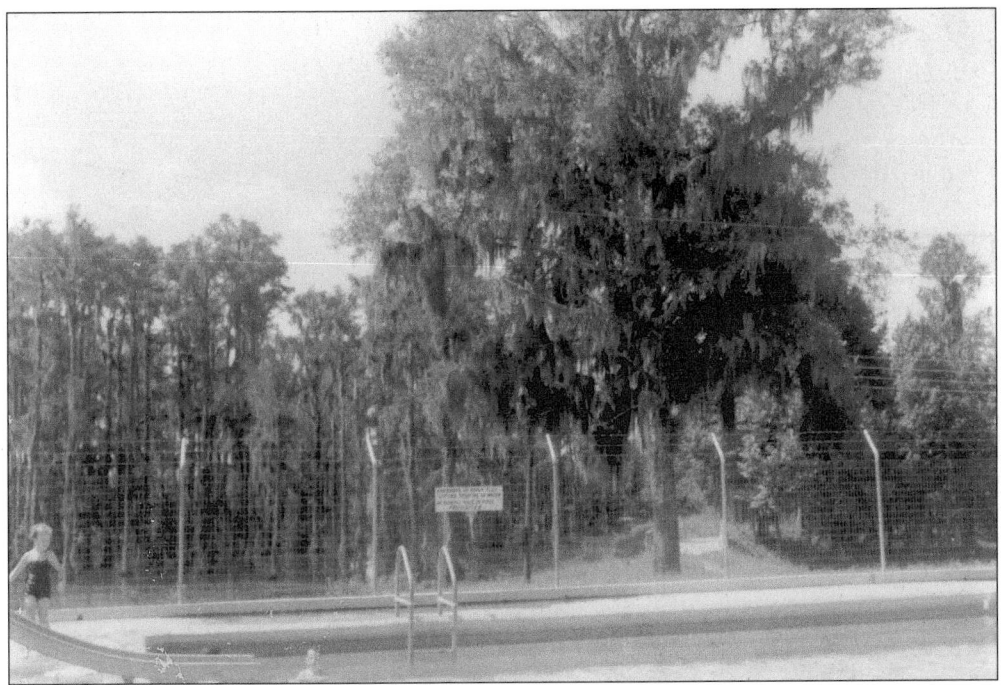

In 1955, the American Legion Swimming Pool at Gaddy's Mill provided a wonderful place to play. (Photo courtesy of Lurline Stedman.)

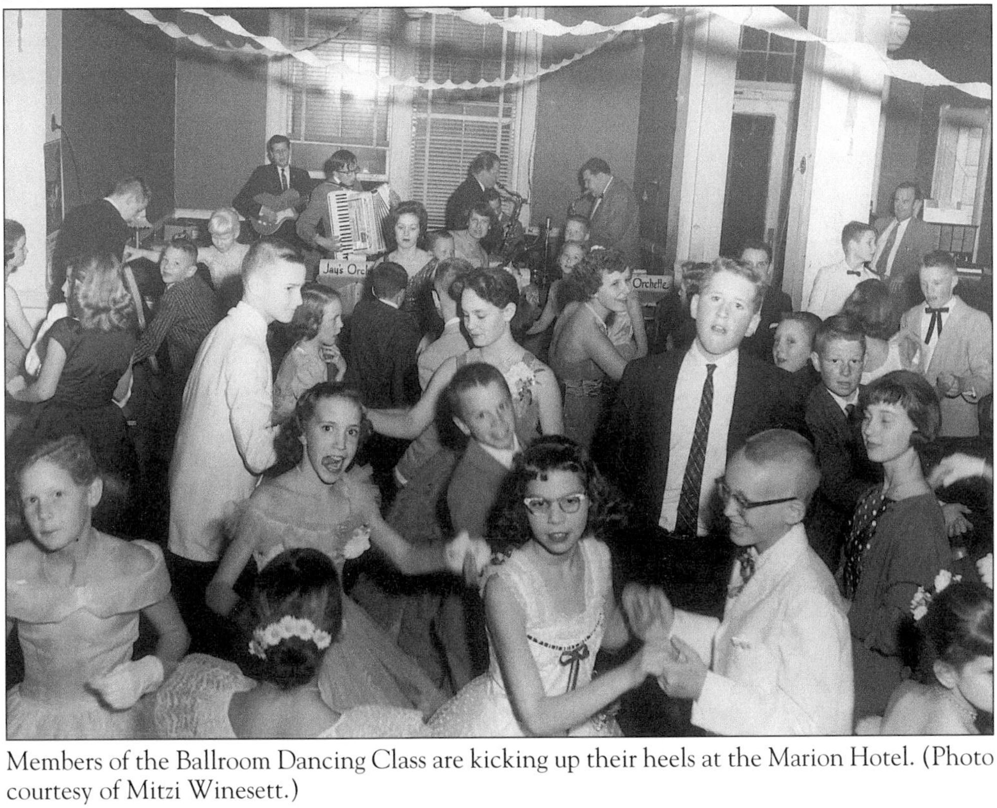

Members of the Ballroom Dancing Class are kicking up their heels at the Marion Hotel. (Photo courtesy of Mitzi Winesett.)

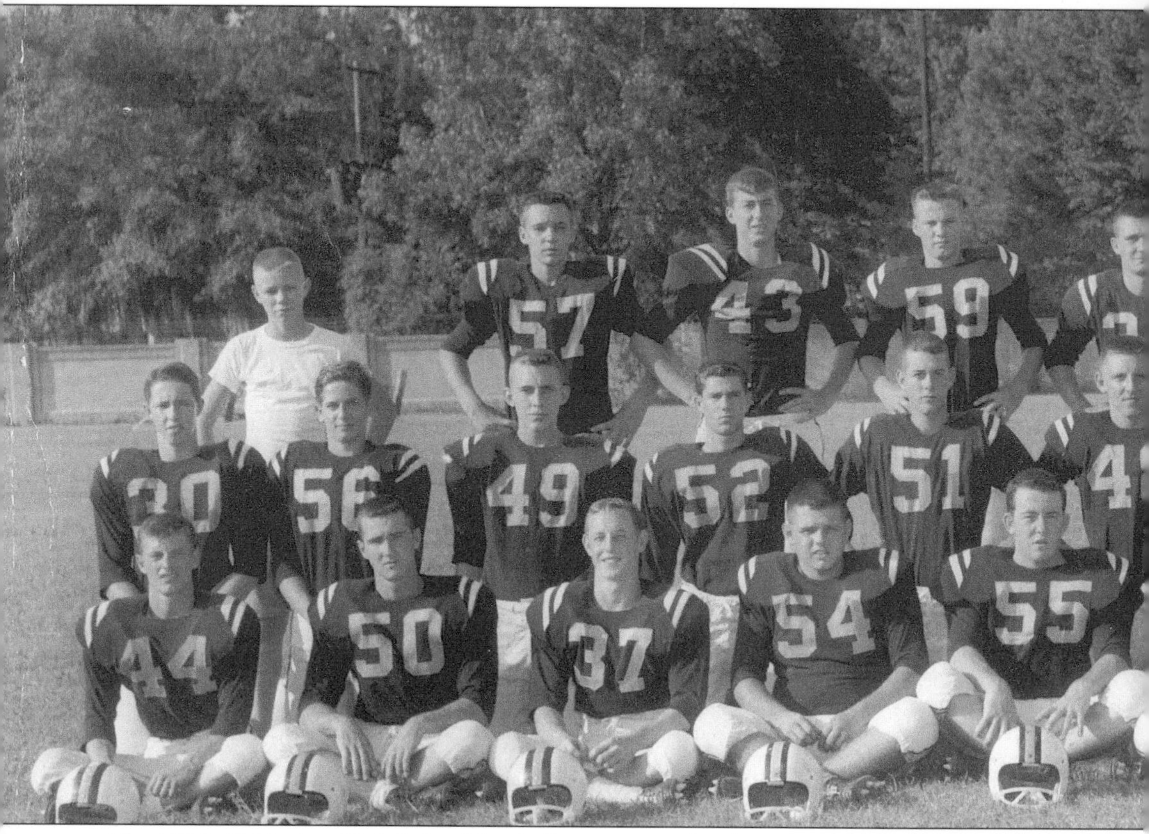

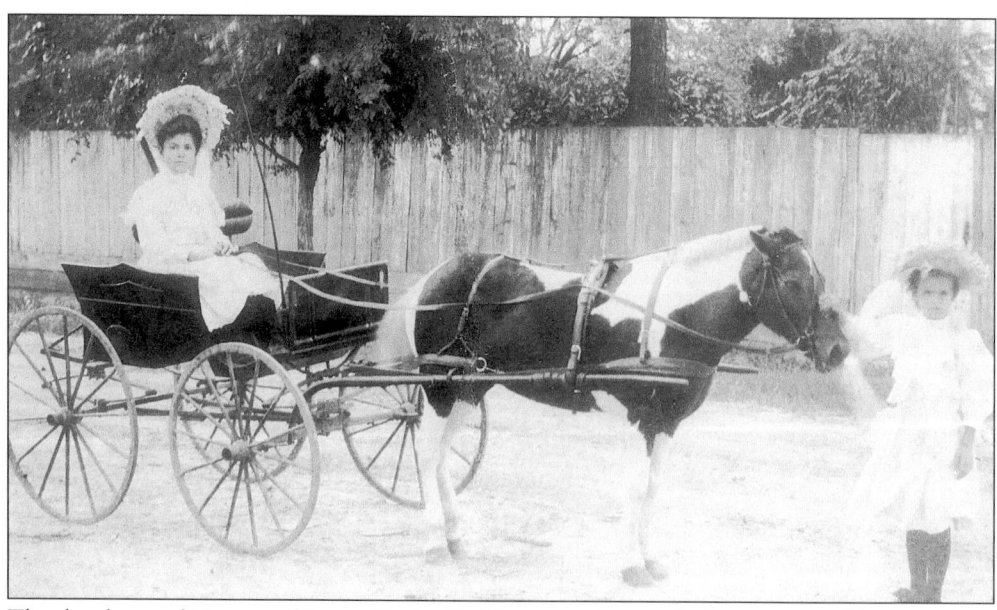

The 1962–63 Marion High School football team poses for the team picture. (Photo by Marion

The daughters of Henry and Laura Dozier Smith are getting ready for a pony and buggy ride in the early 1900s. (Photo courtesy of Lucia Atkinson.)

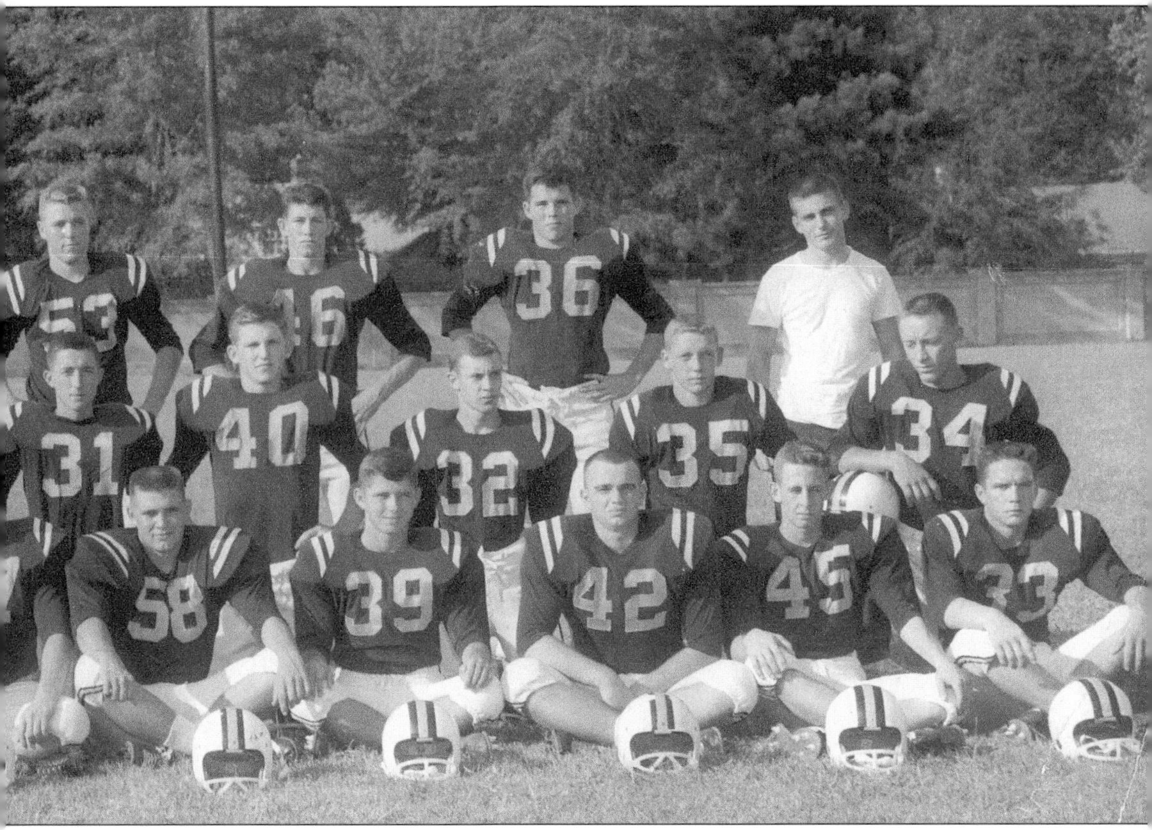

Studios; courtesy of LeeAnne E. Owens.)

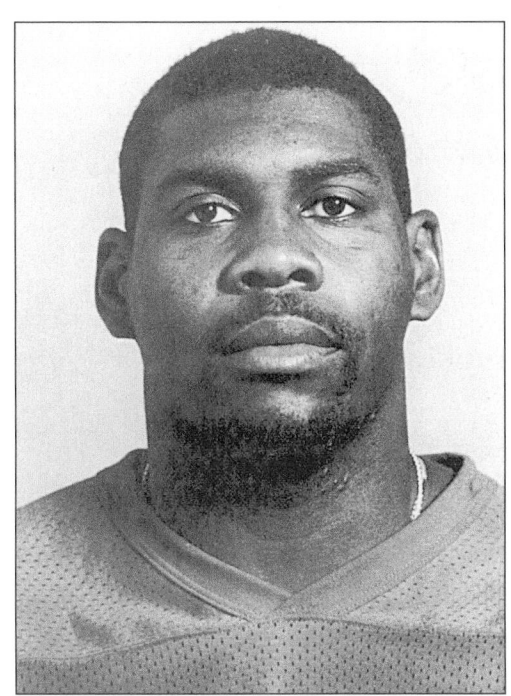

Marion native Louis Cooper played in the National Football League for the Kansas City Chiefs, Miami Dolphins, and Philadelphia Eagles. (Photo courtesy of Annie Mae Hunt.)

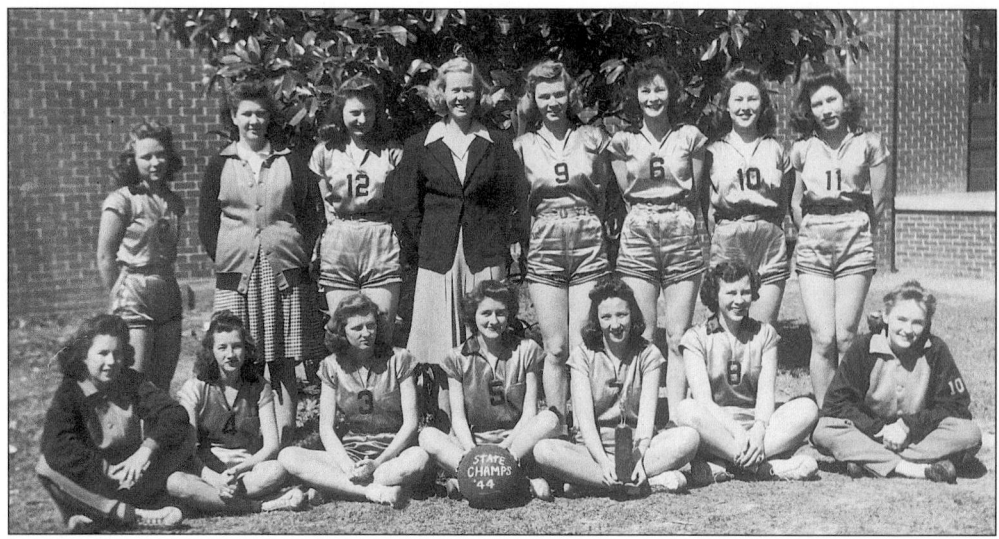

The 1944 State Championship team from Marion High School includes Mary Baker, Bulea Mae Porter, Carolyn Peacock, Betty Thames, Faye Lane, Catherine Ford, Virginia Rose Wallace, Lounita Powers, Jack Stanley, Sara Tanner, Coach Shannon Wilkerson, Jean Foxworth, Jane Blackwell, Margie Boatwright, and Sudie Lunsford. (Photo courtesy of Jane B. Thompson.)

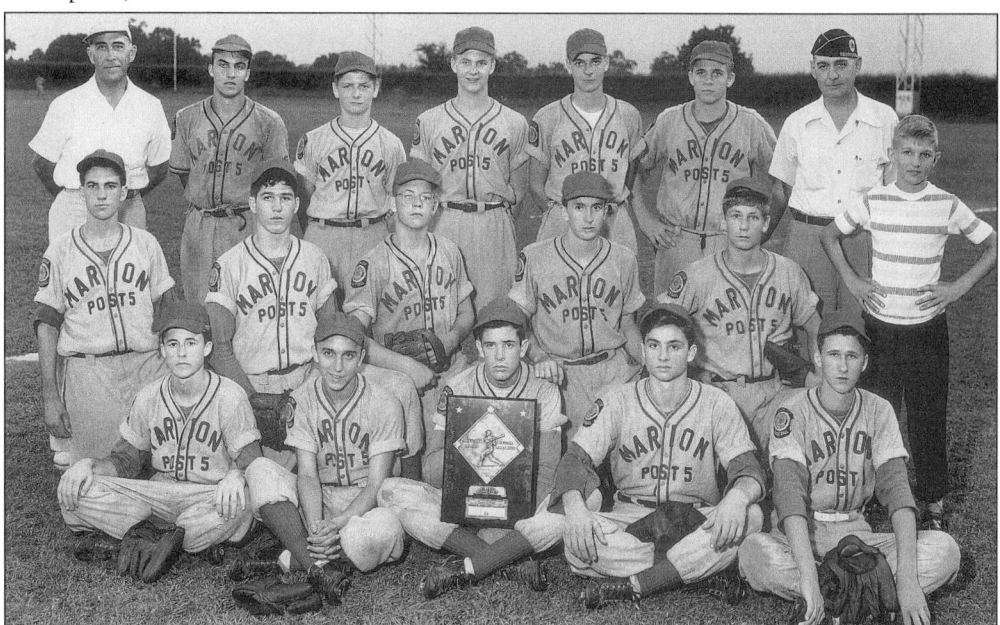

The 1949 Junior American Legion baseball team won the Lower State Championship and became the state runners-up, after they were defeated by Greenwood in the state championship games. Members include, from left to right, the following: (seated) Carlton Sawyer, J.W. "Snout" Hyatt, Frank Ellerbe, Pierce "Red" Huggins, and Billy Hilton; (kneeling) Nelson Carmichael, Milton Morris, Chandler Bryan, Chester Morris, and Cecil Snipes; (standing) Coach N.A. "Bub" McMillan, Gene McLellan, Pete Caulder, Dick Rogers, Mutt Miles, Billy Pope, American Legion Post Five Athletic Director W.M. Dickson, and bat boy Johnny Baxley. (Photo courtesy of Suzanne Gasque McIntyre.)

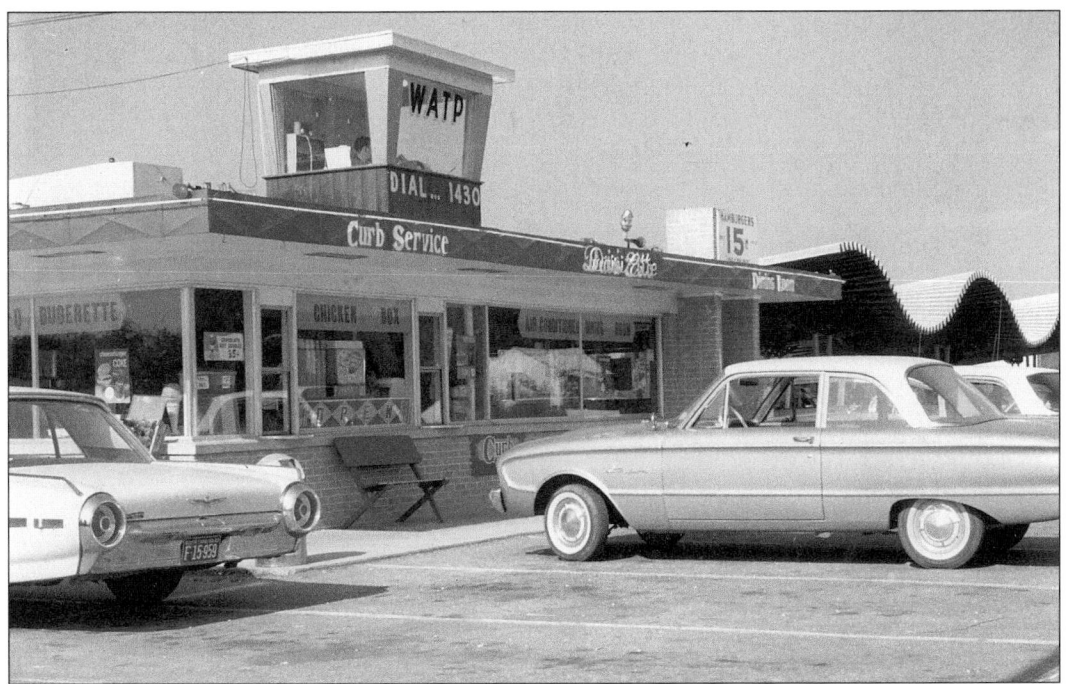

The Dari-ette was a popular gathering spot for teenagers during the late 1950s and early 1960s. Favorite records were played by a disc jockey on top of the building. (Photo courtesy of Arlis West.)

Mr. and Mrs. Cartrell A. Brown worked very hard during their working careers in Marion. Elsie Gallman Brown taught school until 1973 as well as operating Brown's Flower Shop from 1958 until her death. Cartrell A. Brown worked in Marion County from 1948 until his retirement in 1996. In his working career he was the Marion County agricultural agent, coordinator for the South Carolina Rural Development Program, and served as a city judge for the City of Marion. In 1999, the City Court Room was dedicated in his honor. (Photo courtesy of Rita Blake.)

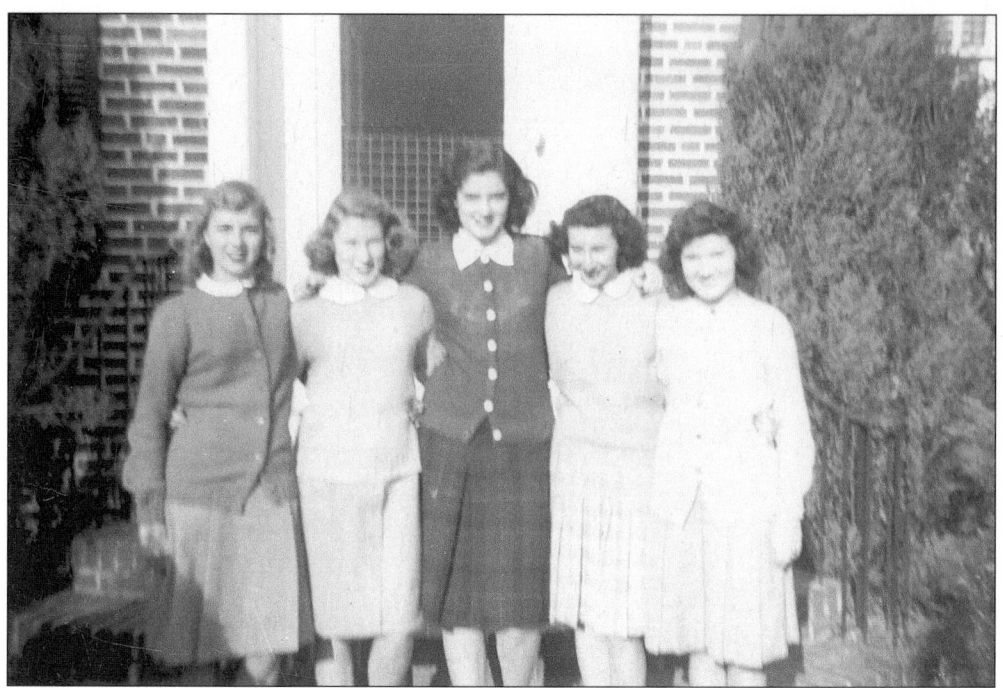

Future careers were not on the minds of these young girls. Pictured are Ann Mace, Betty Wood Moore, Martha Hewitt, Bobbie Boatwright, and Margaret Ledbetter. (Photo courtesy of Ann Mace Hooks.)

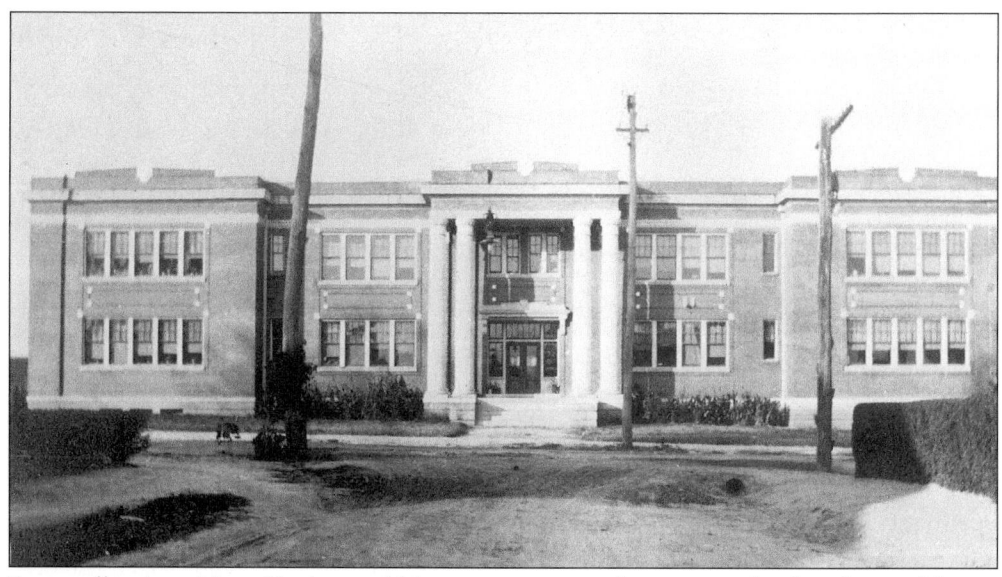

Eventually, Ann Mace Hooks would become a career elementary schoolteacher at Marion Grammar School, shown here facing Second Avenue. (Photo courtesy of Mike Jackson.)

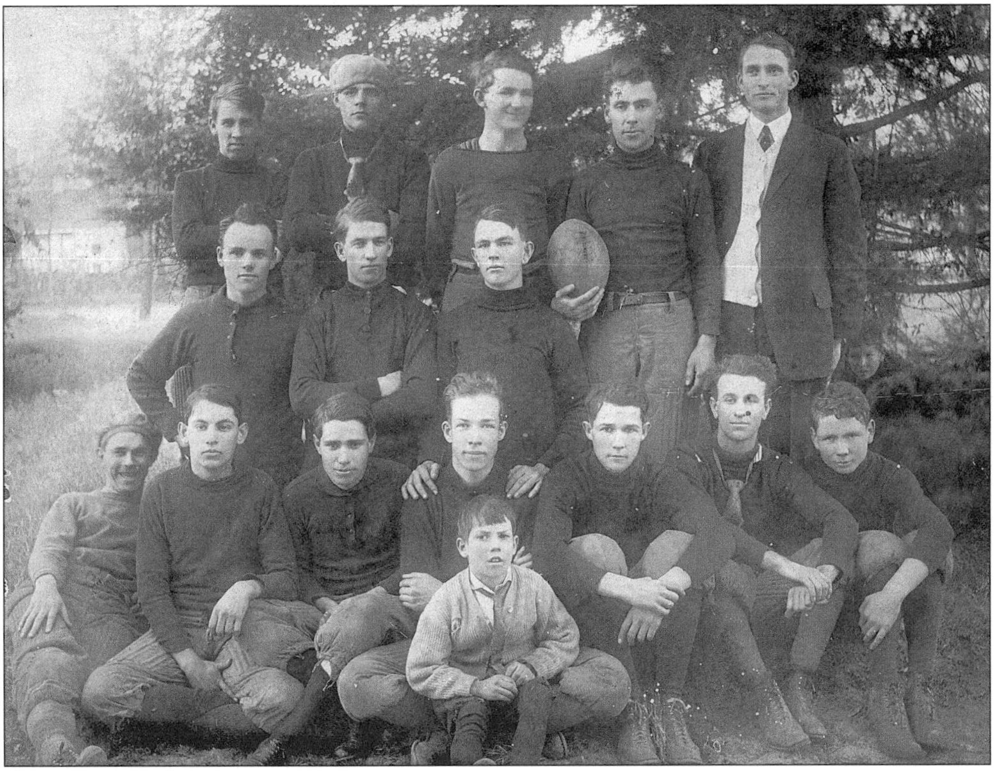

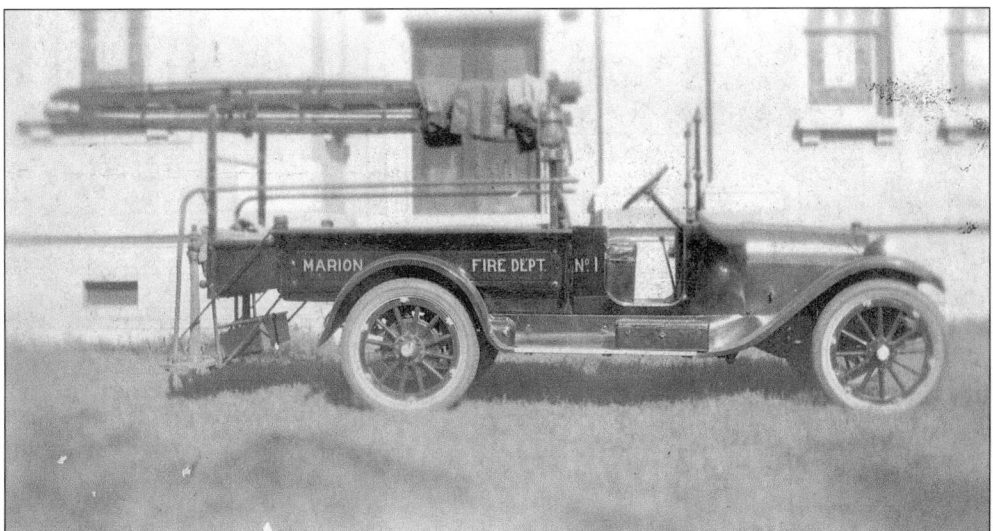

Included in this picture of an early-1900s Marion High School football team is Jones Thomas Hunter. (Photo courtesy of Dorothy Hunter Ellis.)

This is a photograph of Marion's first motorized fire truck. The fire wagon, drawn by two horses, had become outdated. This fire truck was probably photographed in the 1920s in front of city offices located on West Court Street. (Photo courtesy of Mike McLendon.)

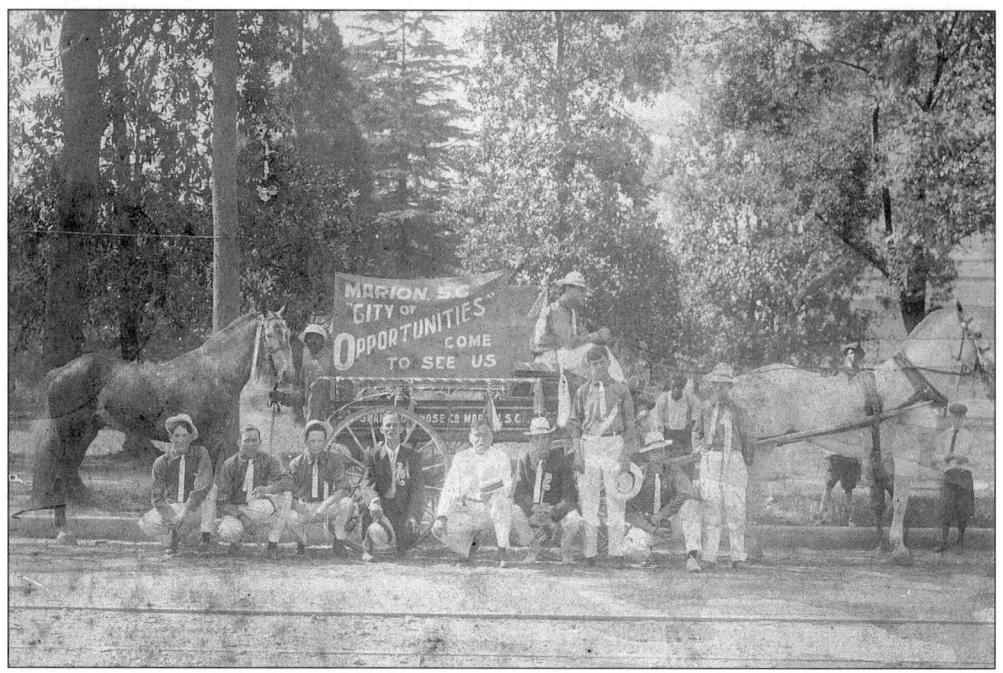

After winning a National Championship Award, Marion proudly displays Herb and Louie, the award-winning fire horses. (Photo courtesy of Suzanne Gasque McIntyre.)

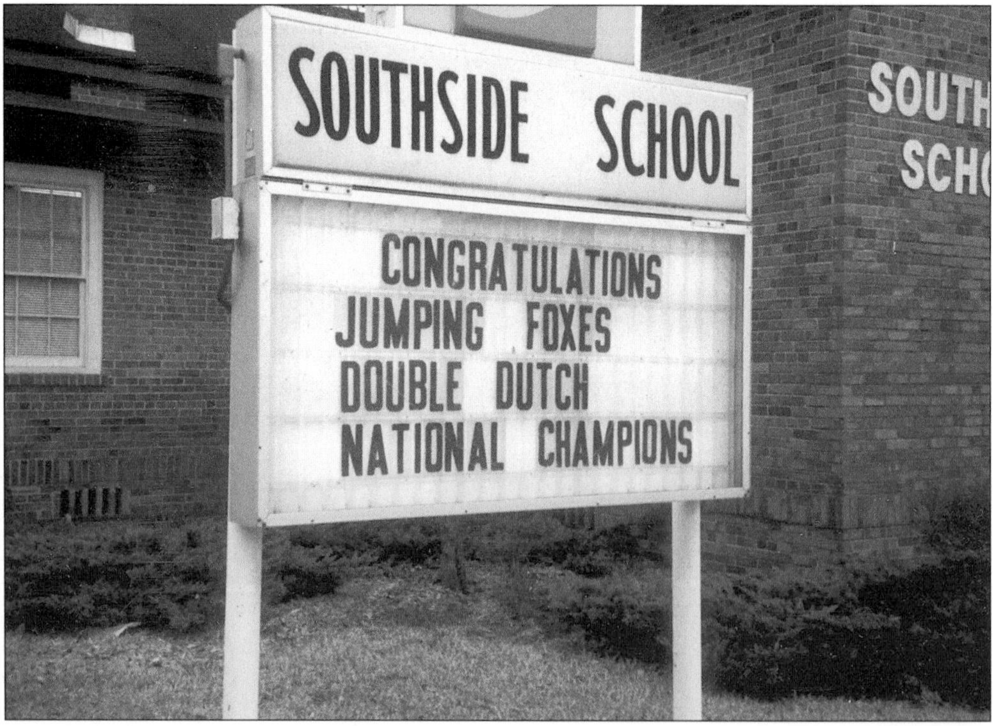

One of a few national championship teams to come out of Marion is the National Double Dutch Jump Rope team from Marion School District One, the Jumping Foxes. (Photo courtesy of Cynthia Drew Faulk.)

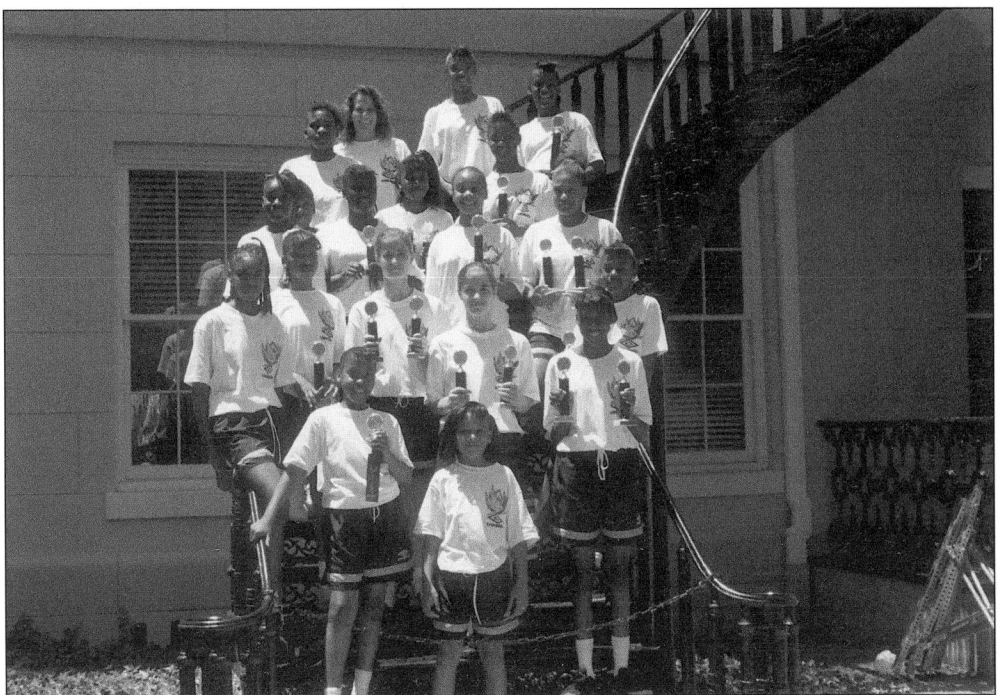

The 1995 Jumping Foxes pose on the courthouse steps after winning trophies as the National Double Dutch Champions. (Photo courtesy of Cynthia Drew Faulk.)

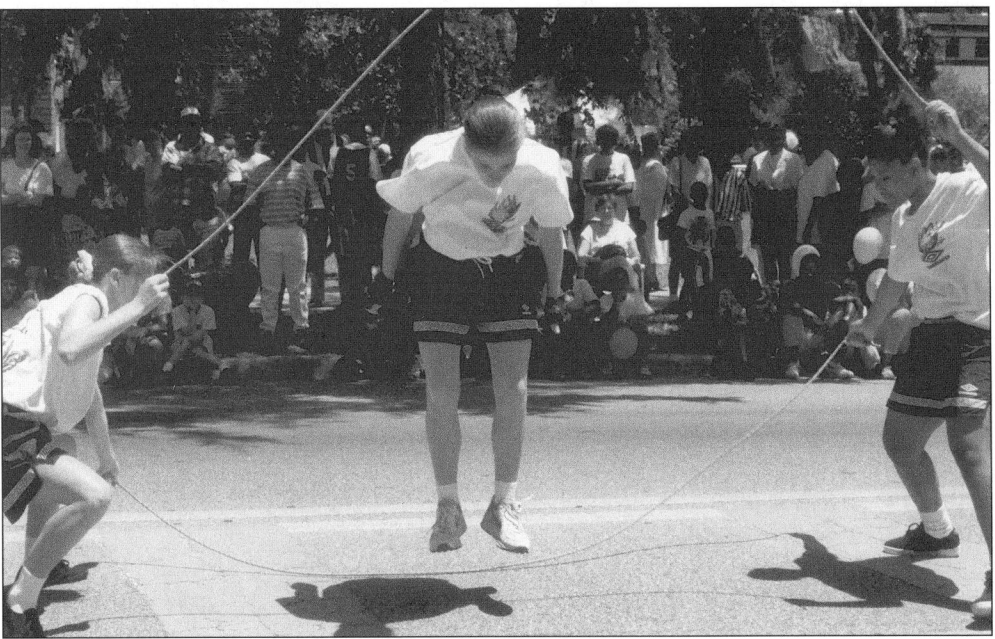

This group of young people worked together for a common goal and achieved success. Here's to our citizenry jumping into the new millennium with this same sense of cooperation, striving to ensure that our town will continue to progress in the future. We have gone from unpaved streets with horses and buggies to a future that still cannot even be imagined! (Photo courtesy of Cynthia Drew Faulk.)

ACKNOWLEDGMENTS

The Historic Marion Revitalization Association (HMRA) was created to restore, promote, and maintain the historic character and viability of Marion for the enjoyment and education of residents and visitors in the area. HMRA has been admitted into the South Carolina Downtown Development Association's Main Street program, which is affiliated with the National Trust for Historic Preservation's National Main Street Center. The foundation of the Main Street program is the preservation and the management of change in the built environment. HMRA is committed to sponsoring programs and activities that fulfill the following purposes: historic preservation, community education, lessening the burden of local government, and combating community deterioration. With the goal of historic preservation and education in mind, the Board of Directors of the Historic Marion Revitalization Association (seen below) gave approval for this historical pictorial of Marion. We would like to thank the Board of Directors of HMRA for its support of this project.

Without the response from the citizens who brought photographs for our use, this book would not have been possible. We would like to thank the following who trusted us with their prized photographs: Judy Alderman, Demont Ammons, Rusty Ammons, Nancy Askins, Lucia Atkinson, Dorothy Bartelle, Laney Baumrind, Pat Z. Bethea, James and Rita Blake, Valerie Baumrind Bonatis, Beaulah and S.A. Bradley, Chamber of Commerce, Billy Cornelius, Mary Lib Dixon, Leslie Dorsey, Martha B. Dozier, Pauline Edwards, Dorothy Ellis, Jeri Evans, Cynthia Faulk, Ernest Fergeson of Photo Arts in Winnsboro, Alma Finklea, Inez Fogan, FoxTrot Committee, Maxcy Foxworth, Doris Gasque, Viola Gibson, Ray Govus, Doris Gregg, Adele Hewitt, Ann Hooks, Annie Mae Hunt, Mike Jackson, Bernard Hubbard, Rawlings Hubbard, Hilda Lemmon, Charlie Levy, Marion County Medical Center, Jackie McGill, Poiette McGill, Dorothy D. McIntyre, Elizabeth McIntyre, Ginny McIntyre, Suzanne Gasque McIntyre, Mike McLendon, Mary and Mike Merchant, Billie Mishoe, Ben and Beth Mullins, James and Nita Neely, LeeAnne E. Owens, Rudy Pace, Shirley Patterson, Mary Pace Proctor, Maggie Riales, Jerry Rowell, Cindi Sloan, Mary B. Smith, Libby Owens Stanley, Lurline Stedman, Jane and William Thompson, USC Caroliniana Library, Arlis West, Gene Wiggins, Joyce Willcox, Mary Elizabeth H. Wilson, Mitzi Winesett, Margaret E. Wood, and F.T. Zeman.

We also would like to thank HMRA's Book Committee, who gave time, energy, and creativity toward the preparation of this book. The book committee has tried to pass on the information given to them with great care. Through the efforts of the committee, important pieces of Marion have been preserved for generations to come. Changes in Marion have come from natural disasters, calamities, and progress. Though changes have taken place, in many ways Marion has remained the same. Architect and town planner Tom Low says, "Unlike many small towns in this country, Marion, South Carolina, has maintained its uniqueness." We hope this book will portray the uniqueness of Marion.